GLOBAL DECEPTION

GLOBAL DECEPTION

THE UN'S STEALTH ASSAULT ON AMERICA'S FREEDOMS

JOSEPH A. KLEIN

World Ahead Publishing, Inc.

Published by World Ahead Publishing, Inc., Los Angeles, CA

World Ahead Publishing's books are available at special discounts for bulk purchases. World Ahead Publishing also publishes books in electronic formats. For more information, visit www.worldahead.com.

First Edition

ISBN 0-9746701-4-6
LCCN 2005933741

Printed in the United States of America

10 9 8 7 6 5 4 3 2 1

To my dear wife Roberta without whose constant love and support this book would not have been possible.

CONTENTS

ACKNOWLEDGEMENTS

I WISH TO ACKNOWLEDGE Eric M. Jackson, Co-Founder and Chairman of World Ahead Publishing, who believed in the mission of this book to expose the deception behind the UN's global governance agenda and its dangers to our constitutional freedoms, and who drove the quality of the work product toward his standard of excellence. I also wish to acknowledge my editor, Wendy Zarganis, who worked very hard to make readable some of my more "legalese" sentences. This book also required much work from people behind the scenes at World Ahead Publishing, including Norman Book, its Co-founder and Vice President, Judith Abarbanel, marketing director, and Brandi Laughey, my cover designer, as well as Cara Eshleman, Sarah Williams, and Jonathan New.

My constitutional law professors at Harvard Law School, Paul Freund and Archibald Cox, helped shape my thinking on the vital role that the Constitution plays in defining the limits of governmental power and protecting our liberties.

On a more personal note, I want to thank my brothers Ken and Robert, and sisters-in-law Paula and Hannah, for their keen interest in my ideas and for taking the time to listen and discuss them. I am also grateful to my cousins Phyllis Bosworth and Nancy and Steve Mendelow for their encouragement and assistance. And finally my daughter Amy always keeps me on my toes and will certainly have a big stake in how the future of the United Nations unfolds.

INTRODUCTION

D URING HIS 2005 confirmation hearings for the UN am-
bassadorship, John Bolton was taken to task for saying
that nobody would notice the difference if we lost ten stories
off the top of the United Nations building. Bolton's opponents
criticized his lack of respect for this internationalist shrine
adorning the East River skyline of Manhattan.

Actually, Ambassador Bolton was being kind. The problem
is not just the UN's pervasive corruption, incompetence and
lack of managerial discipline, which are shocking enough. The
real threat the United Nations poses comes from the zealous,
globalist ideology that has corrupted its founders' original intentions. To reverse Bolton's metaphor, these left-wing globalists strive to add even more stories of UN power, using synthetic materials composed of so-called "universal" or "international norms" that they manufacture at a host of unelected
global forums. Then, they methodically plot to use our own
judicial system to finish their handiwork. They hoodwink
sympathetic internationalists in our federal judiciary to insinuate their ideology into the judges' interpretation of the
U.S. Constitution. The result is to deprive Americans, brick by
brick, of every freedom which the Founding Fathers labored to
write into the Constitution.

As *New York Times* columnist David Brooks put it, the UN
has become the instrument of "elites" and "technocrats" who
want to turn the unelected bodies of the UN and related global
forums into some sort of "supranational authority."[1] (For the

sake of clarity, we'll refer to these elitists throughout as "glob-alists.")

Secretary-General Kofi Annan—and Boutros Boutros-Ghali before him—have actively promoted this ideology, with en-couragement from the majority of developing countries who dominate the UN's General Assembly and stand to gain from the world organization's aggrandizement at the expense of the United States. Sympathetic world leaders like French President Jacques Chirac, prominent liberal "thought" leaders like Bill Clinton and his Presidential aspirant wife Hillary, and the edi-torial board of the New York Times all contribute to giving the globalists a prominent platform on the world stage.

Copious funding from billionaires such as George Soros and Ted Turner keep the globalist propaganda machine whirl-ing away. The globalists' left-wing, anti-American proselytiz-ing is additionally facilitated by the immense resources af-forded them by private, unelected and unaccountable advo-cacy organizations—known as NGOs—including such extrem-ist groups as Amnesty International and Greenpeace.

While the UN's past failures and present travails get most of the media attention, the real story lies in the dangerous di-rection the organization is taking with globalists at the helm. The globalists' tactic: to implement a perverse agenda of eco-nomic regulation, extreme environmentalism, and left-wing social norms. Their strategy: to badger and assault the U.S. through foreign media, politicians, UN bureaucrats and NGOs in order to marshal world-wide support for their gauzy, Hall-mark-card visions of a supposedly benign and just world gov-ernment. Their goal: to neuter the United States Constitution and the nation it defines.

Unfortunately for the globalists, the American people aren't buying it. A 2005 Harris poll reported that by a 44 to 30 percent plurality, this country's citizens don't trust the United Nations. Unable to convince Americans of the worthiness of their goals—or of the trustworthiness of those pushing them—

globalists have turned to stealthier means: infiltrating U.S. courts to chip away at American sovereignty.

This book sounds the alarm on this stealth globalist agenda and exposes it through their own words and actions. The globalists use the UN and its global forums to curse the United States and to light our Constitution afire, with help from their brethren in our own courts. Still, condemning the UN alone is like cursing your lamp for not working during a power outage. Yes, the organization is corrupt and incompetent—maybe hopelessly so. But focusing on the institution's venality and narcissism distracts us from the even more pernicious threat posed by the powerful, pervasive, and "progressive" ideologies that have led it astray.

The globalist movement and its relentlessly left-wing agenda is the true underlying threat to America. The United Nations is simply one element—albeit a highly visible element—of the movement. Lopping off ten stories or leveling the whole thing won't topple the insidious leftist agenda that lurks within and seeks to infect our federal judiciary with foreign jurisprudence.

Whether it is a trillion dollars a year of global taxes that the globalists seek to impose on the rest of us, or regulating everything from gun possession to Internet usage, or creating permanent international courts with unlimited enforcement powers over American citizens, these extremist initiatives imperil our Constitutional liberties and protections. If this momentum isn't reversed, our real democracy will slowly be replaced with a malign form of synthetic global consensus expressed through unaccountable, undemocratic institutions

And the attacks aren't necessarily easy to spot. Experts in PR and well-versed in co-opting media coverage, savvy globalists have adopted a crafty approach that exploits the U.S.'s unelected judiciary to achieve their desired agenda. This strategy includes bringing court cases before sympathetic federal judges who might be willing to incorporate into their interpretations of *our* Constitution loosely worded "international norms" adopted by what we're assured is a "consensus" garnered from some nebulous, unaccountable global forum. Anyone who has actually read the sad document that is the EU Constitution will recognize both the globalists' language and their intent.

The need to protect our Constitutional system of self-government from such over-reaching is self-evident. Yet we can't stop this onslaught just by quitting the UN altogether—satisfying as that might be. Nor can we just withdraw funding, although financial leverage is a vital means of exercising control. The reality is that a "United Nations" in some form or another will remain a reality so long as a majority of the world's governments wants such an institution to exist. It can do more harm to our interests without our participation than it might if we remain a member nation, using our power to moderate its excesses from within.

Being the world's lone superpower brings both rights and responsibilities. There's no doubt that many of this planet's more intractable problems will require transnational cooperation if they are to be even mitigated, much less solved.

There's a big difference, however, between "cooperation" and "coercion." And make no mistake: it's coercion that the globalists have in mind. The United States has the right—and the duty—to thoroughly insulate our Constitutional system from the excesses, contamination and coercive aspects sure to result if globalist initiatives are incorporated into our laws. Contrary to the globalists' most fervent beliefs, a weak United States benefits no one.

Respect for *genuine* multilateral cooperation and *valid* international law requires nothing less than finding effective ways to separate the wheat from the chaff. We must cull the multitude of unaccountable institutions responsible for manufacturing phony "international norms" from the herd, and stop their foolish, superficial rantings from seeping into our own judicial decisions.

Phrases like "Don't be evil" (actually condensed from the mission statement of a major American corporation!) [2] and "Mean people suck" make for catchy bumper stickers, but they are hardly the foundation upon which to build *any* kind of serious government, much less a global one. Yet, as we'll see, trite, juvenile phrases just like these constitute what passes for globalist philosophy.

In short, we may not need to lose any stories from the UN building to keep our Constitution intact, but we surely need to lose the globalist mindset that threatens its basic tenets.

CHAPTER ONE

THE UN IN THE GLOBALISTS' GRASP

A S THE HORRORS of World War II drew to a close, the Allies searched for ways to avoid another conflict like the one that had taken over 60 million lives. They did not want another failure like the League of Nations, which was created after World War I in an effort to foster world cooperation and respect among governments but failed to do either

President Woodrow Wilson was the prime mover behind the Covenant of the League of Nations. An idealist, he refused to compromise with Senate critics who were concerned about preserving the sovereignty of the United States. Senator Henry Cabot Lodge, in particular, wanted to ensure that American troops would not be committed to military action abroad under the Covenant without prior Congressional approval.

But Wilson would not budge. He tried to take his case to the nation over the heads of the objecting senators. Against medical advice, Wilson embarked on a grueling journey to rally public opinion for his near-messianic vision of a universal code of moral conduct, only to suffer a debilitating stroke that effectively stopped him from governing, much less carrying on his League of Nations crusade. When advised to accept

Senator Lodge's reservation just before the Senate vote, Wilson responded: "I have no moral right to accept any change in a paper I have already signed."[1]

The Senate refused to ratify the Covenant and as a result, the United States did not join the League. Not that the countries that *did* took it seriously. For one thing, it was fatally flawed in terms of providing collective security against an aggressor by its voting procedures. Under these procedures, the aggressor nation, so long as it was a member of the League, had the power to veto any punitive actions by the League against itself.[2]

Wilson was an unalloyed idealist who believed that human beings the world over could be "united for peace" by adhering to an overarching universalist moral code. His "supreme spiritual error," wrote the renowned political columnist Walter Lippmann in 1944, was in "forgetting that we are men and thinking that we are gods."[3]

President Franklin D. Roosevelt was not about to travel the same road of self-delusion. He and British Prime Minister Winston Churchill believed strongly in a postwar United Nations dedicated to collective security, and began putting together the blueprint for such an organization even before the conclusion of World War II. But they were realists who wanted the war's victors to maintain control of the world body, with effective procedures in place to deter Hitler-type aggression. FDR and Churchill had no interest in utopian visions of world government.

However, there remained many opinion-makers, including prominent politicians, who wanted nothing less than to create President Wilson's ideal of a universalist moral code. They believed that national sovereignty had to give way to some sort of world government with its own defense force, world parliament, currency and supra-national judiciary. None other than John Foster Dulles—later secretary of state under President Dwight Eisenhower—headed a commission that called for the post-war establishment of just such a "world government" in March of 1942. New York and New Jersey joined with five other states in actually passing resolutions endorsing the idea of a World Federation. The usual self-styled elitists including professors, journalists, literary figures and other committed believers in trans-national government formed citizen lobbying groups to push their agenda. A former *New York Times* journalist named Clarence Streit popularized the idea in a book and founded the Federal Union Incorporated, which started out as an advocacy group for a "Great Republic" of democracies but shortly broadened into a program for universal membership.[4]

These seedlings of the "globalist" ideology soon made their way to Truman's doorstep. Only six days after FDR's death on April 12, 1945, Truman received a very curious letter from one John Ross Delafield, who proclaimed himself a neighbor of Roosevelt's in Hyde Park.

The letter detailed a conversation that Delafield claimed had taken place between himself, FDR, and a visiting Oxford professor. The topic: what an alleged post-war United Nations organization should look like.[5] According to Delafield's letter, FDR had desired nothing less than an international judiciary, funded by a global tax. This global court would have the power to create new principles of its own "in accordance with the common conscience of men" and have the ability to enforce them with its own standing army stationed on the island of Madagascar. It would perform "all the functions classically divided between the three coordinate and equal divisions."

In other words, Delafield claimed that FDR wanted to eliminate the concept of separation of powers between the legislative, executive and judicial branches that is so enshrined in the United States Constitution.

Well, that was one way to try and get Harry Truman's ear, but clearly he wasn't as gullible as, in their opinion, a Missouri upbringing suggested he should be. Thankfully, President

Truman had no patience for such nonsense. One can only imagine "Give 'Em Hell Harry's" salty reaction when he read the letter.

Though committed to establishing a world body devoted to finding peaceful solutions to global problems, Truman was not about to cede U.S. sovereignty or control in the process. Delafield's letter to the contrary, he was confident that FDR would have agreed.

So while not allowing President Roosevelt's death to delay the drafting of the UN Charter scheduled for the spring of 1945, Truman made sure that the representatives he sent kept the United States' interests front and center in the negotiations. Indeed, one of his emissaries to the San Francisco conference, Sen. Tom Connally of Texas, then chairman of the Senate Foreign Relations Committee, put down a rebellion of smaller countries complaining about the Security Council veto granted only to the five Great Powers (United States, USSR, United Kingdom, China and France). Connally ripped up a copy of the draft in front of their representatives and said, "If you want a charter, you can have a charter with the veto or no charter at all." Complaints on that point, at least, ceased.[6]

The small nations were given an equal voice in the General Assembly—a "town hall" type debating society with no real power, meaning that actual control resided with the Great Powers. In order to win final approval in the Senate for ratifying the UN Charter, the United States representatives had to ensure that not even a shred of U.S. sovereignty over decisions affecting its own citizens would be lost. The United States reserved the right, without explicitly saying so in the Charter, to withdraw from the United Nations should it so choose.[7] Indeed, Republican Senator Arthur Vandenburg, whose support was crucial to rallying broad support for the Charter, wrote of the UN organization at the time that it was anything but a wild-eyed internationalist manifestation of a world state.

President Truman did agree to the establishment of the International Court of Justice, but it was a far more modest affair than anything envisioned in that bizarre letter from John Ross Delafield.

In short, the United Nations was founded to bring sovereign nations together for the purpose of cooperating to solve common problems while taking collective action where warranted against threats to international peace and security. In fact, the United Nations Charter specifically recognizes the sovereign status of the member states. It stipulates that the United Nations does not have the authority "to intervene in matters which are essentially within the domestic jurisdiction of any state."

The globalist ideal of a new world order, presided over by wise, benign philosopher-judges rendering binding decisions on behalf of all mankind, appeared to be dead on arrival. Or was it?

The Globalists' Revenge

The globalists may have lost the initial battle for defining the UN's mission, but they never gave up their long-term objectives. The World Federalist Movement was formed in 1947 as a result of a meeting held in Montreux, Switzerland, where 300 participants representing fifty-one organizations from twenty-four different countries held the first "Conference of the World Movement for World Federal Government." Its explicit goal was "to transform the UN and to draw up a World Constitution through a people's convention." The movement blossomed the following year to 150,000 members.

Among other things, the movement supported the conversion of the UN General Assembly into a world parliament. It also advocated the creation of new international bodies with enforcement powers, such as the International Criminal Court.[8]

Dr. Robert Muller, a former UN assistant secretary-general and co-founder and former chancellor of the United Nations "University for Peace" in Costa Rica, is regarded in some circles as a prophet of the global governance movement. Muller has written extensively about his mystical vision of one world government, which he dubs a "United States of the World." This vision remains very much alive today.[9]

And it would be innocuous enough if the globalists confined their activities to harmless New Age natterings and kept their mystical visions to themselves. Instead, they have managed to meld a coalition of New Age followers, environmentalists, human rights activists, peaceniks, anti-capitalists, and other misfits into an odd and dangerous coalition. They seek to convert the United Nations—the tool most immediately at hand—into an instrument of world governance paying homage to the planet Earth, while implementing a hazy but "fair" social justice system world-wide.

Funded in part by celebrities, oddball philanthropists and major foundations, which often have no idea what they're actually paying for, these activists have formed literally thousands of private, non-profit "people's" organizations worldwide that operate outside of the governments of their respective countries. These supra-national organizations, usually referred to as NGOs, or "non-governmental organizations," come in different shapes and sizes, performing a variety of voluntary, private citizen-led activities. By and large, they are free to operate as they wish with *no* public accountability.

NGOs are officially recognized in the UN Charter. The United Nations defines an NGO as "any international organization which is not established by a governmental entity or intergovernmental agreement." These private organizations, operating with no oversight, are deeply encrusted within the UN system. Some even function as handsomely-paid consultants to UN committees.[10]

In fairness, not all NGOs have a globalist philosophy. There are some conservative NGOs, mostly religious organizations, and some that provide truly heroic "on the ground" humanitarian services to the needy around the world, but they are vastly outnumbered by others touting a globalist mind-set.

NGOs like Greenpeace and Amnesty International are among those that have been the most aggressive in forwarding their agendas. Well-funded and blessed with far better press than they deserve, they seek to "empower" the "disenfranchised" by challenging national sovereignty. They want to create "international institutions"—ones populated with zealots and fanatics just like themselves—to deal with their particular issues, figuring that preaching to the choir is far easier than trying to deal with often recalcitrant national governments.

Over the years, globalist NGOs have conjured up a blizzard of schemes seeking to create international institutional frameworks that would govern precisely the types of activities that states have historically reserved for themselves: a universal code of laws and taxes that transcend national borders. Feeding in particular on the jealousy and fear inspired by perceived U.S. hegemony, NGOs have pushed these proposals relentlessly—with the backing of the United Nation's secretary-general, the UN bureaucracy and like-minded leaders of member states.

The NGO hit parade includes: global taxes, strict universal gun control, global economic redistribution, an International Criminal Court with powers to try individual citizens, the exclusive right to declare and preside over military action, and even elimination of Security Council veto power. And the list goes on and on, with increasingly shrill demands for global rules and institutions to replace many of the historical prerogatives that we take for granted as part of national sovereignty and culture.

One of those most outspoken in support of global govern-ance is French President Jacques Chirac. Chirac believes that the free market policies championed by the United States—exactly the policies that have made the U.S. a superpower while Europe languishes—must be challenged by any means necessary. He views the European Union as the first line of defense, although he suffered a nasty setback when the draft EU constitution was decisively rejected by wary French voters in May, 2005.

"In the face of a growing world power that worries the French," Chirac said, "and which is carried by an ultra-liberal current, facing the United States and the large emerging mar-kets such as China, India, Brazil and South America and Rus-sia, the European Union has to equip itself with "useful rules." These powers, we will not face them individually, France does not have that capability. That is why Europe must be strong and organized in order to oppose that evolution."[11]

By "ultra-liberal," Chirac of course means the exact oppo-site of what we might take such words to mean in the States. But whatever the meaning, and whatever the fate of the EU constitution, a global governance structure designed to tame the uppity U.S. is what Chirac is really after. For many years, he has spoken of "globalization with a human face"—the type of Orwellian-sounding phrase that should give any freedom-loving American pause, if not the creeps—and has offered seven broad principles of global governance to achieve it.[12] And he minced no words when he declared that the Kyoto Protocol on global warming was to be the "the first step to-ward global governance."[13]

To advance his personal agenda even further, Chirac has pushed for a new World Environmental Organization as part of the United Nations system. Chirac declared: "In the face of growing ecological hazards, an environmental governance should be urgently established on a world scale...France sub-mitted to her partners proposals for creating a United Nations

Environmental Organization. In order to advance this project, France has brought together a group of countries determined to make headway in this respect with a view to the forthcoming Session of the General Assembly."[14]

On the environmental front at least, Chirac has no doubt been influenced by the ideas of globalists who have long embraced a world-wide environmental regulatory body with enforcement teeth. This author spoke with one of its leading proponents, James Gustave Speth, who is currently dean of the Yale School of Forestry and Environmental Studies Speth is a long-time globalist environmentalist who co-founded the National Resources Defense Council and founded the World Resources Institute. He served as the administrator of the United Nations Development Program between 1993 and 1999. As dean at a major U.S. university, Speth is, of course, in a good position to align students—tomorrow's leaders—with his particularly elitist point of view.

Speth believes that the World Environmental Organization should be set up as a specialized UN agency, incorporating the current UN Environmental Program which he regards as toothless. However, like many globalists who know full well that their true beliefs could never survive the court of public opinion, he was wary about appearing too enthusiastic about his ideas in the interview and refused to discuss his current thoughts on what powers this organization should have. He would not elaborate about the role of a World Environmental Organization (WEO) beyond his prior writings. Fair enough. In his book, *Red Sky at Morning*, Speth spelled it all out:

> There are several models of a WEO, ranging from quite modest to quite powerful...the most ambitious idea would create a world environment agency entrusted with setting international standards and enforcing them against laggard countries. If we are to ever see a WEO, it will probably be essential to start at the modest end of the spectrum and strengthen the new organization over time...[15]

He expressed his enthusiasm for the idea at the Environmental Law Institute Award Dinner Millennium Celebration in Washington, D.C., on October 26, 1999:

> Pollution has gone global; species have gone global; and so must we. Global governance must come to the environment. So bring on the environmental diplomats! Bring on the WEO to match the WTO! Let us have globalization, but globalization with a human face...[16]

Globalization with a human face—the same inane, and vaguely threatening, metaphor invoked by Chirac when describing his seven principles for a new international order. And this from a highly-placed academic in a major American university! Of course, it shouldn't be surprising that so many globalists have found refuge in academia, an incestuous little world with zero tolerance for true diversity of thought.

Talk of global governance, in turn, leads inevitably to the globalists' favorite subject—global taxes. For a group that collectively decries capitalism, they certainly enjoy contemplating how to spend the fruits of other peoples' labors. A number of influential world leaders—or, more correctly perhaps, leaders whom the media consider influential—are putting their weight behind United Nations proposals for global taxes in order to finance a huge increase in the amount of so-called "development assistance" going to the world's poorest nations.[17] Unable to efficiently run *itself*, the United Nations bureaucracy is now jockeying to run this massive wealth redistribution program, designed to fund the "Millennium Development Goals" approved by the General Assembly in its 2000 session.

These quite laudable goals include efforts to cut global poverty in half, improve education, eliminate diseases, and solve the world's environmental woes by 2015. World leaders met to spur these initiatives forward at the kick-off of the UN General Assembly's fall 2005 "Millennium+5" session.

While it's one thing to agree upon a vaguely-worded, feel-good statement committing the developed and developing countries to working together with a sense of urgency to alleviate poverty, it's quite something else to agree on who's supposed to fund it, although it's safe to say that the consensus choice would be the United States. To that end, one subject we can expect to rear its ugly head is global taxes, which UN Ambassador John Bolton vigorously opposes on national sovereignty grounds. But the fight will not be an easy one.

Chirac brushed aside national sovereignty concerns and called for global taxes back in 2003. Once created, Chirac assures us, global taxes "would deliver the precise kind of resource needed to finance human development, one which is both totally predictable and concessional" and would protect "the financing of poverty reduction...from the vagaries of politics and the uncertainties of international cooperation."[18]

Never mind the near-impossibility of implementing these global taxes—billions and billions of dollars worth—in a fair and equitable manner, especially in light of the oil-for-food debacle. And as for accountability when it comes to results and deciding which "worthy recipients" should receive what aid—well, good luck with that.

Of course, United Nations insiders, who already spend member states' money on endless rounds of self-aggrandizing projects and summits, are positively enthralled by any plan to eliminate national sovereignty, thus granting the organization more money to spend—if not steal—with wild abandon.

Secretary-General Kofi Annan himself has been championing this dubious idea since taking office in 1997. Hot on the scent of money without end, Kofi and his UN minions have diligently provided their NGO counterparts with the financial and media resources needed to keep their redistributionist agenda front and center while creating a carefully manufactured "outcry" for more funding. Working with sympathetic world leaders like Chirac, globalists seek what they euphemistically call "innovative sources of financing." They want global taxes to fund an ever-expanding set of grossly impractical initiatives at the expense of each nation deciding for itself whether or not to participate.

Mohamed El-Ashry, a Senior Fellow of Ted Turner's UN Foundation and former chairman and CEO of the World Bank's Global Environmental Facility, told this author that he believes the United Nations is caught in a "circular" situation that is not of its own making. The UN, he said, is blamed for problems that the United States and other powerful member states really caused themselves. It was these member states' fault, he claimed, that there was no coherence among all of the UN's many bodies and agencies world-wide.

El-Ashry also mentioned the frustration he shares with other UN supporters that "talk" about lofty goals to advance human rights, eradicate poverty and protect the environment has not been matched by concrete actions. Part of the responsibility for this failure, El-Ashry asserted with a straight face, lies with the Republican hostility towards the United Nations.

El-Ashry has had many years of experience dealing with global issues, which certainly informs, if not pollutes, his opinions. But in a typical example of circling the wagons, he is attacking the symptoms, rather than the root causes, of the United Nation's problems. An insular culture that encourages moral superiority, entitlement and cronyism has created over the years a bloated, corrupt and self-serving bureaucracy utterly resistant to any real accountability or reform. As for "talk about lofty goals," well, that and generating paper are actually the UN's particular specialties. Perhaps it's the lack of concrete, practical, fact-based and accountable solutions to problems that keeps donor countries in many cases from participating.

But an even more fundamental cause for disenchantment, if not disgust, with the UN is its dubious claim to a moral legitimacy that both history and experience prove unequivocally it does not deserve. Decades after failing to prevail in their attempts to influence the initial design of the UN, the globalists have managed to seize the machinery of the UN establishment. They are using its unaccountable, unelected, and unsupervised forums to advance an anti-freedom agenda in direct contradiction to the organization's original intent.

The result? A lushly funded, unaccountable enemy in our midst, one that stews in its own venom while working to undermine the very Constitutional processes of the democratically elected United States government that have been holding their malign and authoritarian concept of "globalization with a human face" at bay.

"We the World": The Threat to the U.S. Constitution

For the United States to join the globalist parade, we would have to sacrifice a 200-plus year tradition of defining the rule of law by reference to our written Constitution.

The history and identity of this country are bound inextricably with the text of the Constitution and its brilliantly conceived rules for exercising and limiting the power of government through amendment and judicial interpretation. The Constitution is vital to our well-being because it provides a commonly accepted basis for defining how we behave as a political society.

This marvelous document spreads power among the federal government, the states, and among the three branches of the federal government to avoid concentrating power in too few hands. It protects individual liberties from governmental encroachment and requires elected officials to act in conformance with the laws that define the people's sovereignty of self-rule.

The Constitution does *not* separate us from the rest of the world, except as the rest of the world chooses not to embrace its inspired tenets. Yet it should protect *us* from having our core liberties as a free sovereign people undermined by a vague global "value system" determined by a gaggle of un-elected "officials," including some from the most autocratic countries in the world. "We the people," for whom the Found-ing Fathers fought and labored to create "a more perfect Un-ion," will forfeit the unique protections that our Constitution affords us if we succumb to the natterings of world opinion and allow ourselves to be consumed by some sort of global governance structure.

Even if the globalists' goals had something beyond a sort of groovy, feel-good, pie-in-the-sky "evil sucks" appeal, in practice they are impossible to implement. For example, whose definition of "international law" would prevail and through what means would this new structure be implemented?

Here's just one example. In 2004, world Muslim leaders urged incorporation of the moral values of Sharia (Islamic reli-gious law) into international law. "Some western research-ers"—on some American taxpayer-funded college campus, no doubt—"have found out that Islamic principles could be used to develop the international law and incorporate its moral val-ues into it," said Jaafar Abdel-Salam, the secretary-general of the Islamic Universities Association.[19]

It is true that nearly one in five people in the world today claim adherence to the faith of Islam and over fifty countries have Muslim-majority populations. Perhaps on that basis alone, Islam could claim a legitimate moral right to playing a leading role in defining key postulates of international law.

But even if we were to ignore the fanatical jihad elements in the Muslim community who want to impose a Taliban-like fundamentalist society on the world while killing all "infi-dels,"—something that, to be honest, it's a little difficult to push aside—there are still profound problems with this sug-gestion. Islamic religious law does not recognize any distinc-tion between church and state. It contains no tenet of separation of powers. Justice is dispensed by religious rulings, not by the vital principles of due process.

As for the rights of individuals, many of Sharia's adherents do not believe that Western ideas of individual rights, whether religious tolerance or equal rights for women, for example, have any place in a society governed by true Islamic law.[20]

Whatever the peculiar attraction of Sharia to many societies, were the United States were to submit to some form of global governance based on these tenets, we would find ourselves with a governing ideology at odds with the very core of our national identity and historical experience. If this happens, the Constitution that has served us so well for more than two hundred years would enter the dustbin of history, tossed aside as a relic of a bygone era...unless resurrected by the bloody civil war no doubt soon to follow.

Of course, the United States cannot be forced into surrendering its own sovereignty to some global "governance body." We cannot be compelled to replace our own Constitution with a set of vaguely defined "universal principles" and "global values" as defined by the "Mean People Suck" crowd. Even if our political leaders were so foolish as to enter into a treaty that started us down this slippery path, treaties can neither override nor amend the Constitution under the Constitution's "Supremacy Clause." As the Supreme Court has concluded, it would simply make no sense for a treaty, once in effect as a result of the exercise of the President's and the Senate's Constitutional powers, to become the instrument for usurping the legal authority of the Constitution that established those powers in the first place.[21]

Thus, the United States Constitution by definition trumps the UN Charter as the governing instrument for the American people. That charter, and any other treaties we may enter into, is subject to the same limitations upon interference with the rights guaranteed by the U.S. Constitution as would any statute passed by Congress or a state legislature.

So we're safe, right? Not quite. While the Constitution limits the ability of the executive and legislative branches to subordinate our national interests to the UN or any organization like it, there is one branch of government in a position to undermine these protections. *Unless our judiciary adheres to the core Constitutional principles laid down in its own words and historical context, we are at risk from judges who even now are attempting to fuse the Constitution, via creative interpretations reflecting their own predilections, with value systems utterly alien to our political traditions.*

The UN Charter and the U.S. Constitution can be compatible with each other so long as the United Nations does not mutate into a world governance institution that its founders never intended, and the Constitution is interpreted in accordance with its founding principles. But the globalists' ambitious plans for dominance are aimed squarely—and intentionally—at the heart of our Constitutional protections.

In order to preserve these principles, we must first understand who these self-anointed people are, and why they are so intent on circumventing our Constitutional protections, by stealth if necessary. We'll look at what judges must do to protect our core Constitutional principles from globalist assault.

Finally, we'll examine the endlessly malign elements of the globalists' agenda, the better to understand what must be done to stop them from using our nation's own judges to subvert the greatest and most successful constitutional system on the face of the Earth.

CHAPTER TWO

THE GLOBALIST ROGUE'S GALLERY: ANNAN, STRONG AND SACHS

F ROM ITS ONCE LOFTY PERCH , the United Nations has descended into a swamp of corruption, incompetence and power-mad ambition. But you'd never know it listening to its leaders and the globalist groupies who hover nearby.

Day after day, more bad news surfaces on the widening web of entanglements between UN officials and the largest single financial scandal in history—the systematic looting of the Oil-for-Food Program. Nevertheless, the UN's spin doctors pretend that all is well at Turtle Bay and that nothing must distract the United Nations from its vital "work," however that's defined. Of course, the globalists must fend off any and all criticisms, since the UN constitutes the best weapon they have for advancing their agenda. Leading the charge for the globalist brigade is the endlessly agile Kofi Annan.

Oil-for-Food: the UN's "Friends Fly Free" Program

The Oil-for-Food Program was organized under supervision of the United Nations in 1996. It was designed to allow Iraq to sell oil on the world market in exchange for food, medicine and other such commodities. The intent was to provide for the Iraqi people's basic needs despite the international economic sanctions imposed on the government in the wake of the first Gulf War, without letting the country re-arm its military forces.

The UN was, in essence, a middleman. Oil revenues were to be deposited in a UN account and used for approved purchases. However, the secretariat failed miserably at oversight and Saddam Hussein took advantage with abandon. As a grotesque consequence, the Butcher of Baghdad siphoned off more than $20 billion dollars not just to enrich himself but to bribe people in countries such as France, Russia, and Germany—and possibly within the UN itself. Indeed, in papers discovered by Iraqi officials after Hussein's fall, Benon Sevan, Kofi Annan's Oil-for-Food point man, was on a list of individuals who allegedly received oil vouchers at below market prices—a bribe, in other words.

In the third interim report issued on August 8, 2005 by the Independent Inquiry Committee headed by former Federal Reserve Chairman Paul A. Volcker, the committee concluded that Sevan had engaged in "illicit activities." He allegedly received nearly $150,000 in connection with a scheme to divert an allocation of 1.8 million barrels for the benefit of an oil trading company, whose directors included a close friend of Sevan.[1] Sevan denies the charges, but has refused to cooperate with the Volker Committee.

Meanwhile, according to a March 22, 2005 statement from a Kofi Annan spokesman, the United Nations had at one time agreed to accord Mr. Sevan special treatment by reimbursing him for certain of his legal fees out of the Oil-for-Food administrative fund—a decision reversed after it became public.[2] Sevan may yet escape any criminal liability for his actions since, while still possessing UN immunity from prosecution, he fled to his homeland of Cyprus which does not have an extradition treaty with the United States.

The secretary-general has also been less than forthright about the role his own son, Kojo Annan, might have played in the scandal. According to Volcker's second interim report, Kofi Annan "did not pay enough attention" to possible conflicts of interest arising from his son's employment by Cotecna Inspection Services SA as the company sought an inspection contract in connection with the Oil-for-Food program.[3]

Kojo Annan, it turns out, received nearly $400,000 from Cotecna, staying on its payroll past the time Cotecna was awarded the contract it was seeking. The Secretary-General didn't bother to conduct a serious internal investigation when questions about his son's role first surfaced. Yet no matter what the revelations, Kofi Annan's mantra is that he has been fully exonerated by the Volcker Report.

"I was well aware that among the most serious allegations was an insinuation that I myself might have improperly influenced the procurement process in favour of Cotecna Inspection Services, because that company employed my son," he said in an opening statement of a press conference held on March 29, 2005, the day he received the second interim report.

"But I knew that to be untrue and I was therefore absolutely confident that a thorough inquiry would clear me of any wrongdoing. The Committee has now done so after an exhaustive twelve-month investigation. After so many distressing and untrue allegations have been made against me, this exoneration by the independent inquiry obviously comes as a great relief." Asked at the same press conference if he would consider resigning before his term is up at the end of 2006, Annan's terse answer was "Hell, no."[4]

While there have been no findings—yet—regarding personal corruption on the part of the secretary-general himself, the Volcker investigation did find evidence that his former chief-of-staff, Iqbal Riza, ordered that documents potentially relevant to the scandal be shredded, just *one day* after the Security Council established the independent Volcker inquiry.[5]

The Volcker investigation also found evidence that the person supposedly responsible for conducting internal audits of the UN's operations, Dileep Nair, may have abused his position. Nair allegedly steered a crony into a high-level post in his organization—a post funded by the Oil-for-Food auditing committee—even though this individual performed virtually no work directed to the Oil-for-Food Program.[6] Annan had previously cleared Nair of allegations of wrongdoing after a perfunctory internal investigation, but may finally be forced to look again in light of the Volcker Report's findings.

Annan has continually tried to deflect attention from the Oil-for-Food debacle by blaming the usual suspects—the U.S. and Great Britain—for "allowing" Saddam Hussein to evade the oil embargo. Annan has gone so far as to absurdly charge that most of Hussein's thievery "came out of smuggling outside the Oil-for-Food Program, and it was on the American and British watch," conveniently ignoring the fact that Hussein would still be looting and paying bribes to UN officials and others from monies intended for the Iraqi people if it were not for the courageous actions of both countries to finally remove him against Annan's own wishes.(7)

It is not at all surprising to find Annan circling the wagons. Self-preservation is an integral part of the UN culture. From top to bottom, UN bureaucrats believe that their sheer wonderfulness, not to mention the Very Important Work they're doing, simultaneously qualifies them for martyrdom and exempts them from demonstrating anything as prosaic as personal integrity, financial prudence or efficiency.

There is no effective internal mechanism that holds staff members accountable. When questioned, their instinct is first to stonewall, and then to question the motives of the perceived attacker. Theirs is an insular and cliquish world.

With the notable exception of the United States, most member states continue to give the UN leadership a free pass from accountability. Some, like France and Russia, may have plenty to hide in the case of the Oil-for-Food scandal, so their unwillingness to scrutinize Kofi & Company is hardly a surprise.

But of far more relevance is the fact that many member states, despite the organization's overwhelming ineptitude, see the UN as the only practical means by which to bring the United States to heel. Do that, and the thieving and bureaucratic bumbling simply don't matter. "There is no alternative to the United Nations," Chirac declared in a speech to the UN in September 2003. In talking about Iraq, Chirac said in the same speech, "It is up to the United Nations to give legitimacy to this process."[7]

To the contrary, if the UN has any legitimacy at all, it's self-conferred. Much like the Great Wizard of Oz, there's little substance, but a whole lot of ego hiding behind the UN curtain.

All that's there to see is an insular, self-protective, grievance-driven organization managed by unaccountable, self-righteous bureaucrats who in all too many cases love their New York lifestyles while hating the country that makes them possible. Perhaps no one exemplifies this poisoned culture more than Kofi Annan himself.

Born in Ghana in 1938, Annan grew up in a privileged aristocratic environment and received his higher education in the United States and Europe.

He joined the organization in 1962 as an administrative and budget officer with the World Health Organization in Geneva, Switzerland. After a succession of posts abroad, he began his climb at the UN's headquarters in 1987, as assistant secretary-general for human resources management and security coordinator for the UN system. He later served the assistant secretary general in charge of budgeting, followed by a stint overseeing peacekeeping operations. Before becoming secretary-general, he served for more than three years as under secretary general.

Annan was the consensus candidate to succeed Boutros Boutros-Ghali, whom even the Clinton administration, not known for its rigorous oversight of UN affairs, refused to support for another term. Virtually his entire career has been spent at the United Nations, and he became the first secretary-general to rise through its bureaucratic ranks.

Whatever vague hopes might have accompanied Annan's ascension to the top spot have long since been squashed. He did win a Nobel Peace Prize (in 2001)-but then again, the fact that terrorist Yasser Arafat got one in 1994 has gone a long way towards diminishing the award's credibility. Annan's greatest strength, honed by years in the bureaucratic trenches, is his ability to exude a prickly, smarmy sense of self—righteousness designed to deflect any and all criticism.

See No Evil

In Annan's UN, failure will be rewarded with promotions as long as the culprits display absolute fealty to the organization. In the real world, of course, actions have consequences; but in UN-World, incompetents are axed only when spin goes bad and publicity gets too hot to handle. Annan's "see no evil, hear no evil" leadership style has led to the mess in which he now finds himself, his son and his cronies entangled.

By any rational measure, Annan has been a profound failure as an administrator. He over-delegates and won't make decisions, other than to lash out at critics whenever his failings or those of his minions come inconveniently to light. The most glaring—and inexcusable—example occurred while he served as Assistant Secretary-general for peacekeeping operations during the crisis in Rwanda. Not only did he refuse to take charge when he had the chance to head off the slaughter of thousands, but he allowed his confidante Iqbal Riza—the same man accused years later of shredding papers relating to the Oil-for-Food program—on his own authority to override a life-saving recommendation of the UN's commander on the ground in Rwanda, Maj. Gen. Romeo Dallaire.

According to the inquiry, "Of the Actions Which the UN Took at the Time of the Genocide in Rwanda," commissioned by Annan and delivered to the UN Security Council in December, 1999, Annan was criticized because "he did not brief the secretary-general," or the Security Council, about a key cable that Maj. Gen. Dallaire had relayed to UN headquarters containing credible intelligence that Rwandan government extremists planned to exterminate minority Tutsis imminently. The commander recommended a pre-emptive raid by UN peacekeepers to seize a large cache of illegal weapons before they could be used against helpless civilians.

Riza, with Annan's knowledge, directed the commander to stand down and do nothing. Dallaire, of course, turned out to be right and a genocidal campaign that would ultimately result in over 800,000 deaths took place shortly thereafter.[8] Only in the endlessly self-congratulatory globalist world could such heinous incompetence qualify someone to win a "peace" prize.

In a 1999 PBS interview, Riza was asked about his reaction to the Dallaire cable, which, according to the interviewer, clearly "said that the informer had been trained to exterminate Tutsis. That wasn't political, that was a kind of genocide, truly."

Riza said that he was sorry about what happened, but excused his disregard of the cable's warning with this cynical observation:

> Look, since the 1960s, there have been cycles of violence—
> Tutsis against Hutus, Hutus against Tutsis. I'm sorry to put it
> so cynically. It was nothing new. This had continued from the
> '60s through the '70s into the '80s and here it was in the '90s...[9]

According to the Associated Press, Annan blocked several probes to determine who saw the cable that ordered Maj. Gen. Dallaire to give up his plan to intercede. Annan also reportedly refused to allow the commander to testify before a Belgian panel investigating the events in Rwanda because he did not believe it was ``in the interest of the organization.''[10]

Riza was rewarded for his cynicism and misjudgment by becoming Annan's chief-of-staff, a position he held through the end of 2004. In a meeting with thousands of UN staffers held on April 5, 2005, Annan continued to defend his friend Riza as "a man of integrity" and stated that "any of us who know Iqbal Riza could hardly accept" the Volcker committee's claim that Riza pitched countless relevant memos and documents into a shredder the day after the Oil-for-Food investigation was announced. [11]

It is this kind of unswerving—and often misplaced—loyalty that has propelled Annan to the top of the UN heap. Despite paying lip service to requests for management reform at the highest levels, Annan has done little but drag his feet while acting affronted that outsiders have the temerity to make such demands. Even something so obvious as the adoption of rules against nepotism was strongly resisted for years. While a code of conduct was finally adopted, a survey that Deloitte Consulting took of United Nations employees found that "[S]taff members feel unprotected when reporting violations of codes of conduct."[12]

To the surprise of utterly no one, meritocracy has no place within the bowels of the UN. Loyalty to the organization is all that matters. Honest staffers are afraid to come forward and report wrongdoing because of just the "fear of retaliation," the Deloitte survey reported.[13]

And the top brass is duly rewarded, no matter what their level of performance-or non-performance may be. Nearly $1 billion goes towards paying the outsized salaries of thousands of bureaucrats who are entitled, under UN rules, to be compensated at levels equivalent to the highest-paid civil service staff of any of the member states, which at present is... the United States. (At least we're doing something right in the eyes of UN staff.)

Each undersecretary-general—and there are more than thirty — received salaries of $189,952 annually (plus a variety of perks) as of January 1, 2005 according to the UN's own web site and its Office of "Human Resources Management." [14] To put all of this in perspective, the Secretary of State of the United States and other U.S. Cabinet Members received $180,100 for 2005—nearly $10,000 less than what Annan's underlings are paid.[15] Meanwhile, he himself reportedly receives base salary of about $227,000.[16]

Despite their munificent paychecks, program managers are not held directly accountable for meeting program objectives because UN regulations perversely prevent linking program effectiveness and impact with performance. According to a U.S. General Accounting Office status report to Congress on UN reforms, UN officials admitted "that a more mature program monitoring and evaluation system is needed before program managers can be held responsible for program performance."[17]

The United Nations calls its method of determining the salaries of its professional staff the "Noblemaire Principle" In reality, it is an example of the UN establishment's toxic culture of "noblesse" entitlement, the payoff for remaining loyal to the organization at all cost.

Apostles of Arrogance

Just as important as Annan's "circle the wagons" mentality is his endless arrogance, borne firmly on the gaudy wings of self-righteousness and perceived moral superiority. Of course, given the endlessly self-congratulatory environment which has cosseted Annan throughout his career, such beliefs are no surprise. It's from that same foul stew where the concept of the UN as being invested with "unique legitimacy" comes from.

Nor is Annan the only purveyor of such idealistic claptrap. To the contrary, such beliefs run rampant in globalist circles. Two of Annan's most influential senior advisors—economics professor Jeffrey Sachs and businessman-cum-environmentalist Maurice Strong—share them. Both are confirmed globalists who believe in the necessity of redirecting resources—by whatever means necessary—from the developed countries to developing countries in order to "save the world."

Sachs is the director of the Earth Institute at Columbia University and was appointed as special advisor to Kofi Annan. His charge is to devise and implement the largest wealth redistribution plan ever created in the vain and pompous hope of being the man who ended world poverty in one fell swoop, via a vicious bit of whimsy known as the Millennium Development Project.

Ironically, even as Sachs casts himself as the hero in this little morality play, an apostle of truth and righteousness arrayed in lonely splendor against the selfish capitalists of the United States, it's those very same capitalists who endow Columbia University lavishly enough to allow Sachs the leisure time to flog the rest of us with his vacuous utopian nonsense. Oh, the humanity!

Maurice Strong shares Sachs' penchant for shoveling American taxpayer dollars at the rest of the world's problems, but he's been trying to get his hand in the till a lot longer. Strong's connection with the UN started in the '70s. He has worked on many UN projects over the years, organizing a succession of global environmental summits and initiating the infamous Kyoto Protocol on global warming which may yet prove his undoing

Yet another in the long line of shameless hypocrites surrounding Kofi Annan, Strong is a controversial figure, whose many intertwining business and political interests have managed to even entangle him in the Oil-for-Food scandal. Although not found by the Volcker committee investigation to have committed actual wrong-doing in this case, the cumulative effect of Strong's questionable associations and behavior led to a break in his *official* ties to the United Nations in July 2005–although not necessarily a break, as far as can be determined, with his disciple Kofi Annan

Strong's ideas are in synch with Sachs' views. In large part, they provide the dubious intellectual underpinnings for Annan's continuous efforts to expand the UN's traditional role into one of global governance. Though unelected and relatively unknown, both Strong and Sachs believe they have "silver bullet" solutions to the world's social and economic problems, all of which could be solved quickly if only the dastardly U.S. could be pressured into complying with the dictates of the "global community," of which Sachs and Strong consider themselves both charter and Very Important Members.

Never mind that their vacuous and ill-conceived ideas have nothing to do with American priorities, as clearly expressed through our duly elected representatives. With the unrelenting encouragement of anti-American leaders like Jacques Chirac, Annan and his unelected high priests (and priestesses, for gender balance) continually submit, for Learned and Serious Consideration by other unelected elites, sweeping recommendations that cut across the historically accepted tenets of national sovereignty like a buzz saw.

Annan may talk the talk about reforming the UN's operations to make them more transparent and cost-effective, but his interest lies in expansion, not streamlining. Even if there were a shake-up at the top and some cosmetic changes, the momentum behind these proposals will not go away no matter how ridiculous—and dangerous—they are.

Phony Reformer

Annan showed his true feelings about the need for real reforms at the United Nations when he complained at a 1998 press conference, "I think we should be allowed to focus on our work and not face constant harassment of reform, reform, reform. We have done enough. It is an ongoing process. We want to focus on our essential tasks."[18]

At least he's been true to his word. Seven years have passed, and the United Nations still most resembles a bloated, overpaid bureaucracy busy with Tasks so Essential that no mere earthly system could ever measure its performance.

In fact, Annan and his allies have used the reform process to mask their true intentions. The much-heralded report of the panel commissioned by Annan to study reform of the United Nations, issued in December 2004, was a sop to those concerned about a more efficient process but in the end was nothing more than rearranging the deck chairs on the *Titanic*.

This panel, encumbered with the oddly Orwellian title of "High-Level Panel on Threats, Challenges and Change," glided over the UN's failure to provide for the collective security of its members. Nor did it address the issue of whether or not the UN has lost its moral bearings. There are no demands that the veil shielding the UN from public scrutiny be forced aside. Instead, the panel focused on ways to expand the Security Council with the goal of diluting the powers of the current five permanent members.

Despite its blatant omissions, or perhaps because of them, Kofi Annan praised the report, saying it "offers the United Nations a unique opportunity to refashion and renew our institutions," not to mention a unique opportunity to do a possible end-run around the balky United States.

Using this report as the starting point for his own package of recommendations entitled *"In Larger Freedom: Towards Development, Security and Human Rights for All,"* the secretary-general did offer a few grudging concessions to the UN's actual mission.[19] These included defining and addressing the terrorist threat, establishing a "Democracy Fund," strengthening the UN's internal audit function and replacing the scandalous Commission on Human Rights (taken over by the worst abusers of human rights) with a new UN Human Rights Council that is elevated in status and stricter as to which states it will admit to membership. But he also included Professor Jeffrey Sachs' program calling for a massive transfer of wealth from the United States and other wealthy countries to the more undeveloped parts of the world.

The secretary-general wanted all of his recommendations to be accepted at the Millennium+5 Summit meeting as a "package deal with something to offer everyone," as his spokesman Fred Eckhard explained.[20] What the United States gets out of this "something for everyone" deal—besides the shaft—was not clarified. Indeed, the summit adopted a humorously named *"outcome document"* that contained no real outcomes at all for defining terrorism, establishing a human rights commission truly devoted to human rights rather than anti-American propaganda, or instituting budget reforms and an independent audit function.

What *is* clear, however, is that in order to even have a chance of ever getting anything meaningful out of the UN, especially with regards to terrorism or reform, we'll have to pay for the *broader* mandate its supporters want to foist on us—and pay and pay again, via what Jeffrey Sachs calls, in typical globalist doublespeak, "innovative sources of financing."

Kofi's Strong Man

As we've seen, the UN gets plenty of support from NGOs. The relationship between the UN insiders and the NGO outsiders is a symbiotic one.

The NGO phenomenon started out modestly enough. These organizations contributed ideas and research to various United Nations agencies, and assisted them in the implementation of certain UN approved—and legitimate—programs such as emergency relief work and election monitoring.

But in the last decade this focus has changed dramatically. New NGOs have sprung up out of nowhere and have been given official status to participate in UN undertakings. There are now thousands of these groups, not only sitting at the same table with their UN counterparts, but snuffling from the same money trough. This in turn enables the NGOS to form coalitions and networks with *other* NGOs, which allows them to coordinate their efforts to make the UN, fount of so many riches, the foundation for global governance. How convenient is *that?* Perhaps *this* is what Annan's spokesman was referring to with regard to the "package deal with something to offer everyone."

Better yet from their point of view, the supposed "legitimacy" conferred by the NGOs' "consultative status" to the UN allows these unelected groups to exert influence over a multitude of policies that impact U.S. sovereignty.

And nobody has played in this dubious arena with more success than Maurice Strong. For many years, he has controlled a powerful international NGO network, vast sources of funding, top-notch political and business associations and access to the highest levels of the United Nations leadership.

Strong, a native of Canada, started out as, of all things, an oil man. A hypocrite of the first magnitude, he continues to profit from the oil business while advocating any number of radical environmental causes. In the late 1960s, he became head of the Canadian International Development Agency, using this post to advance his internationalist as well as his business interests.

On the business side, despite his apparent hatred for all the oil companies stand for, he has somehow managed to swallow his disdain long enough to climb to the top of a long list of energy and development companies: the Canadian Development Corp., International Energy Development Corp., Strouest Holdings Inc., Procor Inc., Ontarion Hydro, AZL Resources Inc., Canada's Power Corporation, and Canada's national oil company Petro Canada.

When he wasn't in the oil fields or the boardroom, Strong was organizing a globalist power-grab under the banner of environmental protection. After coming to the attention of then United Nations Secretary-General U Thant, Strong was asked to organize the Stockholm Conference on the Human Environment in 1972, which later became the progenitor of the UN Earth Summits. A United Nations-sponsored effort called Earth Watch was set up to coordinate and catalyze environmental observation activities among all UN agencies.

Strong became the first director of the newly created UN Environmental Program shortly after Stockholm. During the 1980's, he was appointed to the post of executive coordinator of the UN Office for Emergency Operations in Africa, where he ran the $3.5 billion famine-relief effort in Somalia and Ethiopia.

Strong used his business connections to support his globalist political agenda while in turn utilizing his political connections to help advance his far-flung business interests. While these two parts of his life would seem to be at odds with each other, Strong himself, with the complete lack of embarrassment that characterizes the dedicated globalist, described himself years ago as "a socialist in ideology, a capitalist in methodology."[21] Talk about chutzpah!

Son of Malthus

Strong is obsessed with the notion that population and economic growth, driven by capital investment, entrepreneurship, efficient production and free trade will inevitably denude the earth of its vital natural resources. Apparently, he has enough to live on and wishes to deprive less worthy individuals of the chance to better themselves via the same methods of exploitation and enhancement of natural resources he's used to such rich effect.

In any event, Strong leveraged his political and business connections to organize the United Nations Conference on Environment and Development—the so-called "Earth Summit"—which took place in Rio de Janeiro in 1992. The attendees included 108 representatives at level of heads of state or government and some 2,400 representatives of non-governmental organizations. An additional 17,000 people attended the parallel NGO Forum.

Strong used the Earth Summit and his own Earth Council NGO to push for the adoption and implementation worldwide of a document that became known as Agenda 21—an 800-page blueprint for "sustainable development" in the 21st century. Added to this was the adoption of legally binding documents on climate, which spawned the Kyoto Protocol on global warming, and on biological diversity addressing a wide variety of living species.

The vaguely titled Agenda 21 consists of forty chapters devoted to environmental conflicts ranging from ozone depletion to deforestation, each outlining specific actions to resolve these problems. Those actions—anti-growth and draconian to boot—consist primarily of using "international instrumentalities" to control population growth, force a slowdown of economic activity in the industrialized nations and to divert, by United Nations fiat, a massive amount of wealth from successful economies—or perhaps we should say, economies that *were* successful before they were forced to slow down growth—to failed ones.

Here we have the globalist philosophy in a nutshell. Instead of exploring creative and practical ways to harness global market forces and stimulate worldwide growth through innovative technologies and free trade, Agenda 21 does the opposite. The preamble states that "[T]he developmental and environmental objectives of Agenda 21 will require a substantial flow of new and additional financial resources to developing countries in order to cover the incremental costs for the actions they have to undertake to deal with global environmental problems and to accelerate sustainable development. Financial resources are also required for strengthening the capacity of international institutions for the implementation of Agenda 21."

Indeed, the secretariat of the Rio Conference Earth Summit "estimated the average annual costs (1993-2000) of implementing in developing countries the activities in Agenda 21 to be over $600 billion, including about $125 billion on grant or concessional terms from the international community"[22]—read, the United States.

The thesis behind "sustainable development," the very core of Agenda 21 and Maurice Strong's own philosophy, is at once simple, breathtakingly naïve, and totalitarian. Unless the current human inhabitants of earth begin to respect the planet and its non-human inhabitants by radically reducing consumption and bringing population growth under control, future generations will be deprived of the basic elements for life on earth.

According to the authors of Agenda 21, "[T]he growth of world population and production combined with unsustainable consumption patterns places increasingly severe stress on the life-supporting capacities of our planet."[23] If this all sounds familiar, it's not surprising. This is no more than a rehash of the discredited theory of Thomas Robert Malthus, the British economist whose 1798 essay predicted that population growth would outstrip the growth of the world's food supply, leading to a catastrophe of subsistence-level living conditions.

At least Malthus, whose name remains synonymous with his discredited theory to this day, died before experiencing the powerful growth engine that is technical change unleashed by a free market economy. The authors of Agenda 21 have no such excuse.

Strong has shown his own Malthusian leanings on repeated occasions, declaring in 1997, for example, that "we cannot afford to be complacent in light of evidence that we continue along a pathway that is not sustainable while the driving forces of population growth in developing countries and unsustainable patterns of production and consumption in industrialized countries persist."[24] Please note that Strong was attacking the very production of energy that he has been profiting from via the slew of energy companies listed above!

Maurice Strong has been a forceful figure pushing for the UN as the manager of sustainable development programs. He has, for example, inspired NGOs staffed by presumably educated people to go forth chanting the mantra of "sustainable development" based on a centuries-old theory that they should know has been continually disproved.[25] He has called for the imposition of a variety of global taxes to pay for "sustainable development," including a tax on air fuel, international financial transactions and even on the use of the Internet in developed countries. Since "sustainable development" programs would result in significantly lower numbers of humans needing food, shelter, etc., one wonders where all that excess tax money is going to be spent.

Strong's Earth Council is an example of an NGO that has acquired enormous influence over the years, developing an international network of tributary NGOs to complement its own "work," while leading the drive to implement Agenda 21 at national levels. Strong has used his leadership of the Earth Council to press for a more powerful United Nations—one that would make his benefactor Kofi Annan even stronger.

However, even Strong isn't delusional enough to think that his airy-fairy-tale vision of a world-wide governance structure, replete with unelected and unaccountable philosopher-kings (and queens), can be installed without overcoming significant and entrenched opposition. In the oddly titled essay *Stockholm to Rio: A Journey Down a Generation*, Strong is quoted as saying:

> Strengthening the role the United Nations can play...will require serious examination of the need to extend into the international arena the rule of law and the principle of taxation to finance agreed actions which provide the basis for governance at the national level. But this will not come about easily. Resistance to such changes is deeply entrenched...[26]

In 1995, Willy Brandt of Germany and 28 other self-proclaimed "global leaders" set up the Commission on Global Governance. This group proposed a "global civic ethic" as a way of subverting traditional ideas of national sovereignty and self-determination. Strong eagerly leapt into the cause.[27]

Strong and his co-commission members came up with a document with the cheerfully child-like title, *Our Global Neighborhood* (sort of like Hillary Clinton's *It Takes a Village* for the globalist set) in which they concluded that "[I]t is our firm conclusion that the United Nations must continue to play a central role in global governance"—a role conspicuously absent from the UN Charter. The commission was not an official body of the United Nations. It was, however, endorsed by Boutros Boutros-Ghali and Kofi Annan and was funded through two trust funds of the United Nations Development Program, nine national governments, and several foundations, including the MacArthur Foundation, the Ford Foundation, and the Carnegie Corporation.

Influenced heavily by Maurice Strong's thinking, the Commission on Global Governance based its recommendations on the belief that human activities have irreversible environmental impacts and that they must be "managed" by bureaucrats steeped in the guiding principles of sustainable development. Among the Commission's recommendations are specific proposals to expand the authority of the United Nations to include many of the globalist tools that Harry Truman wisely rejected—most notably global taxation, a standing UN army, a global court and an end to the veto power of the permanent members of the Security Council.

The Commission on Global Governance conceived "liberty" to be a "core value" of global governance.[28] But its conception of liberty bears no resemblance to the American Constitution's model of limited government and individual freedoms. To the contrary, the Commission's definition of "liberty" means the beneficent hand of global governance compelling richer states, corporations and even families to take mandatory actions to end what the Commission's unelected members have self-defined as deprivation, economic dislocation, oppression based on gender or sexual orientation, abuse of children, debt bondage, and other social and economic patterns. In other words, it's the liberty to pick *our* pockets.

"Just Like Religion," only Strong-er

Maurice Strong does not just operate at the strategic and tactical political level. He considers environmentalism to be a religion. Strong has used his Earth Council NGO to help create and promote his "Earth Charter." In Maurice Strong's own words, the *"real goal* of the Earth Charter is that it will in fact become *like the Ten Commandments..."* (emphasis added)[29] Mohamed El-Ashry, the UN Foundation Senior Fellow and a dedicated environmentalist as well as a close friend of Mr. Strong's, told this author that he viewed the Earth Charter as a set of principles "just like religion."

That Strong would choose to couch his environmental globalism in religious terms comes as no surprise. Strong lived on a ranch in Colorado for several years where he was exposed to New Age thinking. He later integrated this philosophy into his United Nations-related activities.

A World Summit on Peace and Time was convened on June 22, 1999 at the UN-owned, marvelously named University for Peace in Costa Rica—which also happened to be headed by Strong, who was a busy man indeed. Clearly, the participants had some time on *their* hands, which they used to announce, in all seriousness, that the Gregorian Calendar should be replaced with the "World Thirteen Moon 28-day Calendar of Peace."

Their resolution stated that despite over 2,000 years of use by millions of satisfied customers, "[B]y rational discourse and common sense, it has been determined that the Gregorian Calendar does not represent a true or accurate standard of measure or belong to any systematic science of time, and hence, is worthy of reform."[30] Alas, Kofi Annan could not attend this Summit, but he did send a letter of acknowledgment.

No doubt drafted by some of the same great and endlessly profound minds that called for the "Calendar of Peace," the Earth Charter is seen as a way to save the "Sacred Earth" as our planet is sometimes called in the New Age gatherings that Strong attended.[31]

In 1999, Strong gave a lecture in Madras, India entitled "Hunger, Poverty, Population and Environment," in which he laid bare his soul on the need for an Earth Charter:

> One of my disappointments in the results of the Earth Summit was our inability to obtain an agreement on an Earth Charter to define a set of moral and ethical principles for the conduct of people and nations toward each other and the earth as the basis for achieving a sustainable way of life on our planet. Governments were simply not ready for it. They agreed on a Rio Declaration, but, they did not complete the job of agreeing on an Earth Charter, and therefore people are now taking [this up]. The Earth Council has joined with many other organizations to undertake this piece of unfinished business from Rio through a global campaign designed to stimulate dialogue and enlist of the contributions of people everywhere to the formulation of a People's Earth Charter... [32]

The charter itself, which reads like an ode to fuzzy puppies and cuddly kittens written by a dewey-eyed naïf, is good for a laugh, but hardly qualifies as a document from which to derive a serious set of governing principles, such as the U.S. Constitution. Nevertheless, it is this document, one created by unelected New-Age trust-funders, that Strong believes should govern us all. (For your compare-and-contrast convenience, visit http:// www.usconstitution.net/ for an online copy of the U.S. Constitution and http://www.earthcharter.org/files/chart er/charter.pdf to view the Earth Charter.)

But while he talks a good game, Strong's own checkered business career hardly lives up to his own ethical principles. For example, the Earth Charter advocates "[Placing] the burden of proof on those who argue that a proposed activity will not cause significant harm, and make the responsible parties liable for environmental harm."[33]

Yet after he acquired his large ranch in Colorado, Mr. Strong filed a claim for water rights and formed American Water Development Inc., to extract water from underground and sell to Denver. His company fought a lawsuit by local farmers for four years, eventually losing when it was discovered that his plan would have destroyed 25,000 acres of wetland. It would appear that he put the burden of proof and expense on the locals to prove environmental damage rather than accept social responsibility himself at the outset of his project.[34]

Strong's Earth Charter also calls for "[Eliminating] corruption in all public and private institutions" — a pretty sentiment, but not one that Strong has necessarily chosen to implement within his own operations. Coming under investigation by the Volcker committee in conjunction with the Oil-for-Food scandal is not the first time Strong's ethical behavior has been questioned. Strong has come under fire for his dealings with companies on both sides of the U.S.-Canadian border

As chairman of Ontario Hydro, North America's largest utility company, Strong recommended that the company purchase a 31,000 acre Costa Rican rain forest, ostensibly as an offset to gas emissions from oil or coal-generating activities in the area. The local Indian tribes opposed the purchase. Only later was it discovered that the purchase would have promoted ecotourism to the financial benefit of Strong's own hotel in Costa Rica.[35]

Similarly, Strong was on the board of directors of a now—defunct American company called Molten Technology, which became embroiled in a controversy about allegedly improper campaign contributions during our 1996 Presidential elections. Allegations against the company were made at about the same time it was receiving lucrative government contracts. Strong was sued in a securities class action suit following the collapse of the company's stock in October 1996. Apparently, Strong managed to sell some of his shares before the company's collapse and eventual bankruptcy.[36]

Even to this day, Strong is violating the principles of his own Earth Charter as he broadens his business horizons to China. The Earth Charter commands its followers to "[I]nternalize the full environmental and social costs of goods and services in the selling price and enable consumers to identify products that meet the highest social and environmental standards." But this edict has not stopped Strong from getting involved with a venture called Visionary Vehicles that is partnering with Chery Automobile Company, a major Chinese automobile manufacturer, to build cars—including gas-guzzling SUVs—for export to the United States. These cars will be priced 30% lower than their American competitors.[37]

Chery Automobile Company is headquartered in Wuhu, one of China's most polluted cities. Much of this pollution comes from Wuhu's coal-fired power company. Chery has expanded its manufacturing facilities, presumably imposing more power demands on Wuhu's environmentally unsound power system. Strong is the Chairman of Visionary Vehicles' Technology and Environmental Advisory Board.

Given his Earth Charter's philosophy on internalizing all environmental and social costs in the pricing of products and etc., isn't it puzzling that the environmental and social costs to the Chinese people from the increased power demands of Chery's manufacturing facilities do not appear to be internalized in the cut-rate pricing of the Chinese manufactured cars that Visionary Vehicles plans to export to the United States?

Whatever Strong's ethical shortcomings, he has not given up trying to impose his Earth Charter on the rest of us. That it wasn't officially adopted at the Millennium Summit or at the 2002 World Earth Summit wasn't for lack of trying.

In January 2002, the actual Earth Charter document was displayed at the United Nations. It was carried in "The Ark of Hope," a specially-created two-hundred pound hand-crafted chest, the comical nature of which is worth examining in a bit more detail. Globalist activities are sometimes beyond parody.

According to the Ark's very own web site, "The Ark was designed and painted by Vermont, USA artist Sally Linder, built by cabinetmaker Kevin Jenness and lined by fabric artist Beth Haggart. It was crafted from a single plank of sycamore maple from a sustainable forest in Germany. The five painted panels that form the sides and top of the Ark represent the flora and fauna of the world as seen through the images of traditional artists. Each panel visualizes a season, a direction, an element, and a universal symbol. Symbols of faith from traditional religions and indigenous societies surround the top panel of "Spirit" that honors the children and young animals of the world." And most importantly, "The 96" carrying poles are unicorn horns which render evil ineffective."[38]

Yes, you read that right—"unicorn horns which render evil ineffective." And *these* are the people who want—rather, who *demand*—the right to control this nation's destiny?

Apparently so. Kofi Annan's advisory panel issued a statement in February 2002 expressing enthusiastic support for the Earth Charter and recommending that the 2002 World Earth Summit recognize the Charter as an important ethical instrument toward "sustainability." Only at the very last minute did sanity prevail and the reference to the Earth Charter get deleted.

But Maurice Strong's Earth Council and its NGO cohorts press on. Strong testified at a hearing of the United States Senate Committee on the Environment and Public Works and the Committee on Foreign Relations on July 24, 2002, saying that America's preoccupation with the 9/11 terrorist attacks should not "sidetrack or undermine our efforts to achieve economic, environmental and social sustainability and security."

Nor is his advocacy limited to lobbying Congressional representatives who really should know better than to give Mr. "Hi, I'm an evil-deflecting, non-existent mythical creature" Strong the time of day. (Perhaps they're operating on the "World Thirteen Moon 28-day Calendar of Peace.")

A grass-roots effort worldwide is underway to get the Earth Charter adopted at local and national levels, including an active movement among fringe groups within the United States. Strong's wife, who can clearly afford to be a devoted environmentalist, has worked through UN funding networks such as its Development Program to preach to millions of young people what she considers the spiritual and practical dimensions of environmentalism.

According to the executive director of NGO Earth Charter USA, the "Earth Charter has been translated into twenty-eight languages and has been widely distributed throughout the world. It is now recognized by a steadily growing number of governments, organizations, institutions, and individuals..."[39] In addition, through the efforts of such organizations as the Youth and Pedagogy Community Working Groups, the Earth Charter is being utilized as a teaching tool—or more correctly, an indoctrination tool—at all levels in U.S. schools.[40]

As of this writing, the members of the Earth Council NGO and their allies hope to use bottom-up pressure to convince the UN General Assembly to formally adopt the Earth Charter at its fall 2005 Millennium+5 summit session. Chances are they'll fail. But strengthened by their belief in unicorns, the Tooth Fairy and Ostara (the pagan predecessor of the Easter Bunny — no religious icons here, we're activists!) they'll no doubt regroup on some American foundation's dime to try again.

Jeffrey Sachs: The Nutty Professor

If Maurice Strong's Earth Charter seems like the most radical departure from the UN's original mission imaginable, it just means you haven't heard of the UN's Millennium Project.

At the United Nations Millennium Summit in September 2000, some world leaders placed the amply discredited theory of "sustainable development" and its obvious corollary, a massive transfer of wealth from rich to poor countries, at the center of the UN's plate by adopting the Millennium Development Goals (MDGs).

The MDGs set specific targets for reducing poverty, hunger, disease, illiteracy, environmental degradation, and discrimination against women by 2015. A shadowy consortium of agenda-driven NGOs was responsible for "defining" the targets, as usual using opaque methods not open to public scrutiny. And the United States, also as usual, is expected to pick up the lion's share of the bill.

An enthusiastic supporter of anything that will bring more power and influence to the UN, Kofi Annan embraced the Millennium Project, the aim of which was to determine the best means of implementing the amorphous, ethereal MDGs in the developing countries they are supposed to aid.

And of course, there's no one like a left-wing economist to really Get Things Done. Our superhero in this case is Jeffrey Sachs, the former Harvard professor who now heads Columbia's Earth Institute and one of Annan's Special Advisor cronies, just like Maurice Strong.

One of the keys to successful implementation of any program is having available solid, quantifiable information laid out in an impartial, dispassionate and literate manner. It is safe to say that the information provided by Sachs to support the implementation of the MDGs fails on all counts.

Millennium Project's on-going, ideologically-skewed "research" is performed by ten thematically-orientated task forces—sort of a globalist theme park. The task forces are comprised of academics (such self-professed intellectuals are what passes for "regular people" in the globalist world) and other contributors from the public and private sectors, civil society organizations, and UN agencies. Most participants come from outside the UN system and have been self-identified as "leaders" in their fields. Since the MDGs have been created in complete secrecy, there's no way to judge the credentials or credibility of the people involved. But we don't need to know who's specifically involved to conclude that the results have been pre-ordained.

Sachs' Blame-America Bias

In his role as director of the Millennium Project, Professor Sachs is supposed to be objective. But he has displayed his prejudices over and over again, accusing the United States variously of "barbarism" and of being the "developed world's stingiest donor."

In an article entitled "The March to Barbarism," he equated the savage beheadings of innocent people to the isolated instances of abuse at the Abu Ghraib prison. Sachs declared that "[T]he United States seems as capable of barbarism as anyone else, as the abuses at the Abu Ghraib prison make clear. Much of the time the barbarism in Iraq goes unrecorded, as when American tanks sweep into Iraqi neighborhoods and kill dozens of innocents in the name of fighting 'insurgents.' But barbarism is found in many quarters, as the grisly beheading of an American hostage made clear."[41]

Sachs would have us believe that Hitler's Germany was "not uniquely barbarous," but was only responding to tough economic conditions that were not of its own making. "Many historians have argued that German society under Hitler was somehow uniquely evil. False. Germany was destabilized by defeat in World War I, a harsh peace in 1919, hyperinflation in the 1920s, and the Great Depression of the 1930s, but was otherwise not uniquely barbarous," says Sachs.[42]

And the United States, according to Sachs, is guilty of more than barbarism in war. It is immorally selfish as well. He believes that the United States has too much wealth and is guilty of "grossly irresponsible neglect of the world's poor."[43] He also believes that the United States is making itself vulnerable to terrorism by refusing to give away much more money to undeveloped countries.[44] By Sachs' perverse logic, since economic help would have pacified Hitler's Germany, surely the fanatic Islamic terrorists can be made peaceful and productive with some big development grants! A Bin Laden Amusement Park perhaps?

In a speech to the World Bank on March 1, 2004 concerning "Environmentally and Socially Sustainable Development," Sachs sounded like a Strong clone as he discussed the challenges a coerced donor community might face attempting to meet the demands of reducing by half the number of those living under an amorphous and creatively defined "poverty line." The United States is, of course, his main target even though this country provides nearly a quarter of the United Nations' entire budget and is by far the largest contributor of financial aid in absolute dollar terms to developing countries.[45]

Sachs said the Millennium Development Goals are *intended to compel* donor countries *to live up to their "responsibilities" as defined by a shadowy group of non-elected elitists.* While many humanitarians have campaigned for lenders to forgive some third world debts and the world's leading economies including the United States have responded positively to this idea,

Sachs has gone so far as to recommend that Africa should simply ignore its $201 billion debt burden altogether. "If they won't cancel the debts I would suggest obstruction; you do it yourselves," he advised.[46]

Apparently, all that is needed to end world poverty and the world health crisis is a large transfer of wealth via coerced "giving." Who knew? Sachs repeated the demand for compulsory giving at a conference attended by nearly 3,000 NGO representatives in September 2004[47]

In other words, forget the political and economic reform so needed in developing countries. Pouring money down a sinkhole is what it's all about.

The Millennium Project Sinkhole

No surprise then, that the report issued by Professor Sachs' UN Millennium Project in January 2005, entitled "Investing in Development—a Practical Plan to Achieve the Millennium Development Goals," concludes that wealthy developed countries, particularly the United States, *must be either persuaded or forced* into transferring vast amounts of wealth to poorer nations in order to supposedly eradicate world poverty and disease. How did it reach that conclusion? Smoke and mirrors, combined with creative accounting and outright distortions.

Focusing on the costs of achieving all of the Millennium Development Goals at the country-by-country level, each of the ten Task Forces determined the key "interventions" required to meet their particular MDG. Local experts in the countries concerned were asked what they'd need to solve the identified problems, which included building roads, cleaning water, upgrading sanitation, building and staffing health clinics, training doctors, building schools, and educating teachers.

Information was then collected on the theoretical unit costs for meeting the unmet needs. Next, calculations were run to determine what the developing countries would require in or-

der to overcome their gaps in financing these solutions—
calculations based on data provided by self-serving local
sources and enhanced by the self-serving Task Forces. And
developed countries would be expected to foot the bills to
cover these huge financing gaps, more or less on faith.

There was, of course, no critical analysis of whether these
goals were actually achievable given the particular political,
economic, human resource and educational constraints existing in each country, or whether additional aid could even be
absorbed effectively or just wasted, and of course,
zero/zilch/nada accountability. For Sachs the key to solving all
problems is to continue throwing money at them, trusting that
recipient countries—some of them irredeemably corrupt—will
internalize the UN's "feel-good" ethic, strap on their unicorn
horns and get the job done.

As to how much the developed countries are supposed to
pay, well, baby, let the good times roll! Each "donor" country
is supposed to "donate" based on the size of its economy, as
opposed to paying out exactly what's needed. True to his left-
wing agenda, Sachs has hijacked objectivity by manipulating
data to meet his pre-conceived notions. He "proves" why
American taxpayers should pay exponentially more than they
now do to single-handedly lift the world's poor out of their
"poverty trap"—even where the trap is set by their own corrupt, oppressive governments.

Sachs wants to compel each developed country to contribute a fixed 0.7 percent of its GDP (Gross Domestic Product, a
measure of total wealth based on the total value of all goods
and services produced within the area being measured during
a specified period that is very closely correlated with Gross
National Income for comparison purposes) towards global
funding of the Millennium Development Goals.[48] He argues—
incorrectly—that the United States specifically "committed" to
this level of contribution when it signed the 800-page Agenda
21 at the Rio Earth Summit in 1992 that included one para-

graph on the 0.7 percent target. He claims that this target was reaffirmed at a summit meeting held in Monterrey, Mexico ten years later.

Aside from the fact that these were entirely non-binding general expressions of good intentions with no time frame attached, the U.S. went on the record at both conferences to distance itself from *any* pledge to that effect. Maurice Strong, the organizer of the 1992 Rio summit and an eyewitness to what actually happened, conceded that there was no binding commitment. In fact, he complained that "[T]he United States in particular was reducing its foreign aid budget and was adamant that it would not sign on to anything that required an increase in these expenditures."

Alan Larson, U.S. Under Secretary for Economic, Business and Agricultural Affairs, said just before the 2002 Monterrey conference: "First of all, I would like to point out that the U.S. has never been a party to the 0.7-percent agreement target."[49] Indeed, the only specific undertaking by the United States was to increase its development aid to 0.15 percent by 2006. The Bush administration in fact reached that target in 2003—three years ahead of schedule![50]

But of course, as the Wall Street Journal has noted, "The rest of the world is besotted by 0.7%" even though, as John Bolton is quoted saying in the same article, "The levels of ODA (official development assistance) don't necessarily tell you anything about the effectiveness of the development policies of the recipient country. The main thing they need is sound economic policy domestically, not hostile to foreign investment, open to foreign trade and open to international markets."[51]

Rather than acknowledge the U.S.'s ongoing commitment to developmental aid, Sachs continually lambastes the United States for falling far short of his precious 0.7 percent target—a target that continues to exert a seductive aura in the globalists' world, even though it has no legitimate economic underpinning whatsoever. He points out that the United States placed last in order of ranking of the major developed countries when ranked in terms of "Official Development Aid" as a percentage of gross national income. By contrast, Norway receives encomiums from the good professor for already meeting the 0.7 percent target.[52]

This is a classic example of Sachs' manipulating data to support his specious arguments. Using globalist double-talk, Sachs vastly understates this country's strong commitment to helping the world's poor. Again, the Wall Street Journal nails it: "Yet when a fantasy takes place in fantasyland—that is, when the UN talks about 7%—it acquires a kind of plausibility and even the force of necessity, like a magic broom in a Harry Potter novel."[53]

The Organization for Economic Cooperation and Development ("OECD") defines what constitutes Official Development Aid and compiles data on each country's contributions. According to its report for 2003, the United States continues to lead the world in terms of volume, providing 23.4% of the total amount of Official Development Assistance ($69 billion dollars). To put this in perspective, in absolute dollar terms, the United States' Official Development Assistance came to $16.2 billion in 2003, compared to $8.88 billion for the next highest contributor, Japan, and $2.04 billion for Norway.[54]

In relative terms, the U.S.'s share of the total amount of Official Development Assistance (23.4%) is somewhat more than the U.S.'s share of the world's total GDP, which is approximately 21.3% according to GDP estimate figures compiled in the CIA's fact book for 2003 (U.S. GDP—$10.99 trillion dollars; World GDP—$51.48 trillion dollars).

Note too that the United Nations uses a relative metric—a member state's share of the world economy—as the means to calculate what that member state should pay toward the UN's regular budget and not an absolute metric, such as a fixed percentage of each country's GDP.

When such factors as trade, investment, security, and technology assistance are added to the more restrictive categories of expenditures currently used to calculate Official Development Assistance, America's overall commitment to development looks even better. The OECD Development Assistance Committee itself recently reached a consensus to expand its definition of Official Development Aid by including such items as assistance relating to technology, security system reform to improve democratic governance and civilian control, civilian activities for peace-building, conflict prevention and conflict resolution.[55] The United States' significant contributions in these areas will now get the belated official credit they deserve.

And all this, of course, without even acknowledging that the huge amount spent by the U.S. to provide a military shield for much of the civilized world frees up Western Europe and other developed countries to spend as they wish on aid to less developed countries.

Finally, there is the ongoing and massive outpouring of private donations from the American people and organizations—approximately $34 billion in the year 2000 alone, according to former assistant administrator of the U.S. Agency for International Development, Carol Adelman[56]—that should be added in order to get a complete picture of U.S. aid to developing countries.[57]

Consider as one dramatic example the Global Alliance for Vaccines and Immunization. This is a successful public-private partnership which is doing the *real* work of health care that Sachs just talks about, bringing vaccines to the world's poor at very low cost. It has received $1.5 billion dollars from the Bill and Melinda Gates Foundation alone, as well as hundreds of millions of dollars more from the federal government and private donors, not to mention cheap vaccines from U.S. drug companies.[58]

Since it doesn't serve his goals, Sachs downplays the incredible volume of American private giving, saying that much of it consists of income transfers or remittances from family members working in the United States to their relatives abroad. But even if Sachs is accurate on this point—which is questionable—it hardly matters.

Remittances are in fact one of the best ways to improve lives in developing countries. When family members earn enough money in the United States to send financial help to relatives remaining in their home countries, the U.S. economy is enabling the most direct kind of personal giving. Family remittances deliver financial assistance directly from loved ones to those who most need it without any bureaucratic interference. (Perhaps it's that aspect that Sachs objects to.)

Money going directly for food, housing and health care has obvious immediate benefits. But repatriated capital also provides financing for home-grown investments, particularly when funneled through the local hometown associations[59] that emigrants often use to ensure that their private donations are going to finance just the development projects that local communities need most.

Far from being "irrelevant," as Sachs insists, remittances should be encouraged. They are a key part of any sensible strategy to stimulate growth through locally sponsored investments. They reduce poverty and improve living standards in developing countries. The United States is a leading source country for such remittances.[60]

Despite all of the evidence that the U.S. leads the world in total public and private contributions to developing countries, Sachs insists that ours is the stingiest country in the developed world when it comes to providing aid to the world's poor. That is because this self-appointed Very Important Person wants the United States to shoulder the entire burden of the world's problems itself, because anything less is a sign of unconscionable selfishness and of course, as the bumper sticker tells us, Selfishness is Bad.

If Sachs had his way and the United States were required to pay 0.7 percent of the total value of goods and services it produces into some pet project, the United States alone would have paid in excess of $70 billion in 2003—*more than the entire amount contributed by all countries that year.*

Looking to 2015, the year when the Millennium Development Goals are supposedly to be achieved, the United States would be paying nearly $140 billion a year for development assistance under the "0.7% solution"—more than the entire amount all low-income countries would need to close their financial gap of $135 billion in order to meet the Millennium Development Goals, based on Sachs' own projections. After that point, would we get a rebate? Not likely.

Despite overwhelming evidence that the U.S. is doing plenty for the world's poor, Sachs sticks to the trademark globalist mantras of "tax, tax, tax" and "more, more, more." *Does Sachs not realize that that corruption alone has already cost Africa nearly $150 billion dollars a year, according to the African Union?*[61]

Of course, it wouldn't benefit Sachs or his globalist henchpersons to let the rest of us in on what their policies would *really* cost American taxpayers. In his book *The End of Poverty,* Sachs mentions only a $50 billion dollar per year figure, which he suggests could be "easily financed" by a modest rollback in the Bush tax cuts and a five percent income tax surcharge on incomes above $200,000.[62] No problem! But the real truth lies on pg. 256 of the Millennium Project report. "[W]hile we urge all developed countries to commit to a specific year by which to achieve the 0.7 percent target they have set for themselves, *other innovative financing mechanisms may be necessary...Prominent among recent suggestions are international taxation on financial transactions or carbon emissions.*"[63]

Rather than addressing first and foremost how to end the corruption that is keeping existing aid from reaching millions, Sachs uses his report's own dubious statistics and self-aggrandizing "research" to pressure the United States into subsidizing his preferred social policies—and all under the mantle of the United Nations.

Sachs' Simple-Minded "Solution"

The Millennium Project report is, of course, a reflection of reality-challenged utopian thinking. The report assumes that the money extorted from "donor nations" will end up actually benefiting people suffering from hunger and disease, as opposed to corrupt government officials and bureaucrats.

It also usefully overlooks the wasteful military spending of some of the countries supposedly needing the most help. For instance, the report praises Ethiopia's efforts in identifying its needs and points to that country as a model case for much greater support. Indeed, in a 2003 interview Sachs praised Ethiopia as a "well-governed country" and said that development assistance to Ethiopia should be increased five-fold from $1 billion dollars per year to $5 billion dollars per year.

Nowhere in his remarks or in the subsequent UN Millennium Project report is it mentioned that, according to the *CIA Fact Book*, Ethiopia spent what amounted to 80% of the money it's been receiving for "development"—$800 million in fiscal year 2000—on military expenditures, as opposed to giving practical help to its citizens. Nor did Sachs mention the internecine warfare that has killed over 100,000 Ethiopians.[64]

And finally, when does Sachs propose to address the findings of the anti-graft watchdog Transparency International, which in 2003 reported that Ethiopia scored 2.5 on a scale of 10 in terms of governance?[65] Ethiopia is an authoritarian country, with a government that *clearly* deprives its people of basic political and economic rights.

Sachs dismisses the importance of this fact, declaring in *The End of Poverty* that "the charge of authoritarian rule as a basic obstacle to good governance in Africa is passé."[66] Sachs' declarations—so easy to disprove—would be laughable if not for the fact that many people believe the nonsense he spins—and that so many others are suffering because of it.

Indeed, the UN Millennium Project report's focus on more, more, more money as the prime solution to the problems besetting poor countries, particularly in Africa, conveniently overlooks the tribal, racial, religious and ethnic divisions that have spawned killing fields there.

It's not poverty that has caused these various horrors, any more than the Holocaust was caused by problems in the German economy. Sheer hatred breeds an unspeakable evil that neither foreign aid programs nor unicorn horns can prevent, no matter how noble the intentions. And real progress in meeting the basic needs of the peoples of these lands cannot and will not happen until the slaughter stops.

Even beyond the direct casualties of war, such violence destroys the social networks necessary to feed, clothe, shelter and provide health care—right down to the family unit itself. What good are hospitals if staffs and patients are forced to flee while vital hospital supplies are looted? What good is mosquito netting if the homes utilizing it are burned down? True development requires the dynamism provided by personal freedom and a predictable and transparent economic system, sustained and nurtured by honest government.

Sachs overlooks these hard realities, believing instead in his own "big bang" theory of economic reform. Simply go into a country and do something dramatic. Instantly the dynamics of the place will change and, by gum, great things will happen! But this infantile approach to grown-up problems is not just wrong, it has been *proven* wrong, and by Sachs himself.

Government control of resources leads to corruption—a salient fact which Sachs should have learned from his own participation in the Russian economic debacle of the 90's. Perhaps he forgot. More likely, he just can't face his own culpability. When talking about this policy disaster that hurt millions of Russians, Sachs ignores the human toll, instead conveniently focusing on linguistics. He disavows the term "shock therapy" which he says was a journalistic invention. But he sang a different tune in 1994, lauding his own cleverness in an article entitled *Understanding 'Shock Therapy.*[67]

One would think that a "professor" would understand a little psychology, but it's clear that Sachs never even took into account the very obvious and likely possibility that corrupt officials would exploit the chaotic Russian economy to enrich themselves and their friends—including, it's been alleged, members of Sachs' own Harvard Institute of International Development. Sachs himself has not been implicated in any wrong-doing. [68]

Nevertheless, "I still find myself quite shocked at the brazenness of the corruption over a period of many years, and find that the single most disappointing aspect of the Russian reform," Sachs told a radio interviewer in 1998.[69] The naiveté and sheer ignorance on display in that statement is what's actually shocking.

Simply throwing good money after bad does not solve the complex social and political problems deeply rooted in a country's history and demographics. Contrast Sach's shopworn ideas to those of the world renowned Peruvian economist Hernando De Soto, author of *The Mystery of Capitalism: Why Capitalism Triumphs in the West and Fails Everywhere Else.*

De Soto argues for unleashing the potential of capitalism by securing legally recognized property rights for the poor. He believes that instead of focusing only on how many people in the world live on less than $2 per day, the more relevant question is how many people legally own the land they live on and farm, own the businesses they operate and the other tangible assets they use. Without formal title, these assets represent "dead capital."

The best way for people in undeveloped countries to escape poverty, he argues, is not just through the receipt of more aid, but rather through formal legal recognition of their rights to tangible assets that they can then leverage to build wealth. Legal title to property that is properly recorded allows the owners to more easily sell their assets or use them as collateral for loans. In other words, the poorest people in the world may well have trillions of dollars worth of assets in their homes and their businesses that can potentially be monetized for their benefit—*if* they are fully integrated into their own countries' legal systems.

Thus, looking again to Ethiopia as an example, De Soto's approach would address an underlying cause of its peoples' plight. In the words of the *CIA 2003 Factbook*, "[U]nder Ethiopia's land tenure system, *the government owns all land* and provides long-term leases to the tenants; the system continues to hamper growth in the industrial sector as *entrepreneurs are unable to use land as collateral for loans.*"[70] (emphasis added)

Reforming Ethiopia's legal system and giving the peasants formal title to their own land, land that they can invest in and borrow against, is the kind of thinking that, if implemented, would get results. Sachs' repellent old "more money" mantra, on the other hand, will result in nothing more than stabilizing—or further entrenching—a vicious status quo.

In an enlightening UPI interview, De Soto asked why, if Professor Sachs is correct that more aid is the best answer to poverty, "has all the aid in the past 50 years not done much to help?" A comparison of Zambia and Korea is used to illustrate his point. In 1964, Zambia was two times wealthier than Korea. In 2002, Zambia was twenty-seven times *poorer* than Korea—despite receiving billions of dollars in aid.[71]

De Soto's thesis is borne out time and time again by analysis of real-world data. For example, America has provided over $144 billion (in constant 1999 U.S. dollars) in official development assistance to ninety-seven countries between 1980 and 2000. During this same period, these countries' median inflation adjusted per capita Gross Domestic Product *declined.* In another study by former World Bank development economist Bill Easterly, between 1950 and 1995 Western countries gave $1 trillion in aid in constant 1985 dollars, *without any demonstrative link in low-income countries between aid and growth.*[72]

Sachs has acknowledged that De Soto has some "interesting ideas," but criticized him for relying on a single factor to explain the plight of the poor—the lack of legally secure property rights. But alas, it is Sachs who has focused single-mindedly on only one supposed solution to the exclusion of all others—a massive transfer of wealth from developed countries to poor countries. Like the famous Wizard behind the curtain, he's imploring us not to worry about the past sinkholes into which development aid has been poured to no avail. Just keep pumping much more aid for "investments" in infrastructure and human capital and the job will get done, Sachs assures us. Just don't ask how.

Sachs would do well to listen to those who agree with De Soto, such as Mike Moore, Director-General of the World Trade Organization. Moore said that even *"if the United States were to raise its ODA to the United Nations target of 0.7 per cent, it would take the richest country on the planet 150 years* to transfer to the world's poor, resources equal to those they already possess. Unlocking and securing those investments, talent and skill is the challenge."[73] (emphasis added)

Kenyan economist James Shikwati, who, Sachs' preening ego to the contrary, is in a better position to know what would work in his own country, believes that aid to Africa is counterproductive. In a July 2005 interview with Der Spiegel, Shikwati declared that "[M]illions of dollars earmarked for the fight against AIDS are still stashed away in Kenyan bank accounts and have not been spent. Our politicians were overwhelmed with money, and they try to siphon off as much as possible... Huge bureaucracies are financed (with the aid money), corruption and complacency are promoted, Africans are taught to be beggars and not to be independent. In addition, development aid weakens the local markets everywhere and dampens the spirit of entrepreneurship that we so desperately need."[74]

To his credit, Kofi Annan commissioned a report received in 2004 entitled "Unleashing Entrepreneurship: Making Business Work for the Poor." The report was prepared by the UN Commission on the Private Sector & Development, on which De Soto served as a member. De Soto's ideas about integrating the poor into a formal legal structure were included in the entrepreneurship report. Nearly a year later, De Soto was appointed by Annan to chair the UN High Commission for the Empowerment of the Poor, which presumably is supposed to implement the report's recommendations.

Yet it's the Millennium Development Project report, with its nonsensical pie-in-the-sky emphasis on massive increases in development aid, that is getting all the press and enthusiasm. To no one's surprise, Annan clearly prefers Sachs's vision of an expanded United Nations bureaucracy running a massive worldwide wealth redistribution program.

But not even a staunch defender of Annan like former Clinton administration UN ambassador Richard Holbrooke is convinced that Kofi's organization is up to the job. Looking at the UN's track record and its personnel, Holbrooke admitted at a meeting sponsored by the Council on Foreign Relations that he would not trust the UN with the money to run such an ambitious program. He also said that it was a waste to pour more development aid down the well as long as African leadership was destroying itself. Finally, he praised President Bush's own "Millennium Challenge Account" program which links greater contributions from developed nations to greater responsibility from developing nations.[75]

In short, by way of a high-sounding action plan supposedly based on extensive research and to be implemented by the UN, what the architects and supporters of the Millennium Development Project *really* seek is to massively re-align the global economy to the detriment of the United States. They want to force the U.S. government to ignore the will and needs of its own people to subsidize the globalists' own often childlike concept of what should be done to solve very complex problems.

Annan, Strong and Sachs — Leaders of the Globalist Brigade

Kofi Annan, Maurice Strong and Jeffrey Sachs share essentially the same underlying agenda. In addition to be being hypocrites, all are zealots. They want to wield the United Nations as a weapon against the United States, whose wealth, based as it is on the rule of law, capitalism and individual responsibility, is an endless affront to what the British snidely call the "Great and the Good" crowd. Annan, Strong and Sachs are the embodiment of the old joke, "a liberal is a person who's happy to give someone else the shirt off your back," and they want to do so without the consent of the American people.

In Maurice Strong's case, the agenda consists of nothing less than replacing the no-nonsense U.S. Constitution with the utterly nonsensical Earth Charter. In Sachs' case, it is to impose his already discredited worldview — one that mired millions of Russian in chaos and poverty — on the rest of us, by way of a massive wealth transfer via "global taxation" that would do little to help poor nations, but a great deal to hurt the United States economically and politically — no doubt Sachs' real goal, were he honest enough to state it.

The redistributionist, anti-growth agenda advocated by Sachs and Strong is exactly what the globalists mean when they talk about "reform" — which is really just a code word for "redistribution."

In the fevered minds of Annan, Strong, Sachs and others of their dangerous ilk, the UN's number one problem is that it has too little power and too little money. And why is that? Because "antiquated notions" of national sovereignty get in the way. And because, in their view, actually successful countries like the United States and other Western democracies have too much power on the world scene, the limitations President Truman so wisely incorporated in the UN charter must be reversed.

In order to get that process rolling, however, the globalists must operate in secret, with a gullible media standing by to neutralize and spin any unfortunate leaks that might occur. And if Annan, Strong, and Sachs are the generals orchestrating this sordid campaign, the NGOs are the shock troops leading the assault.

CHAPTER THREE

NGOS: A "SPECIAL INTEREST" IN BYPASSING DEMOCRACY

S INCE NGOS SERVE in part to put that oft-cited "human face" on UN-sponsored proposals, ones that often amount to little more than re-inventing the social engineering programs that have worked so spectacularly well in places like the former Soviet Union and North Korea, it's little wonder that Kofi Annan is all for them.

> I see a United Nations which recognizes that the non-governmental organizations revolution—the new global people—power, or whatever else you wish to call this explosion of citizens' concern at the global level—is the best thing that has happened to our Organization in a long time... We can also be strategic partners in policy—in areas where you can persuade your Governments to work through the United Nations.[1]

The number of NGOs internationally has grown nearly four-fold, from 13,000 to over 47,000 between 1981 and 2001. Close to 3,000 of these unregulated organizations have official consultative status with the UN, which means that they can attend UN meetings to keep watch over the negotiations, exchange information with UN agencies, and lobby member state representatives and UN officials.[2]

There are certainly NGOs that hit the ground running every day, taking on the backbreaking and often heartbreaking work of helping the hungry, homeless and dispossessed one-on-one. But in the sleek, glitzy, celebrity-driven world of so many "progressive" NGOs, actually working with *people* is just...well, not done. It's far more fun to hang out with Mick and Bill and Hill and Hollywood's latest flavor-of-the-month at some UN-sponsored blabfest.

Whatever their stated goals, most "progressive" NGOs can be characterized not just by their boorish self-righteousness but by their utter lack of humor and wit. Even their mission statements read like exercises in verbal masochism. The Global Policy Forum, a Non-Governmental Organization with consultative status at the UN, "focuses on the United Nations—the most inclusive international institution, offering the best hope for a humane and sustainable future."[3] Its web site is full of articles sure to interest anyone willing to wade through the sterile, meaning-free language so dear to the politically correct crowd, of which most NGOs are ardent members.

NGOs can thrive financially through UN relationships. Since the bulk of NGO funding comes via participation in "development projects" siphoned through the UN and other multilateral organizations, it only stands to reason that NGOs want to further their pet programs in the hope of feeding more lavishly at the UN trough. In 2000 an estimated $7 billion dollars was flowing through NGOs annually—though flowing *where*, isn't necessarily clear.[4]

Although they have no moral problem with accepting money from guilt-ridden rich people and foundations, many NGO activists want to re-engineer the global economic and political order into a more "enlightened" version of socialism. In an article appearing on the NGO Global Policy Forum Web site, self-described but apparently only partially literate "radical" Michael Albert described his "participatory economics" alternative to capitalism this way (wording and punctuation are faithfully reproduced):

> "Democratic workplace and consumer councils for equitable participation
>
> Diverse decision-making procedures seeking proportionate say for those affected by decisions
>
> Balanced job complexes creating just distribution of empowering and disempowering circumstances
>
> Remuneration for effort and sacrifice in accord with admirable moral and efficient incentive logic
>
> Participatory planning in tune with economics serving human well being and development"[5]

Take *that*, Thomas Jefferson! It's just a sample of the convoluted thought processes motivating the kind of "new global people" that Kofi Annan thinks are "the best thing that has happened to our Organization in a long time."

The globalist NGOs are not a bunch of do-gooder civics organizations holding town hall meetings and writing letters to their UN Ambassadors. They are instead a highly coordinated international network of activist influence peddlers, largely peddling on behalf of "progressive"—read left-wing-causes. They use the Internet and other networking tools to magnify their voices and influence many-fold.

One group called the Association for Progressive Communications is dedicated to this very purpose—to "empower and support organizations, social movements and individuals in and through the uses of information and communication technologies to build strategic communities and initiatives for the purpose of making meaningful contributions to equitable human development, social justice, participatory political processes and environmental sustainability."[6] This association enables the networking of thousands upon thousands of NGOs worldwide in order to raise funds and craft common messages and lobbying techniques, the better to descend like money-seeking locusts on every UN conference.

The Global Policy Forum is another example of an NGO that relies on networking and coalition-building, stating on its web site that it "uses a holistic approach, linking peace and security with economic justice and human development, and we place a heavy emphasis on networking to build broad coalitions for research, action and advocacy." One can only imagine how many of these NGOs represent duplicative efforts, trying to force their drone-like visions of "peace and justice/justice and peace/no peace without justice" and etc. onto a wary world.

All this networking and interaction and hanging out at elaborately staged UN cocktail parties has, at least, produced one well-articulated goal—tame the big, bad United States by any means necessary. As Professor Peter Willets, a leading British observer of NGOs, put it, "the major UN conferences produced an unprecedented scale of global public engagement with intergovernmental events. In addition, the secretariats of the UN and other intergovernmental organizations sought to overcome the crises generated by the unilateralism of United States administrations and the failure of Congress to deliver U.S. financial obligations, by appealing to global civil society as a source of legitimacy for international co-operation."[7]

Globalists use NGOs to legitimize the vision of the U.S. as the heartless villain mocking the rest of the world's noble desire for cooperation and civility. That "the rest of world" consists in large part of vicious totalitarian regimes and kleptocracies seems to have eluded these worthies. But of course, why let truth derail a potential gravy train?

NGOs are generally staffed by earnest, if not completely obsessed individuals. And because *they're* obsessed with some pet cause, the rest of us are expected to hop-to. Obsessions, of course, can trigger delusions, and one of the bigger delusions infesting the NGO universe is that these groups speak for "the people." They believe that they have a monopoly on the truth, which makes it easy to reject the legitimacy of organizations that might *also* want to participate in UN conferences but have—gasp—different points of view.

For example, caucus members were shocked—*shocked*—to discover that, while preparing a statement for the United Nations 2002 General Assembly Special Session on Children, they'd been outvoted by pro-family members representing a more conservative point of view. The "progressives," so used to getting their own way on the UN playground, simply walked out.

At a preparatory session for the United Nations-sponsored follow-up meeting (meetings are clearly another obsession for these groups), feminist NGO observers who had dominated the proceedings in Beijing were outraged that pro-family advocates, wearing red buttons that read "Motherhood," had the temerity to actually state their own point of view. The following week, these pro-family spokespeople further offended the "progressives" by daring to wear buttons bearing the word "family" and praying during the meeting.[8]

Rather than try and compete with other points of view in the marketplace of ideas—where failure is almost guaranteed—the "progressive" NGOs try to shut out their opponents altogether by branding them as extremists. So much for their belief in the democratic process and tolerance

In reality, the globalist NGOs whose agendas have so dominated the public's dialogue with the United Nations represent only a small hardcore group of committed activists. They lack public accountability and so any legitimate claim to speaking for society at large. In a functioning democracy, it is the elected government that rightfully has that role.

Of course, NGOs have every right to lobby the elected officials of each of their countries just like any other special interest group. But that's all they are—special interest groups. They have neither the right to shut out competing viewpoints nor to by-pass a functioning democracy's elected officials by trying to move policy issues with "global impact" to unaccountable UN bodies for resolution.

The Kyoto Kabuki

Ah, the environment. Few issues inspire such passion in the humorless, or such a demand for a never-ending stream of costly initiatives and summits (and of course, carbon-spewing travel to exotic locations.)

As we've seen, Maurice Strong, the oilman, was largely responsible for setting the Kyoto Protocol in motion at the UN 1992 Earth Summit in Rio de Janeiro. He then used his Earth Council NGO and others, including Greenpeace, to push relentlessly for ratification. Greenpeace, the group which initially won the world's heart by coming to the defense of baby seals, has now become notorious for using aggressive and borderline illegal tactics in support of its obsessions.

Some environmentalists hailed Kyoto as "a good start," but only a start. Whether or not the label of "junk science" applies here has, of course, been completely ignored in the headlong rush to: a) excoriate the U.S. and b) open the money floodgates. In any event, the more extreme NGOs weren't sated at all. On the day the Kyoto Protocol officially went into effect, Greenpeace stormed the trading floor of the International Petroleum Exchange to demonstrate their belief that Kyoto was way too modest in scope.

One of Greenpeace's spokesmen proudly proclaimed: "The reason we did this is that the Kyoto accord, which comes into force today, has modest targets to cut greenhouse gases. We need huge cuts if we are going to divert dangerous climate change. This madness has to end, it's that simple. As Kyoto becomes law, we ask the world to take a deep breath and consider where our oil addiction is taking us."

The traders were not impressed, and in fact had the invaders forcibly removed, which led to the inevitable whining we've come to expect from such groups when confronted with a divergent point of view. "I've never seen anyone less amenable to listening to our point of view," said one of the Greenpeace protesters. Perhaps they should work on their presentation skills.[9]

To environmentalists, the U.S. is of course Enemy Number One, and much time and effort is spent on condemning us for refusing to toe the party line. The fact that the United States would have had to shoulder two-thirds of the total cost of complying with the Kyoto Protocol makes our rejection of the treaty that much more frustrating—all that money, being spent under the direction of American taxpayers instead! The hyperbole and hysteria of the "sky is falling" contingent makes so much more difficult any rational discussion of the actual, and clearly important, issues involved.

Sadly, the Kyoto Protocol zealots have reduced complex, multifaceted, real-life environmental issues into a simplistic paradigm that pits predatory man against the "sacred" Earth. Given legitimacy via media coverage of an endless succession of global summits, operating under the sound-bite friendly banners of "sustainable development" and "Earth Charters," the UN agencies and globalist NGOs, by default, have received a free pass to set the agendas on vital and serious issues such as population control, management of natural resources, fish and forest resource depletion, greenhouse gases, acid rain and oil spills.

And in its rapacious quest for dominion over the Earth's "common spaces" in the seas, land and air as well as over energy policy, the UN bureaucracy and its suppliants are looking for ways to tax as many uses of the Earth's resources as it can find.

The Kyoto Protocol is part and parcel of the ritualized "dance of the globalists," seeking to shift blame for all the world's problems to the United States. What the Kyoto Protocol has always been about is curbing the economic growth of industrialized countries just because a cadre of well-funded, self-selected, unelected "activists" and obsessives say so. Which lends an even more sinister tone to Jacques Chirac's comment that the Kyoto Protocol was intended to be "the first component of an authentic global governance."[10]

The European Union, led by France, saw the Kyoto Protocol as a means of indirectly taxing the United States for its energy consumption through a formula that overwhelmingly penalized the U.S. *vis-à-vis* the EU. What Europe couldn't achieve in the marketplace of ideas and productivity, it tried to achieve by typically underhanded means—in this case, by setting a target of reducing carbon emissions among industrialized nations during the commitment period 2008-2012 to at least 5% below 1990 levels.

Each country or region was given its own target. The United States was "assigned" a reduction target of 7%. The European Union agreed to a collective target of 8%, which the EU member countries could divvy up any way they wished.

By using 1990 as the baseline, the EU gave itself an easy target because collective emissions were quite high in 1990 due to existence of inefficient, pollution-producing industries in communist-controlled Eastern Europe—the vast majority of which have been shut down. It was a cheap way to enable the entire EU to meet its Kyoto target.

On the other hand, the U.S. already had relatively low carbon dioxide emissions in 1990. Its annual carbon dioxide emissions per dollar of GDP had fallen by 15% since 1990. In 1998 and 1999, U.S. greenhouse gas emissions had grown by just 1%, while the overall GDP had grown by 8%. Even though the efforts to increase energy efficiency and implement new technologies had begun to "de-link" economic growth and greenhouse gas emissions, an economy the size of the U.S. that continued on a path of robust growth would by definition still take a big hit if forced to cut emissions 7% below 1990 levels.

Moreover, the Kyoto Protocol includes neither binding targets nor timetables for developing countries. Places like China and India could continue their rapid growth while emitting greenhouse gasses without penalties, in effect voiding the sacrifices the U.S. would have to make to hit its target reduction.

Had Kyoto not been rejected, the U.S. would have been financially crippled. The global cost of the Kyoto Protocol was estimated at $716 billion (as of 1999.) The United States would have borne almost *two-thirds of the global cost* had rationality not prevailed,[11] carrying nearly 66% of the economic burden of carbon reduction for the whole world even though it produces a little under 22% of the world's GDP and accounts for no more than 25% of global emissions of carbon dioxide!

Estimates by the Energy Information Agency show U.S. GDP losses averaging as high as 4.2% annually by 2010 had we allowed ourselves to be ensnared by this anti-growth agenda. Job losses alone would have ranged anywhere from 1.3 million to 2.4 million by 2010.[12]

China and India, of course, ratified Kyoto Protocol because they stood to gain from it. Here's how the Indian Government put it in a press release issued the day after it ratified the Protocol:

> India is not required to reduce emission of Green House Gases under the Protocol under which basically the developed countries were required to reduce emissions of GHG by an average of 5.2 per cent below 1990 level by 2012...India will benefit from transfer of technology and additional foreign investments when the Kyoto Protocol comes into force. Additional investments will come into renewable energy, energy generation and efficiency promotion and forestation projects... the Kyoto Protocol enables India to take up clean technology projects with external assistance in accordance with national sustainable development priorities.[13]

President Bush wisely declined to submit the Kyoto Protocol to the Senate for ratification. Nevertheless, with Russia's decision to join, the Kyoto Protocol went into effect on February 16, 2005 for the signatory nations.[14] (Tony Blair pulled the plug on the UK's participation in September 2005, stating that "No country is going to cut its growth.")[15]

Still, with the Protocol's commitments to reduce carbon emissions scheduled to expire in 2012, NGO zealots are already touting a "new and improved" version that would extend its binding obligations to the developing countries (referred to as Kyoto Mark II).

But in this case the United States is already one step ahead of its enemies. At yet another in an endless line of conferences—this one held in Buenos Aries in 2004—the U.S. allied itself with China and other developing countries in opposition to "Kyoto Mark II." This time, China and India knew that they would suffer economically if they went along with the Kyoto expansion.

Fearing stunted economic growth, they found a common interest with the United States in creating a different route towards greenhouse gas reduction policy. And instead of waiting until international "consensus" hardened into a treaty—one driven by the NGOs, the UN and their handmaidens in the press—the Bush administration engaged in some pre-emptive multilateralism of its own.

According to a former Australian ambassador to the General Agreement on Trades and Tariffs, "[I]n Buenos Aires the Bush administration has practiced artful multilateral diplomacy, comprehensively outflanking the EU. The framework for determining international climate change policy is no longer based on the European world view, but on a Pacific world view. The U.S. and China want climate change policies that do not undermine growth and that are rational."[16]

We are already seeing some dividends from this approach. As reported in the *Wall Street Journal*, European Commission

President Jose Manuel Barroso supports less environmental regulation in the EU and the use of a cost-effectiveness test for any new regulations. Most significantly, he wants the EU Commission to work more closely with the U.S. on environmental issues. Similarly, at a joint climate-control initiative for China and India, the director general of the Italian Ministry of Environment, Corrado Clini, stated, "[T]he first step in going beyond Kyoto will be to join up with the U.S. and get the World Bank and other international institutions to support investments."[17]

Here's a clear demonstration of the path the U.S. should follow when dealing with issues that transcend national boundaries. Instead of mechanically invoking the UN as a participant, the U.S. can and should enlist *coalitions of the willing* charged with devising rational and fair solutions to shared problems while respecting the national sovereignty of each country involved.

When voluntary arrangements are entered into for the purposes of tackling common problems, parties not only have a strong incentive to participate, but will be more willing to enact and enforce their own laws. Each country could decide its own spending priorities and whether to deal with problems such as energy consumption through taxes or some other means—or not at all.

This approach is in keeping with the UN Charter's original mandate—to achieve solutions to global problems through *cooperation* among sovereign nations rather than through *compulsion*. Global interdependence *can* co-exist with national independence. The world does not need some supra-national rulemaking or judicial behemoth run through the United Nations or a spin-off international body.

Unwilling to be confused by the facts, the reaction of the globalist NGO ideologues is always the same—don't try to reason with the big bad United States or show any respect for its democratic processes. Punish the American people instead, through trade and other economic reprisals and press on with even more radical proposals. (One would think that reading these vacuous proposals would be punishment enough for most people.)

Five Steps To A Binding International Norm

Let's examine the process by which those radical proposals might be implemented. In the case of The Center for Reproductive Rights, which has received funding from George Soros, the process has five distinct steps:

Step one: Bind States to International Standards
Step two: Impact Committee Reviews
Step three: Help Implement Outcome of Country Reviews
Step four: Legislate and Litigate
Step five: Follow Up and Evaluate Progress

Step five begins with lobbying for treaty ratification in each member state without any reservations and then proceeds to assemble NGOs and professional associations of lawyers, judges and law professors to "advise" governments on how to "harmonize" national laws and judicial interpretations with international standards. Governments must "actively incorporate these standards" into its laws—"standards" being the pronouncements of unelected UN committee members who put their own gloss on vaguely worded treaty language.

Step two, of course, involves a lot of meetings. "Impact Committees" made up of UN committees, NGOs and the usual "local experts" are formed, the better to determine how best to cram these new "reproductive rights standards" into existing law on a country-by-country basis. (The word "impact" here, of course, doesn't refer to what might happen when it begins to dawn on the citizens of a sovereign nation that their elites are selling them out—but perhaps it should.)

Step three? Well, that's implementation. In this case, the Center for Reproductive Rights will begin to "monitor" the actions of legislatures and courts to see whether the new "standards" are being utilized without further prompting. If they're not, as is inevitable when concepts of *fairness* and *standards* have no meaning, there's always...

Step four, which puts the lie to the UN Charter's principle of non-interference in the domestic affairs of each member state. Here, the UN committee on "reproductive rights" would "instruct states' parties to revise specific laws and policies or adopt new ones that comply with a given treaty." In plain English, this means using some unelected UN committee, which has spun its own unaccountable interpretation on a vaguely worded treaty, to "instruct" Congress as to what laws it must pass in order to comply with this interpretation—completely interfering with our own Constitutional processes of self-government.

But the Center for Reproductive Rights won't even be satisfied with all *this*.

No, the Center wants the legislature "to *mandate specific regulations and guidelines* to accompany reformed and new laws to ensure they are *interpreted and enforced in accordance with treaty obligations and committees' general comments and concluding observations*." (emphasis added)

Furthermore, the Center intends to "assist in *reforming the judicial system to ensure that it addresses issues consistent with international standards* on reproductive and sexual rights as specified by the treaty, and by the general comments and concluding observations of the committees." (emphasis added)

And finally, it plans to "[M]onitor court decisions, prosecution and conviction rates, and severity of sentences for crimes that *constitute violations of reproductive and sexual rights as articulated by the committees*."[18] (emphasis added)

This same breathtaking arrogance and certitude permeates the belief systems of all too many NGOs. Certainly the pattern is clear. First, marshal biased research in support of your cause, and then work with the UN bureaucracy to advocate that particular point of view. Next, lobby to get the policies formally adopted in the form of a treaty-like instrument mandating an "international norm" of conduct that the member states are obligated to follow—and enforce—against their own citizens and businesses.

Then, establish a permanent committee within the UN, with your NGO's active participation (naturally), to issue interpretations of the "international norm" and to "monitor member state compliance." Of course, if member states don't fall into line, you'll need to find plaintiffs willing to litigate in the domestic courts with the objective of getting sympathetic judges to incorporate the "international norms," as defined by the permanent UN committee or other forum, into their Constitutional law interpretations: but hey! No problem!

It's a remarkably insidious and dangerous process, and one that's taking place under our noses every day.

The NGO globalists and their UN familiars are in reality attempting a coup. They want to move away from state-to-state dealings and in their stead, create a body of international law prescribing their debatable visions of "universal rights and obligations," enforceable in global forums open to anyone claiming that their "rights" have been detrimentally affected. The global forums would be vested with authority to assign individual liability to defendants and to generate enforceable remedies. Sovereign nations would have no ability to protect either their citizens or their businesses from capricious litigation, international-style. Think the lawsuit problem is bad here in the U.S.? You ain't seen nothing yet.

To achieve their objectives, globalists frame their pet issues in the kinds of overtly politically correct ways that allow them to dominate the moral high ground. Sure, it's an approach that's both vile and cynical, but since the viewpoints of so many NGOs cannot withstand any kind of intellectually rigorous scrutiny, it's the only one they can take. Find enough equally daft citizens in enough countries, and they may yet find a way to get national governments to cede authority to faceless global "institutions."

Globalist Plans for UN Expansion

Global treaties are the most obvious way to accomplish the transfer of policy-making and enforcement authority from national to international institutions. A treaty can be defined as a formal agreement between two or more states (for example, to terms of peace or trade), or as the document in which such an agreement is set down.

Treaties have built-in limitations. Historically, neither individuals nor groups such as NGOs have standing to initiate enforcement action. This is of course unacceptable to the overweening egoists infesting many NGOs, so they are pressing for a new kind of treaty that will break with the tradition of exclusive state-to-state interaction by giving NGOs and individuals direct access to an enforcement mechanism. The world needs centralized dispute resolution agencies replete with effective enforcement mechanisms open to individual plaintiffs and NGOs, their arguments go, because nations will always find ways to side-step inconvenient commitments. Actually, the world needs centralized dispute resolution agencies replete with effective enforcement mechanisms open to individual plaintiffs and NGOs like it needs, well, a hole in the head.

Treaties, of course, are merely paper documents. It's when they create an actual forum that's accepted by a critical mass of member states that they become empowered to render actual opinions. One ugly example is the International Criminal Court.

Although not technically a UN entity, the ICC may as well be for the loving support it receives from the UN Mother Ship.

This "court" remains in business despite the United States' well-founded opposition. But it is only the tip of the iceberg.

For example, the "World Federalist Movement"—yes, it's an NGO and no, the name was *not* taken from a *Star Trek* episode—has declared that the "International Criminal Court (ICC) is a harbinger of what is ahead—the global expansion and crystallization of environmental and human rights, access to justice, and universal application of the rule of law..."[19]

But wait, there's more. "[F]or some time, proposals have circulated regarding the establishment of an international environmental court, under the auspices of the UN, or a world environment organization that could coordinate the efforts of various agencies, as well as states and environmental NGOs." (Ah, those *circulating proposals*, always in motion, moving from NGO to NGO to UN committee and back again and somehow never coming into contact with a regular person imbued with one ounce of common sense.)

What the "World Federalist Movement" wants is an enforceable legal system based on "universally recognized environmental rights and obligations for private entities" and "global environmental standards of care." As a result of this brave new world, environmentalist NGOs and individuals claiming to be harmed by the conduct of a "transnational" corporation could sue the company directly.[20] If ever a prescription was created for laying waste to an economy, this is it.

In order to get things started, globalists must first organize a world environmental organization. This body would create the rules and regulations for *any* activity impacting the environment. Then a global environmental court would be set up to enforce the rules, possibly along the lines recommended at the 2004 *Conference of the Americas for the Environment and Sustainable Development.*[21]

The fact that globalists want to use the United Nations in ways that clearly exceed the bounds of the UN Charter does not bother them in the least. *They* know what's good for us, and that's good enough for them. It's that kind of logic that allows NGOs to continually pollute international discussions about complex problems with their global governance proposals run amok.

The UN and its agencies can, of course, perform all of the studies and make as many recommendations as they want as long as all this busy work resides within the budgets they are allotted. But it's violating its own governing rules when it involves itself, via side treaties, in enforcing mandates that interfere with member-state sovereignty.

Demonstrating little understanding, but a great deal of wishful thinking, Agenda 21 improperly confers upon the General Assembly the role of the "supreme policy-making forum that would provide overall guidance to Governments, the United Nations system and relevant treaty bodies."[22] Under the UN Charter, of course, the General Assembly is supreme in nothing and certainly does not have policy-making authority. Only the Security Council, with its five permanent veto-bearing member states, has *any* defined policy-making role, and even that role is confined to collective security matters. The General Assembly can discuss and recommend till its collective head explodes, but that is the extent of its powers.

There is, however, a process for amending the UN Charter in order to broaden its authority, one which the proponents of expansion have not followed for reasons that will become obvious. In order for an amendment to take effect, Article 108 of the Charter says that it must be adopted by a vote of two-thirds of the members of the General Assembly and ratified in accordance with their respective constitutional processes by two-thirds of the members of the United Nations, including all the permanent members of the Security Council. Good luck with that.

So, knowing that the United States will always exercise its veto when it sees clearly that its sovereignty is being trod upon, the globalists instead disguise their actual intent using the subterfuge of separate treaties, protocols or covenants to enlist the all-too-willing UN establishment as partners in their schemes—even though Article 103 of its Charter plainly states that the United Nations cannot impose obligations upon a member state that are more onerous than the UN Charter itself imposes, whether or not provided for in another treaty.

If you still have doubts about the globalists' intentions, the Center for Reproductive Rights again provides an instructive example. Several internal memos found their way to Congressman Chris Smith, a Republican from New Jersey. He, in turn, submitted them to the Congressional Record. They speak volumes about where the globalists are headed, and where they intend to drag the rest of us, willingly or not.

> As interpretations of norms acknowledging reproductive rights are repeated in international bodies, the legitimacy of these rights is reinforced...*there is a stealth quality to the work*: we are achieving incremental recognition of values without a huge amount of scrutiny from the opposition. These lower profile victories will gradually put us in a strong position to assert a broad consensus around our assertions...." (emphasis added)[23]

Stealth, litigation, and staking the moral high ground as a way of avoiding scrutiny are the globalists' chief weapons. Voiding the U.S. Constitution is the ultimate goal. And with multi-billionaire handmaidens like Soros and Ted Turner providing the funds, the opportunity for mischief—and far, far worse—is virtually endless.

CHAPTER FOUR

JUDICIAL SURRENDER OR DEFENSE OF OUR LIBERTIES?

A S LONG AS the United States take its national sovereignty seriously, this country remains the globalists' chief obstacle. Without U.S. participation, key initiatives such as the Kyoto Protocol and the International Criminal Court are basically meaningless. And with President Bush's timely reelection and Congress in Republican hands, designs for an "International Environment Court" won't get far either. With their legislative options cut off, those who've designated themselves our moral superiors must employ subtler methods to force this country to abdicate its world leadership role.

As usual, we need look no farther than to our own universities for suggestions about how best to bring the U.S. to its knees. University of Georgia law professor Peter Spiro, for example, suggests organized foreign economic retaliation against Americans until the government is forced to cry "uncle" and concede its sovereignty to what one assumes is a '"higher power." Spiro actually goes so far as to attack those he brands as the *new sovereigntists*, urging the amorphous but oft-cited "international community" to give up negotiating with the federal government and to take direct action "against key U.S. actors"—individual states and corporations—if they do not adopt "international norms." According to Spiro, the globalists "can directly discipline U.S. entities, circumventing and constraining anti-internationalist federal policymakers in the process." That way, "the Constitution will have to adapt to global requirements sooner or later."[1]

European Union member states—so many of which exist only because of American sacrifices during WW II—are already giving serious consideration to Professor Spiro's ideas. Some are advocating, for example, trade sanctions against the United States if it continues to spurn the Kyoto Protocol, believing that the World Trade Organization would support trade restraints imposed to enforce international environmental norms.

Because Americans are cold towards their new-age totalitarian gibberish, our betters are continually trolling for other ways of getting what they want. And thanks to people like Peter Spiro, they've hit on one—our Federal judiciary.

Once international courts and other forums are established, via the UN or other means, and once they develop a set of legal "norms" that meet with broad "consensus" across developed and developing nations (nations that in many cases have nothing to lose—or a lot to gain—by neutering our ability to chart our own course), the globalists are hoping that sympathetic federal judges will adopt the international "legal norms" in their decisions.

Rather than blatantly imposing one unified legal system from a supranational world court and risking a revolution, the global laws would gently seep through the porous layers of our own judiciary, eroding our Constitution in the judicial equivalent of osmosis.

As Dean Anne-Marie Slaughter of the Woodrow Wilson School of Public and International Affairs at Princeton University puts it so charmingly, "[H]uman rights lawyers are more likely to develop transnational litigation strategies for domestic courts than to petition the UN Committee on Human Rights."[2]

Globalists look for federal judges who are enthusiastic about imposing their own new and novel Constitutional interpretations. (It's old, after all, and written by dead white men who didn't invoke Gaia and Mother Earth into their pronouncements. How meaningful can it *be* in this hip new era where anything goes?) Their legal strategy is to dust off the decades-old Supreme Court doctrine of "incorporation" which Justice Hugo Black used to explain, in our own unique federal—state context, is the mechanism for applying the federal Bill of Rights to the states through the due process clause of the Fourteenth Amendment.

It's through just this mechanism that federal judges might incorporate into the words used in *our* Constitution, the meanings assigned by *international forums*. The mantra, of course, is that the United States courts must end their judicial "isolationism" if only because a bunch of lawyers from other countries have said so.

The globalist Spiro told this author what he thinks will happen to U.S. law, explaining that the "pressure on the United States to bring our law into conformance with international law" is an "insinuating process by which international law makes itself felt through incorporation" into U.S. law— that in a conflict between an "international norm" on which there was a manufactured global consensus and a conflicting U.S. norm, the U.S. "would give one way or the other in the face of "international norms."

These new interpretations of familiar Constitutional words and phrases will be barely visible at first, much less fathomable or meaningful to most of our elected representatives. (As we saw during the recent John Roberts confirmation hearings, a significant number of our elected Senators—including the lawyers—have little or no understanding of the Constitutional guarantees they have been elected to uphold, which hardly bodes well for the future.)

In any event, we'll first see the effect in the number of lawsuits filed against municipalities, states and the federal government—they'll increase exponentially. Next will come an erosion of our nation's vital checks and balances system, which places limitations on government interference with individual liberties and the historical pillars of our national sovereignty.

Suppose, for example, that a new International Economic and Social Human Rights Court is established and rules that "adequate housing," as some Oxford or Harvard graduate student defines it, is a "universally recognized human right" that individuals are entitled to "demand" from their governments as the providers of last resort, no matter what their individual circumstances or culpabilities. The logic, of course, is that when people can't or won't provide themselves with adequate housing, then the State, as guardian of the common good, must do so.

Suppose further that this new International Court also decides to define the minimum standard of adequacy as no lower then the mean of private housing in the applicable jurisdiction. A human rights NGO then brings a federal class action suit in a U.S. District Court on behalf of every person presently living in the United States who is either homeless or deemed to be living in vaguely defined poor housing conditions. The suit would claim that until the federal government pays to "adequately" house these individuals, they are being deprived of their Constitutional right to life, liberty and property without due process of law.

In other words, the globalists would argue in court that an "internationally accepted norm" of adequate housing for all must be incorporated into the interpretation of the Constitutional words in the Fifth and Fourteenth Amendments prohibiting the government from depriving its people of life, liberty and property. A supposed "right to housing" that nowhere appears in the U.S. Constitution would require Congress and/or the state legislative bodies to provide adequate and appropriate housing for all the people residing in the country.

And since all "persons" are guaranteed this right, illegal aliens would be included in the class seeking relief. This interpretation converts a *negative right* to be left alone from unreasonable governmental interference into an *affirmative duty* on the part of the federal and state governments to underwrite housing for millions without involving any political branch of government in the formulation of this policy—except to demand that they find a way to pay for it.

Sound far-fetched? It's already happening in the United Kingdom. In 2004, a British high court ruled that the government's "refusal of accommodation" for three asylum seekers was illegal. The court held that the three destitute asylum seekers should have been given housing support, concluding that "shelter of some form from the elements at night" is a "basic amenity" and that destitute people, not currently given state assistance, have a case for claiming that their human rights have been breached on the grounds of homelessness.

By not offering state help, the government had subjected the three asylum seekers to "inhuman or degrading treatment," contravening Article 3 of the European Convention of Human Rights. This kind of bizarro-world logic is just the sort of thinking that is preventing the British government from deporting known terrorists![3]

American judges, even at the Supreme Court level, have demonstrated a disturbing willingness to base decisions on foreign legal sources—*disturbing, because the focus has been on matters that include defining the scope of fundamental Constitutional rights.* In many ways, the U.S. Constitution is a conservative document—conservative in the best possible sense—but this didn't stop members of the Supreme Court from citing and incorporating far more liberal laws from other countries into their opinions on a death penalty case.[4]

In an opinion written by Justice Kennedy, it was held that the Constitutional prohibition of "cruel and unusual punishment" embodied in the Eighth Amendment required the banning of the death penalty for juvenile offenders below the age of 18 convicted of murder, no matter what the circumstances. Justice Kennedy wrote that *"the express affirmation of certain fundamental rights by other nations and peoples*...underscores the centrality of those same rights within our own heritage of freedom."

Former Justice O'Connor dissented from the Court's ruling, but agreed with the Court on the relevance of "foreign and international law to [our] assessment of evolving standards of decency." But as Justice Scalia observed so sagely in his dissenting opinion, "[W]hat these foreign sources 'affirm', rather than repudiate, is the justices' own notion of how the world ought to be, and their diktat that it shall be so henceforth in America."

This was certainly not the first time that Justice Kennedy turned to foreign law for answers to his questions about the U.S. Constitution. In trying to figure out what the Constitution has to say about de-criminalizing homosexual conduct, for example, Kennedy cited the opinion of the European Court of Human Rights. He also referred approvingly to the "friend of the court" brief submitted by Mary Robinson, former United Nations high commissioner for human rights, as if her opinion on protection of sodomy under some vaguely defined mantle of global liberty was more important than what the duly elected state officials intended their anti-sodomy laws to accomplish. Of course, our Constitution says nothing about gay rights, but Kennedy used foreign law to help fill in the gaps. "The right the petitioners seek in this case has been accepted as an integral part of human freedom in many other countries," he said. "There has been no showing that in this country the governmental interest in circumscribing personal choice is somehow more legitimate or urgent."[5] Will the Supreme Court next declare a Constitutional right to same sex marriage, citing Canadian and Spanish law allowing such marriages to support their interpretation?

Without the discipline of judicial restraint, we may find more and more federal judges basing their decisions on foreign sources and the musings, whims and obsessions of "human rights" advocates, environmentalists, and globalist law professors like Peter Spiro, rather than on the traditional roots of the Constitution. Indeed, Spiro admitted as much, saying to this author that "within the Supreme Court itself there is an incorporation process" with respect to the application of international law to U.S. Constitutional cases since the Supreme Court is "more comfortable and aware of international law" than it was twenty or thirty years ago. Proving his point, Justice Ginsburg, the strongest voice for this approach, remarked proudly in a speech to the American Constitutional Society that what she called the Court's prior "Lone Ranger mentality" was giving way to an attitude on the part of the Justices that was "more open to comparative and international law perspectives."[6]

This blithe, contemptuous attitude provides precisely the entre that globalists are looking for. If the goal is to break down Constitutional barriers to international governance, then Supreme Court Justices like Ginsburg and Kennedy are working overtime to accommodate them. And once they have fused our Constitution with "global charters" and incomprehensible "international norms," they will have destroyed everything that makes this country unique and a light unto the world. It may take some time, but much like jihad organizations which some resemble in their single-minded 'take-no-prisoners' approach, NGOs have a lot of funding, a perverted and endlessly self-renewing sense of their own righteousness, and so a lot of patience.

The best defense against this intellectual jihadism is to demand that judges at all levels exercise judicial restraint—that they follow an objective standard for interpretation rooted in the Constitution itself. As Alexander Hamilton said, "The rules of legal interpretation are rules of COMMONSENSE, adopted by the courts in the construction of the laws. The true test, therefore, of a just application of them is its conformity to the source from which they are derived."[7]

What are the tenets of such restraint? Common-sense interpretation begins with the actual words and structure of the document being interpreted, the better to understand the underlying principles at the document's core. The judge's task is to identify and apply the enduring principles embedded in the text, not to invent new ones.

Since the precise words of the Constitutional text alone may not provide a definitive answer to their meaning, judges are obligated to look next to the Founding Fathers' own thoughts and beliefs as expressed in their writings, deliberations and speeches.

The Declaration of Independence, the document that Thomas Jefferson called the "soul" of American law, provides the context of values needed to construe the Constitution's purposes. The Federalist Papers provide solid evidence as to the intent and meaning of Constitutional language. There are records from the Constitutional Convention that shed bright and penetrating light on just what the Constitution's drafters had in mind. The correspondence of Thomas Jefferson, James Madison and the other Founding Fathers reveal patterns of thought on fundamental issues that seem fresh and contemporary even today.

Judges must then study prior cases that deal with the same issues for valuable guidance. However, since these precedents are one step removed from actual primary sources, they can't be treated with reverence, lest they be proved wrong. The *Dred Scott* decision sanctioning slavery and the *Plessy v. Ferguson* case upholding segregation of public schools as "separate but equal" are examples of terrible precedents that were rightly overturned.[8]

Finally, judicial restraint requires that judges consider the *practical consequences of the decision*. After all, he or she is making a determination that may well affect future generations. It's here where the temptation to impose a subjective interpretation on what the Constitution says or "should have" said can become overwhelming. After all, who *doesn't* want to make a decision that guarantees you'll be the featured guest speaker at the next bar association meeting? But judges must truly assess whether their egos and the desire to impress their law biz friends should take precedence over the words and intent of the U.S. Constitution. The answer should be self-evident. Unfortunately, in all too many cases, it isn't.

In summary, *we must always start with what the Constitution actually says and intended to achieve*. It's the best way to set objective boundaries around judicial discretion. Oddly enough, judges to both left and right of center have endorsed this kind of approach, at least in theory. Justice Stephen Breyer commented,

> Individual phrases make up a single document. The document embodies general purposes. And those purposes inform the interpretation of the phrases. By openly and clearly referring to those general purposes, courts can help to create harmonious relationships both among different individual provisions and among the several general constitutional purposes...[9]

Justice Breyer went on to say that a judge should be "disciplined in emphasizing, for example, constitutionally relevant consequences rather than allowing his own subjectively held values to be outcome determinative." [10] It's too bad that Breyer has strayed from this approach himself. Referring to human rights issues, Breyer told lawyers assembled at the ABA's 2005 annual conference: "To decide [those cases] correctly requires lawyers and judges who have some familiarity and ability to reach out and find out about certain areas of foreign law."[11]

Justice Breyer had previewed his admiration for foreign decisions years before in his bizarre dissent to a decision denying review of their death sentences by long-time death row inmates who had stayed on death row for so long because they kept filing frivolous appeals. Breyer actually cited the Supreme Court of *Zimbabwe*—one of the most repressive regimes in the world. The United States, he said, should pay heed to the fact that "[A] growing number of courts outside the United States—*courts that accept or assume the lawfulness of the death penalty*—have held that lengthy delay in administering a *lawful* death penalty renders ultimate execution inhuman, degrading, or unusually cruel." (Emphasis in the original) The courts of Zimbabwe and Jamaica are given as examples along with the European Court of Human Rights.[12]

The globalists, of course, salivate at every such opening. Judges like Breyer, Kennedy and Ginsburg are little more than tools being used by elitists to circumvent our democratic process by imposing, via the cloak of "Constitutional interpretation," their chosen "international norms." Thanks to our own oblivious—or actively participating—judiciary, unelected and unaccountable activists are achieving through litigation and stealth what they could never achieve through vigorous, open debate in the political arena.

Extremist Judges Gone Wild

When judges lack restraint, they perform intellectual acrobatics with the Constitution. The late Justice William Douglas, an ardent environmentalist, went so far as to say that inanimate objects like trees should have their own standing as plaintiffs in lawsuits to protect the wilderness, stating that "[c]ontemporary public concern for protecting nature's ecological equilibrium should lead to the conferral of standing upon environmental objects to sue for their own preservation."!13 Maurice Strong must regret that Justice Douglas is dead. He would have been just the guy to elevate Maurice Strong's nonsensical Earth Charter to the level of the U.S. Constitution—or better yet for Strong's massive ego, the Ten Commandments.

But maybe Strong shouldn't worry. The environmental extremists have found the federal courthouse door wide open in California. U.S. District Judge Jeffrey White granted the NGOs Friends of the Earth and Greenpeace the right to take two federal development agencies to court for financing overseas projects that allegedly add to global warming.

Remember that the United States has not ratified the anti-global warming Kyoto Protocol. Neither our duly elected President, nor the Senate, have shown any appetite to support its compulsory anti-growth provisions. Our democracy has spoken through its elected representatives. Nevertheless, an unelected federal judge—in a precedent-setting decision—is allowing two globalist NGOs to get around this roadblock to their agenda. He is letting them sue two duly authorized agencies of the U.S. government for pursuing overseas development programs because somehow they allegedly speed up climate change. If the globalists succeed, American taxpayers will pick up the bill, and overseas economies that might have benefited from the development projects will suffer.

There's an entire cadre of extremist judges out there who believe that what the Constitution actually says doesn't matter at all. Believing themselves smarter than the Founders, they *know* that every generation must re-write the Constitution to fit current social and political conditions. The Founders? Dead centuries ago! Why be bound by precedents that are so "clearly" archaic and irrelevant?

These self-declared legal geniuses either don't understand or don't care that they are "standing on the shoulders of giants." Imbued by their own cleverness, happily buying into the myth that attending law school—particularly an "elite" law school—proves them that much smarter than everyone else, they are simply not content to treat the Constitution as a document animated by a set of enduring principles. Where's the glamour in working within the text to adapt these vibrant principles to circumstances that the Founding Fathers could not have anticipated? How will that get you invited to Bill Clinton's next "Global Initiative Meeting" where you might meet some really hot actress?

So, looking towards *their* futures, they treat the Constitution like a lump of clay they can mold to fit their concept of what the Constitution *should* say. The Founding Fathers, prescient as ever, warned that such an attitude would turn the Constitution into a useless piece of paper, since no fixed principles would remain to constrain the passions, obsessions and fads of the moment. All too many of today's judges give proof to that warning.

Unless this trend is stopped dead, we're opening ourselves up to the risk of nothing less than having a socialist agenda foisted upon us, one that will move this country in a direction that is thoroughly inimical to our identity as a sovereign people ruling ourselves under a written compact that defines— and limits—governmental authority.

Here's an example of the Founders' reasoning. Let's look for a moment at the perennial court battles over innocuous displays of traditional religious symbols in public settings. It's argued that such displays offend the First Amendment's prohibition of the making of any law "respecting an establishment of religion."

However, the meaning, structure and history of Constitutional text clearly belie such an interpretation. The words "establish" or "establishment" are used several times in the context of instituting or creating a body, enacting a law or making an appointment-usage that conformed to the common understanding of those terms *at the time.*

The drafters expressly rejected alternative language that would have omitted the word "establishment" and said simply that "Congress shall make no laws touching religion."[14] Indeed, it was reported that during discussions in the House of Representatives, one Mr. Huntington was particularly concerned that Amendment be drafted in such a way so as "to secure the rights of conscience, and the free exercise of religion, but not to patronize those who professed no religion at all."[15]

It was reported that James Madison assured him on this point. The Amendment's intent was only to address the fear that "one sect might obtain a pre-eminence, or two combined together, and establish a religion, to which they would compel others to conform." A judge well-versed in constitutional law—and one not interested in creating law herself—should clearly interpret this to mean that traditional displays are legal, since such displays are compelling no one to conform.[16]

The Supreme Court has ruled that the Ten Commandments cannot be displayed in public schools at all, and has recently issued two concurrent opinions on the display of the Ten Commandments in other public places. Interestingly enough—and so much a testament to the dynamism and relevance of the Constitution—these two decisions actually reached *diametrically opposed results* that depended on the specific context in and purpose for which the Ten Commandments were displayed.

This led Justice Scalia to observe in his dissent to the opinion banning the display of the Ten Commandments on certain courthouse walls (but not banning its display at the Supreme Court itself where the context is considered largely secular!) that "[W]hat distinguishes the rule of law from the dictatorship of a shifting Supreme Court majority is the absolutely indispensable requirement that judicial opinions be grounded in consistently applied principle."[17]

We are not secular Europeans for whom the very presence of religion in public is an offense. Nor is this one of the Muslim countries whose religious leaders run around dictating how people go about their everyday lives-and punish them severely if they don't conform.

Instead, our attitudes towards religion are a product of our peculiar history and are reflected in the core Constitutional value of *religious freedom*. But religious freedom should *not* mean depriving the majority of Americans who believe in God the right to freely acknowledge their country's religious foundation in the public square. *Atheists are not compelled to believe or do anything of a religious nature, but the Founders never intended for this group's private and personal rejection of faith to prohibit fellow citizens from recognizing theirs in a public manner.*

Consider the irony here. The Ten Commandments, bedrock of the Judeo-Christian tradition upon which this country was founded, can be barred from display in public schools and other public arenas. Meanwhile Maurice Strong's lachrymose, preachy and semi-intelligible Earth Charter, which stands equivalent to the Ten Commandants only in his own fevered mind, can be displayed everywhere and no one objects. Of course, few thinking people have ever bothered to read the thing, so perhaps that lack of protest is understandable.

And while we're on the subject of irony—how ironic is it that even indirect government funding of traditional faith-based initiatives is continually challenged by the ACLU and other hostile groups, but there's nary a peep from the same quarters when U.S. taxpayers' money is redistributed to the UN to support its religious initiatives? The UN provides a forum for "The United Religions Initiative," offering official accreditation to the "Bureau of the Committee of Religious NGOs at the United Nations" which is composed of organizations which define their work as religious, spiritual or ethical in nature.[18]

On the other hand, UN bureaucrats seem even more partial to the earth religion "Gaia" (Greek for *Earth Goddess*) which of course "inspired" Maurice Strong in his environmental crusade. Contrary to what you might think, "Gaia" is not just a trendy name for hipster dogs, but the title of a quasi-religious "movement" that encompasses a wide range of valid—and not so valid—environmental theories. Gaia material frequently finds its way into UN offices (and, one must surmise, into New York City dumps. Oh, the wasted paper! Shameful.) Still, the London—based 'Gaia Foundation' holds their press conferences in normally restricted UN press rooms.[19]

And all this while the UN bureaucrats often demonstrate hostility towards traditional monotheist religions. For example, at the 1996 Istanbul Conference, the then-director general of the World Health Organization reportedly told a press conference that "the three great monotheistic religions are not compatible with the New World Order."[20] Evidently God is not a globalist.

Terrorists With Benefits

It's bad enough that some of our most highly placed judges are rendering decisions that strike at the heart of our traditional religious heritage, but this is hardly the only example of courts showing utter disdain for the Constitution—and for the safety of the American people. Judges getting all huffy and puffy about Ten Commandments displays is one thing, but creating new "rights" for the enemy combatants in our midst is quite something else.

This issue here involves the right of an enemy combatant prisoner to petition for a "habeas corpus" proceeding. The writ of habeas corpus (literally, "you have the body") means that anyone arrested has the right to be brought before a court to determine whether there is sufficient cause to continue holding that person.

Long enshrined in English common law as a way to prevent arbitrary arrest and unjust imprisonment at the whim of the King, the colonies adopted the writ of habeas corpus in the seventeenth century. For the Founding Fathers, it was exactly the kind of pillar of personal liberty that the Constitution was designed to protect. Without this fundamental protection, individuals could be imprisoned and held without charge indefinitely with no possible recourse.

However, habeas corpus is *not* an absolute right that must be made available to detained individuals no matter the circumstance. Article 1, Section 9 of the Constitution says flatly that "The privilege of the writ of habeas corpus shall not be suspended, *unless when in cases of rebellion or invasion the public safety may require it.*" (Emphasis added.)

Moreover, the right to a habeas corpus proceeding does *not* mean an automatic right to a full-blown trial. It simply means that there must be access to a neutral body that stands between the imprisoned and the imprisoning authority to determine whether continued imprisonment is just under the circumstances.

In June 2004, the Supreme Court ruled that enemy combatants swept up in the war in Afghanistan and detained at the Guantanamo Naval Station in Cuba were entitled to a hearing on the legality of their detention. In so doing, the Court extended the ancient right of habeas corpus to individuals allied with a stateless terrorist network who were operating at will, outside the normal conventions of war, against American soldiers and civilians alike.[21] In a companion case, a plurality of Justices held open the possibility that the habeas corpus requirement could be satisfied by independent review of properly constituted military tribunals.[22]

The Bush administration did not fight the Supreme Court's extension of authority in this area. But it tried to find a balance between the Court's considerations and the need to protect this country from further attack. Keeping citizens safe is the first duty of the President of the United States. And, as Commander-in-Chief, the President is vested with Constitutional responsibility for the handling of the war, which necessarily involves making decisions of life and death regarding enemy combatants.

President Bush did not seek to push the outer edges of his powers. He went nowhere near the extreme and instructive precedent set by Abraham Lincoln. Instead, the Bush administration established a new Combatant Status Review Tribunal where the prisoners could question witnesses, call their own witnesses and testify themselves. The Tribunal's standard for reaching a decision was by the "preponderance of the evidence." A determination beyond a reasonable doubt was not appropriate since guilt or innocence of a crime was not at issue.

And even if a prisoner should lose this round and continue in detention, there would be opportunity for subsequent review on an annual basis, where the prisoner can present additional evidence to prove that he no longer poses a threat.
But these protections were clearly not enough for one federal judge.

A Yemeni prisoner, Salim Ahmed Hamdan, had been charged with, among other things, transferring weapons to al-Qaeda security and helping Bin Laden escape on a number of occasions. He also allegedly received weapons training in Afghanistan.

Hamdan was not being held indefinitely without any prospect of review of his case. The Status Review Tribunal had already determined that Hamdan was an enemy combatant in league with al-Qaeda. And he was set to have a military trial before a military commission, where he would be granted the presumption of innocence and could only be found guilty with proof beyond a reasonable doubt. The military commission's procedures had been approved for fairness by outside legal experts, including former Nuremberg prosecutor and law professor Bernard Meltzer. There was also an opportunity for appellate review by a panel that included civilian lawyers.[23]

In other words, this alleged al-Queda operative's fate was not left up to the President's whim. A process consistent with habeas corpus—an opportunity for Hamden to gain his freedom by having his case heard without interference by his arresting officers—was being scrupulously followed.

Into the middle of this stepped federal district judge James Robertson, who twisted the use of habeas corpus to stop the trial before it ever began because "there is nothing in this record to suggest that a competent tribunal has determined that Hamdan is not a prisoner-of-war under the Geneva Conventions. Hamdan has appeared before the Combatant Status Review Tribunal, but the CSRT was not established to address detainees' status under the Geneva Conventions. It was established to comply with the Supreme Court's mandate, to decide 'whether the detainee is properly detained as an enemy combatant for purposes of continued detention...'"[24]

And yet, as we've already established, *the U.S. Constitution is superior to and takes precedence over any treaty*. The Supreme Court had already declared what was necessary to meet the habeas corpus requirements in this case—and the Geneva Conventions were not on the list. Yet one judge felt it was his right to replace the Constitutional standard for habeas corpus with an extraneous reference to an international instrument— the Geneva Conventions treaty.

And even if the Geneva Conventions were to be taken into account in some fashion, the protections accorded to soldiers fighting for a state and wearing uniforms or other military insignia to distinguish themselves from civilians *do not apply* to an alleged terrorist like Hamdan. Judge Robertson found nothing inherently wrong with the Status Review Tribunal procedures themselves. But he put all evidence and common sense aside and held that Hamdan's rights had been violated by not having a formal determination of whether he was a "prisoner of war" and so entitled to all of the Geneva Convention's protections.

The Bush administration has continued to contest the proposition that Al-Qaeda, Taliban and foreign insurgents captured in Afghanistan or Iraq should be treated as "Prisoners of War" under Geneva Convention III. This certainly doesn't mean that we can do whatever we want with the detainees—basic principles of humane treatment apply. But under Geneva III, combatants are entitled to the additional protections of POW status if they meet the following conditions:

- They are members of the armed forces; or of a militia belonging to a party to the conflict.

- They are organized under a command structure.

- They have a fixed distinctive sign recognizable at a distance.

- They carry their arms openly.

- They conduct their operations in accordance with the laws and customs of war.

As anyone who watched in horror on 9/11 as everyday Americans leapt to their deaths from the flaming World Trade Center can tell you, Al-Qaeda and other terrorist detainees do not even begin to meet these minimum qualifications. Terrorists deliberately target innocent civilians in violation of the most elementary laws of war. They set off bombs, impersonate civilians or police, hide among civilians, and use mosques as sanctuaries.

At the same time, the terrorists mock the "infidel UN laws" and the other often touchy-feely "international laws" that naïve human rights activists are invoking to protect the terrorists themselves! Can any rational person argue that such individuals are entitled to the kind of special prisoner status designed for wars in which both sides agreed to observe the most basic rules of civilized behavior?

And yet, Judge Robertson has done just that.

If we were to throw common sense to the wind and accede to the demands for conferring POW status on all detainees for Geneva III purposes, they'd be effectively out of bounds for any type of effective interrogation: "Prisoners of war who refuse to answer may not be threatened, insulted, or *exposed to unpleasant or disadvantageous treatment of any kind.*"(emphasis added)[25]

And as a Prisoner of War under Geneva III, Al-Qaeda detainees would have to be treated as if they were in the U.S. military, with the same living conditions as our own military forces. That means good medical care at Uncle Sam's expense, better than many American citizens receive. They'd also have plenty of opportunity for recreation as well as at least one week of paid vacation every year.[26] That's something for the Al—Qaeda recruitment brochures!

It's just laughable to think that denial of POW status as defined under Geneva III to certain enemy detainees equates to inhumane treatment. To the contrary, it means only denying special privileges to individuals who refuse to abide by even the most minimal set of civilized norms, not to mention the same norms set forth in the Geneva Accords themselves. No terrorist comes even close nowhere to qualifying for such special treatment.

As a humane society, we can agree that physical torture of even the most despicable class of human beings is out of bounds. As a rational society, however—and not one governed by the whims of that dewey-eyed 14-year old who could have written the "Earth Charter"—we should also be able to agree that denying a detainee dentures, special recreational facilities, a week of paid vacation is neither torture nor inhumane.

And finally, as a rational society, we should be able to agree that being "exposed to unpleasant or disadvantageous treatment of any kind" in the course of an interrogation that might extract information which could easily save innocent lives is not torture, but rather a reasonable burden imposed on a foreigner caught in connection with hostilities aimed against the United States. Yet Judge Robertson defied rationality by requiring imposition of Geneva III POW standards on the U.S. military for *all* detainees without distinction—against the wishes of Congress and the Commander-in-Chief.

In a single decision, this unelected federal judge put himself *above the President*, who has the Constitutional responsibility as Commander-in-Chief to determine how best to protect the public safety against further terrorist invasions.

Not all past presidents have trod so lightly as George W. Bush. President Abraham Lincoln actually suspended the privilege of the writ of habeas corpus on his own authority toward the beginning of the Civil War. Why did Lincoln take this extreme step?

Just days after a confrontation between the Sixth Massachusetts Regiment and an angry Baltimore mob that left 12 dead—an incident with great implications for the physical safety of Washington D.C.—Lincoln expressed his fears in an April 25, 1861 letter to General Scott. Lincoln was concerned that the Maryland Legislature could take action to arm the state's citizens against the United States. Were that to happen, Lincoln said, the Commanding General must be prepared to take extreme actions including "the bombardment of their cities—*and in the extreme necessity, the suspension of the writ of habeas corpus.*" (emphasis added)[27]

On April 27, 1861, Lincoln suspended the habeas corpus privilege without prior Congressional authorization in the corridor between Philadelphia and Washington. This allowed Union generals to apprehend anyone deemed a threat to "public safety," with no right for such detainees to a trial. This included one John Merryman of Maryland, who was imprisoned by military order. Chief Justice Taney—the author of the infamous *Dred Scott* slavery decision—condemned Lincoln's suspension and issued the writ of habeas corpus after receiving a petition from Merryman. But President Lincoln disregarded the order.

Two years later, with more time to reflect on what he had done, Lincoln explained his rationale in more detail. His explanation focused on the *inability of the courts to deal with imminent threats to the public safety*:[28]

> Ours is a case of Rebellion—so called by the resolutions before me—in fact, a clear, flagrant, and gigantic case of Rebellion; and the provision of the Constitution that 'The privilege of the writ of Habeas Corpus shall not be suspended, unless when in cases of Rebellion or Invasion, the public safety may require it,' is the provision which specially applies to our present case. This provision plainly attests the understanding of those who made the Constitution, that ordinary Courts of justice are inadequate to 'Cases of Rebellion.'

Congress passed the Habeas Corpus Indemnity Act on March 3, 1863, which stated that "during the present rebellion, the President of the United States, whenever in his judgment the public safety may require it, is authorized to suspend the privilege of the writ of habeas corpus in any case throughout the United States or any part thereof."

Lincoln faced a threat to the Union's very existence, one unparalleled in American history. He believed that once the immediate threat of civil war was removed, the country would be restored to full civil liberties. He never intended his extreme measures to become the norm for defining Presidential powers—nor have they.

Of course, today we do not face an immediate threat of the Union's dissolution. There is no armed rebellion tearing the country apart. But we do face our own unique crisis. We were attacked on our own soil by a global terrorist network whose members purposely targeted innocent civilians for murder. Bin Laden declared war on the United States and followed up with devastating effect, and the threat of more attacks on our home soil continues unabated.

9/11 certainly qualifies as the type of "invasion" and threat to "public safety" that might justify a temporary suspension of the Constitutional privilege of writ of habeas corpus. Our soldiers went into Afghanistan to uproot Al-Qaeda's principal sanctuary. We faced an enemy who did not wear military uniforms, who did not fight under any official state banner, and who did not distinguish between military and civilian targets. Prisoners taken into custody had information that might be key in preventing further attacks. If released, a prisoner could return to combat or engage in more terrorist attacks against civilians in this country and elsewhere.

In such circumstances, the President as Commander-in-Chief must be able to order the detention of foreign combatants who are fighting along side our mortal enemies, and who have taken up arms against us, for as long as necessary. In wartime, this requires a military-based judgment of the danger of releasing such combatants, and the likelihood of extracting whatever information they may possess about those planning further harm.

Even though courts are not really placed to deal with imminent threats to public safety, they do have an important role to play in preventing the abuse of power. However, they shouldn't overplay it either. Judge Robertson crossed way over the line. Fortunately, in this particular case, the Court of Appeals for the D.C. Circuit did ultimately reverse Robertson and ruled that the Geneva Convention POW rules did not apply to alleged terrorists such as Hamdan.[29]

Even so, Robertson's actions demonstrate the mischief—and far, far worse—that might be caused by just one judge who ignores the Constitution and instead sets out to make up new laws in the hopes of earning kudos at the next bar association meeting. Robertson's kind of judicial over-reaching plays directly into the hands of the globalists, because it bypasses just those two branches of government—the legislative and executive—whose members must be elected.

Turning the Constitution Upside Down

Should the globalists succeed, they will neuter the four organizing principles that have evolved from our history and political traditions:

- The separation of powers among the three branches of government to legislate, to execute, and to adjudicate, respectively, where the courts have an assigned role to interpret but not to make the law;

- The protection of individual liberties from governmental encroachments;

- The expression of the political will of the people through their elected representatives, constrained by the limits placed upon the exercise of legislative and executive power that are fixed in the Constitution and interpreted by the judiciary;

- The Constitution as the supreme law governing the United States.

If those like Judge Robertson have their way, each of these organizing principles will be turned on its head. The judiciary will become in effect a super-legislature, nullifying the separation of powers. Individual liberties will be subordinated to the "norms" of the world community, as translated by the globalists-cum-jihadists, and incorporated into our Constitution by sympathetic judges sitting like tribunes pontificating on what's good or bad for the rest of us.

Of course, according to Maurice Strong, we are all global citizens first—whether we want to be or not. "Global governance" could easily transform this country into exactly the kind of hell that countless millions have fled here to avoid.

And make no mistake, the danger is here. A majority of the Supreme Court Justices have expressed a strong inclination to internationalize the Constitution on controversial issues, ranging from abortion to the death penalty to gay rights to affirmative action. Leading by example, Justice Ruth Bader Ginsberg based her vote to uphold the use of race in college admissions in part on international treaties that expressed the "universalistic norms" of a global society.

She cited the "International Convention on the Elimination of All Forms of Racial Discrimination," which the U.S. has ratified, and the "International Convention on the Elimination of All Forms of Discrimination against Women," which the U.S. has not, because they promote "temporary special measures" aimed at accelerating *de facto* equality. She also drew upon what she called the "international understanding of the [purpose and propriety] of affirmative action."[30]

Not even Justice Scalia would suggest that federal judges shut their eyes completely to legal developments occurring around the world. But to make ever-changing "international norms"—ones established not by duly elected representatives, but by the mealy-mouthed trust-funders, hacks and single-topic fanatics that so infest the NGOs and their primary enabler, the UN, the basis of for decisions that affect the American people, is nothing less than a vile and direct threat to this country.

Fortunately, as we've seen, the UN's ongoing arrogance and increasingly anti-American tone are turning Americans off. Traditionally, we've been very supportive of the United Nations. Polls taken in the 1990s show that a majority thought that the UN was making a "very" (25%) or "somewhat" (51%) positive contribution to world peace and health.[31]

But a January 13, 2005 Harris poll tells a different story—that by a 44 to 30 percent plurality, Americans no longer trust the UN. That in Europe the result was essentially reversed should tell us all we need to know about our so-called European "allies."(29) Aided by the indispensable Volcker Reports and the few intrepid reporters not entranced by the UN's endless glad-handing, America-bashing and sleazy Kumbaya sensibilities, people are waking up—and not a moment too soon.

The United States has the world's longest-running Constitutional democracy. Our unparalleled economic, military and humanitarian might should be proof to all that our system, if diligently applied, works. But if we're not careful, our own courts may yet sow the seeds of our destruction.

CHAPTER FIVE

LOTS OF TAXATION, NO REPRESENTATION

JOHN HANCOCK had no qualms about leaving his large signature on the Declaration of Independence. Like the other brave Founders, he'd already put his life on the line to defend the proposition of no taxation without representation—the concept that taxes imposed by the British Parliament had no standing in America because lawfully elected representatives here had not approved them.

At great risk to his own safety, this New England businessman turned into a revolutionary. Along with 80 others, he disguised himself as a Mohawk Indian and instigated the Boston Tea Party. But this was hardly his first brush with the British over taxes.

Five years earlier, Hancock had been involved in a skirmish over customs duties for wine imported on his sloop *Liberty*. When the crew refused to pay duties for the entire shipment, the customs commissioners seized the sloop, which led to a crowd reaction violent enough to drive the customs commissioners out of town. A suit for penalties was later brought against Hancock in the Court of Admiralty but was not pursued. Word of the *Liberty* confrontation spread through the colonies and it became a rallying cry for defiance against British taxes.

Hancock was a marked man because he challenged every English taxation plan as a direct affront to American colonists' liberties. He was one of many brave Colonial leaders branded as "incendiaries." British officers were instructed to arrest this "terrible desperado" for treason. And there were plots afoot to not to bother with a trial, but instead to look for the right opportunity to take his life on the spot.

Hancock was almost assassinated in March 1775, on the fifth anniversary of the Boston Massacre. British officers were, as the saying goes, "monitoring" Dr. Joseph Warren's "Oration" to the Boston crowd in the hopes that several firebrands on their colonial hit list might be attending. The officers decided that if Warren said anything that could be considered inflammatory against the King, a soldier standing near the speaker's platform would throw an egg in Warren's face as a signal for British officers to draw their swords and kill Hancock, Adams, and hundreds more.[1]

The plot never hatched, but rumor of it spread widely. There was no turning back. The British had already made clear their belief that the Parliament of England had every right to impose taxes on the colonists, and that their opponents were "zealots of anarchy."[2]

General Thomas Gage, the military governor of Massachusetts, was ordered to arrest Hancock and Adams. He headed towards Lexington to fulfill the order. But the Americans found what General Gage was planning, and "The shot heard 'round the world" was fired at Lexington's village green in April 1775.

The Second Continental Congress convened in Philadelphia on May 10, 1775 with John Hancock elected as President. Defiant in the face of British threats, Hancock declared that matters were moving rapidly to a crisis point and condemned the "Tyrant of Britain and his Parliament."[3] The decade-old battle over taxes and lack of representation soon escalated into the Revolutionary War.

The Founding Fathers certainly differed in their beliefs about the form the newly formed United States government should take, and they didn't hesitate to express those differences publicly, and in often strident terms. But on the principle of no taxation without representation, the Founders were united.

According to Mr. Gerry, a Constitutional Convention delegate: "Taxation & representation are strongly associated in the minds of the people, and they will not agree that any but their immediate representatives shall meddle with their purses."[4] In Article 1, Section 7 of the Constitution, the delegates invested with the House of Representatives the power to originate "[A]ll Bills for raising Revenue."

As James Madison said, "[O]ur forefathers brought with them the germ of Independence in the principle of self-taxation. Circumstances unfolded and perfected it."[5] The principle of no taxation without representation has stood the test of time since the Constitution's ratification. Enter the globalists, who seek nothing less but to negate the very concept upon which this country was founded.

The Drive For Global Taxes

Hancock fought the good fight. But more than 200 years later, the fruits of his victory are under attack by do-gooders, Earth-firsters and the usual contingent of one-issue fanatics whose battle cry is "Global Taxes!" They need such taxes in order to underwrite their alternately grandiose, naïve and dangerous schemes. A massive, forced redistribution of wealth from productive to unproductive countries? No problem!

And make no mistake, it will take a *lot* of money to implement both the legitimate and the hare-brained ideas floating around "NGO-World". It's estimated that it would take $625 billion a year to implement the "sustainable development" programs of the Earth Summit's Agenda 21 *alone*, requiring the euphemistic "transfer" of at least $125 billion a year from developed countries.[6]

Think about that for a minute: A billion dollars is a huge amount just on its own. Multiply that by 125 and all of sudden you're talking about real money—money being forcibly sucked out of our economy. Money that will essentially go to underwrite a UN slush fund, one administered by the same cadre of UN bureaucrats and buffoons who have already proven themselves in some cases to be morbidly stupid, if not outright corrupt.

And of course the money to fund "sustainable development" and all its attendant bells and whistles would constitute only a fraction of what our so-called "betters" want us to pay for. The list, already seemingly endless, is refreshed and renewed every time some UN "forum" convenes.

In other words, the globalists want the UN to become a world taxing authority, one that can generate revenue sources free of any political constraints—an arrangement that's as far away from John Hancock's beliefs as you can get. Indeed, former Secretary-General Boutros Boutros-Ghali bluntly remarked in a BBC interview in 1996 that generating revenues for the United Nations through global taxes would free the UN from being "under the daily financial will of the Member States."[7]. Boutros-Ghali elaborated further in a lecture at Oxford University the very next day:

> As the immediate financial emergency is addressed, and system-wide reform is pursued, it is time to seriously address the need for a United Nations that can operate on a secure and steady independent financial foundation. Measures for consideration could include: a fee on speculative international financial transactions, a levy on fossil fuel use (or its resulting pollution); earmarking a small portion of the anticipated decline in world military expenditures, utilizing some resources released by the elimination of unnecessary subsidies; resources

generated from a stamp tax on international travel and travel documents, or a levy on global currency transactions. Finding the right formula will be a project of vast importance for the future of the international community.[8]

Wasn't the Revolutionary War fought in part because of a stamp tax?

Greedy to share in the perceived spoils, many NGOs are, of course, poised to jump right on board this gravy train:

> In an ideal world, we would all be concerned with the state of the global commons to create and sustain a livable world. New forms of resource generation including taxation and tax shifting are needed, *which might be collected nationally but which would be available for collective use.* (emphasis added) In this regard, we must better access resources that are available for sustainable development. Many of these ideas relate to other global objectives; the recommendations here concentrate primarily on ways of raising money for sustainable development.[9]

No longer would foreign aid be considered a discretionary policy decision made at the national level by elected officials accountable to the people they serve. No, our high-minded moral superiors plan to totally bypass the democratic process so that an unelected "global body" can have free rein to pick our pockets 24/7 with no accountability whatsoever. They would be thieves, naturally, but since they'd be "thieves with a human face," that should presumably make it palatable.

Yes, our busybody betters are constantly hard at work refining Boutros-Ghali's ideas for global taxes into a practical list they can impose on all of us:

- Fuel taxes, including carbon and aviation fuel taxes (annual revenues of about $643 billion)

- International financial transactions (annual revenue of about $300 billion).

- E-mail/Internet services (annual revenue of about $70 billion)

- World trade (annual revenue of about $37 billion)

- International arms trade (annual revenue of about $1.2 billion)

- International flights from Organization for Economic Cooperation and Development (OECD) countries (annual revenue of
  about $2.2 billion).

Revenue estimates for a number of these taxes are taken from "Global Taxes for Global Priorities."[10] Of course, The Great and the Good are not satisfied with just taxing the gas productive people use to drive to work every day, which is horrendous enough. They want to tax us every time every time we send an e-mail, too!

Add it all up and potentially *a trillion dollars a year* will line the coffers of UN-controlled agencies to spend as they wish. And that's just for starters.

Other ideas for global taxes or mandatory fees on the drawing boards include royalties on minerals mined in inter-national waters, parking charges for satellites placed in geosta-tionary orbit, charges for fishing international waters, charges for use of the electromagnetic spectrum (e.g., television, radio, mobile phones, etc.) in OECD countries, a tax on traded pollu-tion permits, a tax on the profits of transnational corporations, and a tax on international advertising, just to name a few. These taxes would then (in theory) be used to accomplish the various amorphous social policy goals of the unelected, unac-countable globalists.

Sound far-fetched? Some form of global taxation is closer than you might think. The idea of taxing financial transactions, for example, has been circulating for years and has gone from academic exercise to serious proposal in many world capitals. As usual, the NGOs have gotten the ball rolling by lobbying officials in their respective countries. Unsurprisingly, consider-ing the depths to which such organizations have sunk, even the World Council of Churches and the AFL-CIO have voiced their support.

The "International Innovative Revenue Project," sponsored by the California-based "Center for Environmental Economic Development," has a web site promoting excise taxes on cross-border currency transactions. These are called "Tobin Taxes," after Nobel-prize winning Yale economist James Tobin, who first proposed them during the 1970s. (Just to keep things in perspective, remember that Yasser Arafat and Kofi Annan are also Nobel Prize winners.)[11]

Hundreds of parliamentarians from six continents—many from countries that have absolutely nothing to lose, but plenty to gain—have signed an international appeal favoring the tax. It has received high level government endorsement in such countries as France, Belgium, Finland, India, Brazil and is being studied seriously in many others, most notably the United Kingdom.[12] In Congress, a resolution was introduced in 2000 endorsing the Tobin Tax, although it was never passed.[13]

Ever eager to expand his portfolio, Kofi Annan has taken up the mantle of his predecessor, Bourtro-Ghali. In December 2000 Annan appointed a High-Level Panel on Financing for Development chaired by Ernesto Zedillo, former President of Mexico, that included Robert Rubin, long-time Treasury Secretary for President Clinton. In June 2001 the panel issued a 72-page document consolidating ideas for global taxes under the seemingly inoffensive heading, "Innovative Sources of Financing." It seriously recommended establishing an "International Tax Organization."[14] Watch out, IRS—you've got competition!

The UN's current leadership is, of course, working overtime to popularize the global tax idea as a way of funding the Millennium Development Goals, which— as we've already seen— are based on specious data and thoroughly devoid of anything resembling cost controls and measurement criteria. In the lead-up to the Millennium +5 General Assembly summit session, the UN Secretariat commissioned the pretentiously titled "United Nations University World Institute for Development Economics Research" to undertake a study of "innovative sources of finance." This, of course, is nothing but UN-speak for global taxes as a new source of revenue, one that might indeed free the UN from laboring financially under the "daily will" of the member states.

This study, sonorously entitled "New Sources of Development Finance: Funding the Millennium Development Goals," was completed in September 2004 and presented to the secretary-general and the General Assembly. It specifically included discussion of a global environmental tax and a currency transactions tax among its list of "innovative sources of financing" for "development." Even more to the point, this UN study waxed eloquent about how global taxes would benefit a hypothetical "world government" :

> How far can we bring to bear on the funding of the Goals accumulated knowledge in the field of national public finance? One interesting point of departure is to consider the taxes and transfers that might be instituted by a world government. There is no possibility of such an institution being created in the relevant time frame, but it provides a reference point to illuminate the actual policy issues. It may also serve as a moral challenge. *If such a global government were to act in the interests of world citizens as a whole, then global welfare maximization is likely to imply substantial positive taxes on almost everyone in richer countries and substantial transfers to the majority of people in low-income countries.* (emphasis added)[15]

The General Assembly then adopted a resolution in which it decided "to give further consideration to the subject of possible innovative and additional sources of financing for development from all sources." No doubt, calls for global taxes will not abate any time soon—at least not until every flight, stock sale, and e-mail message is "generating revenue" for the Robin Hoods of Turtle Bay.

Before we turn to the Constitutional objections to global taxes, let's consider just how the UN would handle the billions of dollars that global taxes would put under its control. If the UN's past record is any guide, it won't be a pretty picture.

More Money To Burn

The United Nations did not have any internal oversight function to speak of until 1994—nearly fifty years after its founding. The Office of Internal Oversight Services (OIOS) was set up to oversee the UN's world-wide operations by conducting audits, recommending internal controls and investigating misconduct within the organization. However, the *OIOS was allotted only $20 million* in the Secretary-General's regular budget of approximately $2.63 billion during 2002-2003, a little over a half of one percent. Compare this with the $39.2 million which the General Assembly authorized for numerous projects in the Secretariat's Development Account.[16]

To get an idea of how low the internal audit function is on the list of the UN bureaucracy's real priorities, consider that the secretary-general has been authorized to spend *$26 million during the 2004-2005 budget cycle to complete the design work on refurbishing the UN headquarters building,*[17] currently taking up space on some of the most valuable real estate in the most expensive city in the country.

Remember that "Earth Summit" in Rio de Janeiro that Maurice Strong organized in 1992? It cost the United Nations more than *$65 million dollars.*[18] Multiply that figure by the number of forums, meetings, and summits the UN sponsors every year, and you've got a good idea why the audit function *must* be important in the overall scheme of things. The fact that it *isn't* should ring more than just a warning bell.

As of August 2003, nearly ten years since its establishment, only a third of OIOS's critical recommendations regarding UN budget controls had actually been implemented, as the United Nations General Assembly Budget Committee admitted itself.[19]

Interestingly, the OIOS's audit from 2003 that uncovered significant problems with the Oil-for-Food Program was addressed to none other than Benon Sevan, the former *head* of the program, who of course did little about it.[20] Sevan was later found to have engaged in alleged "illicit activities" of his own in connection with Oil-for-Food—the same program he was supposed to administer.[21]

The OIOS audit found that literally millions of dollars were unaccounted for—and that was just tip of the iceberg. The OIOS had spent considerable time looking into the UN's dealings with Cotecna, the Swiss-based company that employed Annan's son Kojo as it prepared its bid for an oil-for-food contract.

Shortly after Kojo ended his consulting assignment with the firm, Cotecna received a $4.8 million dollar contract to conduct inspections of goods purchased with the oil-for-food revenues.[22] Evidence has subsequently surfaced that Kojo *continued* to receive money from Cotecna after his formal consultancy arrangement ended. Apparently Annan Sr. simply looked the other way while his son used his family connection to the UN for personal gain.[23]

Besides the question of possible nepotism in the awarding of the contract, the OIOS found serious irregularities and overcharges in connection with the actual contract itself, reporting that the required inspections were non-existent or basically useless. The audit also concluded that the Oil-for-Food administrators at the UN had known about the problems for years but ignored them. No one even bothered to monitor the Cotecna agents operating in Iraq.

Nevertheless, completely ignoring the findings of its *own* Office of Internal Oversight Services, ever-vigilant UN bureaucrats signed yet *another* multi-million dollar contract with Cotenca.[24] *Put another way, the United Nations awarded at least $14.6 million to a non-performing company with ties to Annan's son Kojo—an amount equivalent to seventy percent of the entire annual* *budget for the OIOS's worldwide audit functions!* The findings of the second Volcker Report, which laid out substantial evidence of Kojo's wrongdoing and the fact that his father ignored it, has made this sordid mess all the more damning.[25]

Adding insult to injury, UN auditors refused to release their internal audits to investigators at the General Accounting Office (GAO) who have been probing the Oil-for-Food scandal.[26] Even though we cover about 22% of the United Nations' regular budget, our elected representatives were stonewalled in our efforts to determine just what was going on. Only now, with the full dimensions of the scandal coming inconveniently to light, has the UN decided to honor us with the release of a few audit reports. And of course, who knows what evidence the intrepid Iqbal Riza, Kofi Annan's former chief of staff, might have shoved into the shredder?

All this is just a glimpse of what the future holds if funding sources shift from member state contributions to a broad global tax base. UN leadership, already unable to account for millions, will have even less reason to be accountable. They'll feel no pressure to cooperate with member state investigations. American taxpayers will still pick up, directly or indirectly, a significant piece of the bill under any and all global tax schemes, but they will have *absolutely no say* on how their money is spent—and on who is spending it.

Global Taxing Of American Citizens Is Unconstitutional

The United Nations is an organization of sovereign countries according to its Charter, not a sovereign entity unto itself. When a sovereign government, particularly a functioning democracy, imposes taxes on its own people, it is accountable to those people for how it raises and spends this money. The UN is only accountable to its member states from which it receives its funding in the form of dues and voluntary contributions, again as provided for in the UN Charter. There is simply no extant authority under which the UN can derive revenue through global taxes imposed on individuals or companies, *because the UN has no legal jurisdiction whatsoever.*

The UN remains subject to the fiscal control of its member states—unless its Charter is amended. As mentioned previously, this would require a vote of two-thirds of the General Assembly. Such a change would then need to be ratified in accordance with their respective Constitutional processes by two thirds of the members of the United Nations, including all the permanent members of the Security Council. Thankfully, that's a high hurdle to jump.

Still, a legal foundation for global tax extortion could be created via ratification of a separate treaty among a "critical mass" of nations. Knowing the political obstacles—particularly in the United States—the globalists will employ their usual stealth strategy.

After assuring us that "it's for the children/environment /homeless, etc.," they'll start small, with "modest" tax proposals that might hit only the relatively well-to-do—a tax on airline tickets, or some sort of "luxury tax" on vehicles. Of course, they won't call them taxes, because that term has a negative connotation and no one actually *likes* the tax collector, even if he has a human face. Indeed, Kevin Baumert, a former intern at the Global Policy Forum, urged proponents of these taxes to describe the taxes very carefully in non-offensive terms:

> The very word 'tax' is loaded with negative connotations and is often synonymous with political death. For this reason, couching proposals in terms of a fee, levy or charge will be decidedly more palatable to policymakers.[27]

To provide the illusion of national authority over taxing decisions, the treaty would turn member states into tax collectors for the UN, passing an agreed-upon portion of the revenue over to some international institution acting under the UN

Secretariat's direction, for spending on whatever NGO's project is "flavor of the millennium."

Does this all sound just too cynical? It is. While globalists try to co-opt the high moral ground via whatever their personal obsessions are, their ulterior motives are clear. Helping "the people" is merely a sideline—and for some groups, a mere distraction. What they really want is power, and the ego-boosting prestige that comes from being a professional do-gooder. They want money, the more the better, and no oversight please, we're activists so of course you can trust us. And most of all, they want to tame the United States and its citizens who, despite socialist-type inroads, remain too rich, too free, too clever, too gung-ho, too well-armed and just too much of everything to be willingly controlled by this high-minded gang that has such low intentions.

But of course, even if our government refuses to go along with what's in essence organized extortion, the globalists would see to it that U.S. businesses pay indirectly through surcharges and levies imposed by countries that are part of, let's say, the "global carbon tax regime"—a form of multilateral trade retaliation for not joining the global tax bandwagon.

Under our Constitution, Congress cannot delegate the power to enact new taxes. Only the House of Representatives (not the Senate) can originate bills to raise revenues. For example, it is a violation of the separation of powers between the legislative and executive branches for Congress to pass a resolution giving the President discretionary powers to institute new taxes, or to modify old ones. If it did so, Congress would be handing over to the President a legislative power—exactly what the Founding Fathers ingeniously designed the Constitution to prevent.

So if Congress can't hand over taxing authority to a co-equal branch of the U.S. government, it *certainly* can't delegate taxing authority to a global body that has no Constitutional status whatsoever. Nor does it matter if the Senate ratifies a treaty with a global tax provision, if the treaty itself violates the Constitution by giving to an unaccountable foreign institution a non-delegable power that only the elected representatives can exercise.

But hey, why worry? The globalists aren't! They'll get around all this by calling their taxes by another name, claiming that their main purpose is not to raise revenue but to fund protection of the environment/children/old people/animals/_____ (fill in your own cause.) That way, the issue of taxing authority is irrelevant, because we are not dealing with an actual revenue-raising tax to start with. But of course, this is sheer spin. We're talking taxes—we know it, and the NGOs know it. They've issued way too many documents over the years confirming their real intent to deny it now.

"The power to tax is the power to destroy," Supreme Court Justice John Marshall said during the early years of this country's history. Marshall's maxim is truer than ever today. In Congress alone are all Americans represented in connection with the taxes they are required to pay—with Congress' power tempered by the checks and balances that the executive and judicial branches provide in the exercise of their respective Constitutional powers.

There is no room in this brilliantly constructed system for some unaccountable global institution. The Constitution—properly interpreted—places beyond the reach of the United Nations or any of its greedy minions all those powers which are conferred *by* the people of the United States *on* the government of the United States alone. Successfully imposing any sort of "international tax" on Americans would be the first step towards destroying our ability to govern ourselves— the way we see fit— through history's most successful Constitutional structure.

If this happens, the Kofi Annans, Maurice Strongs and Jeffrey Sachs of the world would be free to run rampant through the U.S. Treasury, spending our money in ways that would likely be contrary to our own interests—and, frankly, to the interests of the world. Americans would have less money to spend as they see fit, which of course is part of the point. Damn the consumer! Never mind that the true engine of prosperity is private enterprise, and that if Americans have no money, there won't be anyone to buy whatever it is that's being produced by the developing countries in question.

Jobs would be destroyed as yet another layer of taxation is added to existing burdens—who in their right mind would continue to run or start a business under such conditions? Any notion of enforcing budget controls or operational transparency on the United Nations would be destroyed because the UN would have a huge tax base of its own to draw from and wouldn't have to make its case every year for contributions from member states. What a pretty picture!

"The price of freedom is eternal vigilance," said Thomas Jefferson. Congress, thankfully, has taken a good first step towards avoiding the above nightmare by prohibiting the use of appropriated funds to pay any voluntary contributions to the UN, should the latter make an effort to impose taxes on U.S. citizens for the purposes of raising revenues for itself. [28]

But the problem is that our vigilance is stalled there. The UN is pushing harder than ever to impose global taxes and instead of cutting off funding in response, our elected representatives are instead excoriating the tough-minded John Bolton for daring to question Kofi Annan's motives.

"The power to tax is the power to destroy." The price of maintaining the freedom to tax ourselves under a representative system of government also requires vigilance against treaties that emanate even a whiff of "global tax" stench. Again, Congress took a first step, at least with regards to taxing the Internet, one of the greatest engines of freedom and free enterprise every created: "[N]one of the funds appropriated or otherwise made available in this Act for the United Nations may be used by the United Nations for the promulgation or enforcement of any treaty, resolution, or regulation authorizing the United Nations, or any of its specialized agencies or affiliated organizations, to tax any aspect of the Internet".[29]

But of course, this is just one of the myriad tax schemes the UN and its supporters have on hand to bludgeon us with. They also have a whole morass of "treaties" and "agreements" out there, some of them signed merely as good-will gestures, that may yet come back to haunt us. We should be eternally grateful that John Bolton is at least temporarily wielding a sharp red pen and deleting dangerously broad wording from UN and NGO "agreements" as fast as their advocates can write them.

But Bolton and his team are just the first line of defense.

The President and Senate must keep an eye out for any attempt to slip a "global tax" into an otherwise benign looking treaty and stop it in its tracks.

Finally, vigilance extends to making sure we have federal judges who are not fooled by the smokescreens and endlessly benign language that globalists use to confuse their opponents. We need judges who are not afraid to strike down an unconstitutional tax when they see one—even one that may have slipped under the radar in a treaty ratified by the Senate. And we must be just as diligent about appointing federal judges who understand that their judicial role is NOT to impose expensive "global programs" as Constitutional mandates that will wind up being funded through additional taxes—effectively legislating from the bench the equivalent of global taxes through the back door.

Let us remember the words of the *Liberty Song*, the tribute written shortly after the confrontation between the British custom collectors and the crew of John Hancock's sloop Liberty:

> Come, join hand in hand, brave Americans all, And rouse your bold hearts at fair Liberty's call. No tyrannous acts shall suppress your just claim or stain with dishonor America's name.[30]

Were he alive today, John Hancock would be again rallying the *Liberty* cause against those who would try to impose their venal and oppressive global taxes on us without the consent of our elected representatives.

CHAPTER SIX

THE GLOBALISTS TAKE AIM AT LAWFUL GUN POSSESSION

I T'S A BAD SIGN when a British "human rights" organiza-tion tells Americans how our Constitution should be inter-preted. Apparently, some British folks have forgotten from whom we won our freedom-and why we sought it in the first place.

This NGO called International Alert has shown no com-punction at all in boldly declaring that "the U.S. Constitution does not guarantee individuals the right to possess or carry guns. The Second Amendment only protects 'the right to form militias under the control of state authorities.'"[1]

Sorry, guys, but it ain't that simple, even though the inter-pretation of exactly what the Second Amendment is supposed to protect is very much up in the air right now. It is true that some federal courts, particularly California's liberal federal Ninth Circuit Court of Appeals, have bought into the theory that the Second Amendment does not protect individual rights and was meant only to serve communal needs for self-defense. However, the Fifth Circuit Court of Appeals has come out squarely on the side of the individual's right to lawfully possess firearms for his or her protection.

In an exhaustive and welcome review of the literature and precedent, the Justice Department also recently concluded that the Second Amendment was intended to protect the rights of individuals to keep and bear arms for their own use.[2] Some legal scholars remain uncertain on the subject. Harvard Law professor Laurence Tribe, the usually liberal constitutional law expert, observed that there was an individual right to "possess and use firearms in the defense of themselves and their homes" but it was "admittedly of uncertain scope."

In response to his scholarly discussion of the issue, "I've gotten an avalanche of angry mail from apparent liberals who said, 'How could you?'" Tribe was quoted as saying. "But as someone who takes the Constitution seriously, I thought I had a responsibility to see what the Second Amendment says, and how it fits."[3]

The almost overwhelmingly left-wingers who are intent on curbing gun possession worldwide have no interest in scholarly debate, or in approaching Congress for an up or down vote on their proposals. They want the UN to somehow magically conjure up enforceable "international norms" strictly limiting, if not prohibiting, what firearms individuals may possess for their own defense. They then want to see those "norms" incorporated into the interpretation of the Second Amendment by judges who are willing to erase, also like magic, the protection of individual rights altogether.

Under the cloak of yet *another* conference—the "UN Conference on the Illicit Trade in Small Arms in All Its Aspects"— the globalists are seeking to end all civilian possession and use of small arms and light weapons. They insist that civilian possession of ordinary firearms poses a threat to "human rights" and that there is no general right to civilian access to arms under any international instrument, which apparently are the only "instruments" that count.

One could ask whose "human rights" they are seeking to defend—those of the prospective victim using a gun in self-defense, or those of the criminal preying on the defenseless?—but there's a sense in which even the question is irrelevant. As is so often the case with elitist do-gooders, individuals count for nothing. It's the group, the class, the oppressed, etc., that counts.

As we have seen in the case of the Earth Charter movement, well-funded NGOs are taking the lead in trying to deprive us of our God-given right to self-defense. The International Action Network on Small Arms (IANSA) is the global network of NGOs working to stop the proliferation and "misuse"- read, any use-of small arms and light weapons.

Founded in 1998, IANSA claims that it has more than 500 participant groups in nearly one hundred countries and is composed of organizations "concerning themselves" with small arms, including policy development organizations, national gun control groups, research institutes, aid agencies, faith groups, victims, and of course the ubiquitous "human rights" and "community action" organizations. The British-based International Alert, self-proclaimed experts on the U.S. Constitution, is part of this global network of small-arms ban activists.

As such groups always seem to be, IANSA is well funded, receiving money from the British, Belgian, Swedish and Norwegian governments, as well as a large number of U.S.-based foundations, many of whom seem increasingly intent on underwriting any and all initiatives that seek to compromise U.S. sovereignty. These include multi-billionaire George Soros' Open Society Institute, the Ford Foundation, Rockefeller Foundation, Compton Foundation, Ploughshares Fund, John D. and Catherine T. MacArthur Foundation, Samuel Rubin Foundation and Christian Aid.

The IANSA plans to "strengthen the network of organizations committed to stopping small arms proliferation" and "to

continue to play a leadership role in the UN Small Arms Conference process, promoting NGO participation in the meetings,
and keeping pressure on UN member governments to create
effective and binding measures against the proliferation and
misuse of small arms and light weapons at all levels."[4]
IANSA's use of the word "proliferation" is, of course, its
euphemism for any gun possession by private individuals.
IANSA's ultimate objective is to take all guns out of the hands
of private individuals—or, as they call it in the endlessly pre-
tentious language so many NGOs favor when honoring the
public with their pronouncements "creating norms of non-
possession."[5] (emphasis added.)

The director of IANSA is Rebecca Peters, an activist who
assumed this post in 2002 after working for three years in New
York for George Soros' Open Society Institute. Conveniently,
IANSA also has a UN liaison officer on staff. Peters is a gun
prohibitionist who is not content with just tracking the sale of
firearms or even with the licensing of gun owners. Apparently
not worried about the proliferation of nuclear, biological and
chemical weapons that might kill millions in coordinated terrorist attacks, Peters sees ordinary guns as the real menace to
be eradicated.

And she said so, too. "Governments, preoccupied with a
search for nuclear, biological and chemical weapons in their
fight against terrorism have essentially ignored *the real weapons
of mass destruction—small arms*. So they continue to proliferate,
at the cost of hundreds of thousands of lives."[6] (emphasis
added)

In 1998, Peters told the UN Commission on Crime Prevention and Criminal Justice that "the international effort to restrict the flow of guns across borders must be accompanied by
efforts to restrict the build-up of arsenals in private homes."
She went on to say that "gun ownership is not a right but a
privilege."[7] Of course, she didn't bother mentioning that this is
merely *her* opinion on the subject.

Pointing to her own country Australia's 1996 gun prohibition law as a model to follow in creating an "international norm," she failed to observe that according to Australia's own statistics, murders went up about 3% and armed robberies up 44% during the year after the enactment of Australia's draconian law. With some fluctuations, they've continued to rise. The United States, meanwhile, experienced declines of 8% in the murder rate and a 17% drop in armed robberies during the same period.[8] And more right-to-carry and concealed-carry laws in this country should contribute to even greater decreases in years to come, something that IANSA should applaud—but won't. The UN first got involved with the small arms issue under Secretary-General Boutros-Ghali. In his 1995 report to the UN Security Council, Boutros-Ghali called for new efforts in the field of what he exquisitely termed "microdisarmament." The General Assembly established an ad hoc Panel of Governmental Experts on Small Arms, which released a report in August 1997 analyzing the small arms trade and recommending ways to control it.

IANSA kept up the pressure for more UN involvement and, smelling both a funding opportunity and a chance to tweak the United States, Boutros-Ghali's successor enthusiastically took up the cause. Control of small arms became a permanent fixture on the UN agenda when Kofi Annan created yet another working group, the "Group of Governmental Experts on Small Arms" and called for—wait for it—*several conferences* to devise global curbs on firearms.

The UN came very close to codifying an "international norm" curtailing civilian access to firearms. A draft version of the "Programme of Action" adopted during the 2001 Conference on the Illicit Trade in Small Arms in All its Aspects made explicit reference to the "need" for states to regulate civilian possession and use.

However, this draft was not adopted by the member states. The president of the Conference, Camilo Reyes Rodriguez of

Colombia, expressed his "disappointment over the Conference's inability to agree, due to the concerns of one State, on language recognizing the need to establish and maintain controls over private ownership" of small weapons.[9]

Who could that one State be? Why, the United States of course, which once again refused to suborn its citizens' right to self-defense to yet another grandiose, unenforceable "norm." Rebecca Peters, still with George Soros' Open Society Institute at the time and reeking with typical self-importance, was far more vociferous in her condemnation of the United States' refusal to buy into her scheme. Clearly peeved with our right to petition the government on matters that concern us—as opposed to matters in which she has chosen to insinuate herself—she said:

"It's unbelievably selfish that the most powerful nation in the world, that produces more than half of the small arms in the world, is prepared to jeopardize the safety of millions of people in other countries purely for the sake of pandering to its own domestic lobbying interest."[10]

And selfishness is bad, as we've noted before, in this instance because it allows law-abiding citizens to make their own decisions as to whether or not to arm themselves for self-defense.

Peters and her fellow globalists insist that no effort to combat illicit trafficking of small arms can succeed without full controls on civilian sale, possession, and use of firearms. Despite overwhelming empirical evidence that supports the old adage that "when guns are outlawed, only outlaws will have guns," Peters and her fellow travelers will continue to press their cause until they secure an international treaty or protocol that invalidates any individual right to possess and use of firearms except under very strict controls imposed by the "global community"—a "community" which we can safely assume won't be instantly available to help individual Americans being mugged or threatened in their own homes.

In 2006 IANSA will try again to revive the "Programme of Action" at yet another conference. This provides a great opportunity for IANSA to press the member states to expand their commitments to the very Orwellian-sounding "global norms of good behavior" on small weapons controls.

At the advance Preparatory Committee meeting in which NGOs can participate, IANSA will try to influence the negotiations over any text to be agreed upon through the creation of "a binding implementation plan," or "programme of work," to be appended to the existing "Programme of Action."

Such picayune and nit-picking attention to detail is exhausting even to read about, but it's what enables IANSA and others of its ilk to find subtle ways of insinuating binding language into treaties and agreements. As we've seen again and again, globalists excel at using vague, neutral, non-threatening language to disguise their intentions, but when zooming in on an opportunity to hog-tie a developed nation, they rarely miss a linguistic beat.

In any event, IANSA has put out the call that it will reintroduce "the issue of regulating gun possession by civilians." The United States successfully kept this item out of the Programme of Action back in 2001, but IANSA intends to push for it once again.[11]

Constitutional Armor Against Dangerous "Norms"

Can our Second Amendment continue to protect law-abiding gun owners in this country? The globalists are counting on sympathetic federal judges to use their interpretation of the rights conferred by deferring to "international norms" against gun possession. Which would, of course, make a mockery of what a judge is supposed to do—examine the Second Amendment's text, history and intended purpose and then decide accordingly, whether he or she approves of the outcome or not. A judge who takes the task of interpreting the

Constitution seriously would pay no attention at all to what a UN "Programme of Action" might say or what some George Soros lackey sees as an appropriate "international norm."

Instead, a diligent judge would start with the text of the Second Amendment itself, which is only one sentence long— "A well regulated Militia, being necessary to the security of a free State, the right of the people to keep and bear Arms shall not be infringed." The judge would note that the three key phrases in the clause are "Militia," "keep and bear Arms" and "people" and that the phrase "to keep and bear Arms" is used in the context of a "right of the people."

As the recent Justice Department memorandum astutely observes, "the phrase 'keep arms' was commonly understood to denote ownership of arms by private citizens for private purposes. When that phrase is read together with its subject, 'the right of the people,' the evidence points strongly toward an individual right."[12]

Those arguing that no protection of individual rights was intended by the Amendment's drafters claim that the people collectively could only bear arms as part of an organized militia—a small sub-set of the population. In this reading, the "people" were only a group of citizens serving in a state-run "Militia." But if this were so, why is the right of the people to bear arms included as one of the ten amendments constituting the fundamental Bill of Rights? The same word "people" is used elsewhere in the Bill of Rights, and in virtually every instance it is given a much broader interpretation.

Consider, for example, the First Amendment's "right of the people peaceably to assemble, and to petition the Government for a redress of grievances," and the Fourth Amendment's "right of the people to be secure in their persons, houses, papers." The Founding Fathers considered the "people" as distinct from, not subordinate to or in the service of, the government.[13]

As explained by the Supreme Court in its only decision dealing squarely with the scope of the Second Amendment back in 1939, the term "Militia" as used by the drafters of the Second Amendment meant the entire adult population, not an organized military unit.[14] While considered outdated today with the National Guard being the contemporary version of the militia, the meaning of "Militia" to our Founding Fathers was co-mingled with their idea of an essential liberty—that of enabling individuals to protect themselves, their families and their property without being beholden to an oppressive government.

Alexander Hamilton described the militia as made up of "the great body of the yeomanry".[15] James Madison emphasized the "advantage of being armed, which the Americans possess over the people of almost every other nation" and pointed out that "notwithstanding the military establishments in the several kingdoms of Europe, which are carried as far as the public resources will bear, the governments are afraid to trust the people with arms."[16] Only by letting all law-abiding citizens keep their own arms would the citizenry be safe from a repeat of their experience with the British, whose soldiers had seized weapons from those same law-abiding citizens while in charge of the colonies.

So from even a cursory study of the text and its history, the Second Amendment's meaning and relevancy should be quite clear to a judge who has done his or her homework—the people, from whom the militia must be taken, shall have the right to keep and bear arms. Civilian possession and use of firearms are not "privileges" for which law-abiding citizens need special permission from the government—they are rights.

Unfortunately, the lower federal courts did not find much guidance in the Supreme Court's Second Amendment decision. It straddled the key issue—whether there was an individual right to keep and bear arms that went beyond the needs of a very broadly defined citizens' militia. In any event, the

Supreme Court has not ruled directly on the scope of the Second Amendment's protections since 1939.

Since then, the most ardent Supreme Court justice unambiguously opposing private gun ownership was Justice Douglas, who said in a dissenting opinion, "[T]here is no reason why all pistols should not be barred to everyone except the police."[17] The strongest statement from a Supreme Court justice on the other side of the issue has been Clarence Thomas who said, "The First Amendment...is fittingly celebrated for preventing Congress from 'prohibiting the free exercise' of religion or 'abridging the freedom of speech.' The Second Amendment similarly appears to contain an express limitation on the government's authority."[18]

Other current Supreme Court justices appear to show mild support for the individual right approach, but they have done so via side comments and have not had to deal squarely with the issue. How they would come out in a case directly calling for a Second Amendment interpretation in today's world is far from certain.[19]

As to the lower federal courts, particularly since Congress' passage of the Omnibus Crime Control and Safe Streets Act in 1968, most have rejected the individual right interpretation of the Second Amendment. However, this view is not unanimous. In 2001, a majority of a Fifth Circuit Court of Appeals panel adopted the individual right view, following a careful analysis of the Second Amendment's text and history.[20]

Since the issue appears wide open, globalist gun prohibitionists are jumping into the breach (metaphorically speaking, of course.) The apparent judicial confusion over the meaning of the Second Amendment makes it vulnerable to those judges willing to be seduced by the globalists' siren call to incorporate "international norms" into their interpretations.

And much like the proverbial camel with his nose in the tent, once our betters secure the wording they seek on curtailing private gun possession, they will argue that this "international norm" should be incorporated into any interpretation of the Second Amendment, *converting a constitutionally protected individual right into a government-bestowed privilege*—in part because some woman named Rebecca Peters who doesn't even live in this country says that's the way it should be.

Those opposing the individual rights interpretation have argued that the Second Amendment was the product of "anachronistic" assumptions about the balance between federal and state powers.[21] Since the military and police professionals have assumed responsibility for our collective defense, this view holds, the idea of a people's armed militia is quaint but no longer relevant.

But these arguments miss the point. If the Constitution is to be changed, the proper and legal way is through the amendment process, a process which would require the kind of "debate in the public square" that globalists simply can't abide—not only because their behind-the-scenes machinations would be exposed, but because their arguments are often so simplistic and childish as to be unsupportable when brought to light.

The Constitution is a compact between "we the people" and the government to form a "more perfect union" that establishes a shared responsibility for our common defense. Nothing is more basic—or more sacred—than self-preservation, the right to ensure one's own personal security. The Constitution provides assurances that our own beings and property will be protected, both against arbitrary intrusion by our government and from invasions and domestic violence.[22]

And the Second Amendment codifies the right for the people to keep their own arms and use them in their own defense when necessary. It's basic. It's obvious. It's a right articulated by brilliant thinkers who had seen war and social upheaval, and whose intellects and sheer guts in defense of their beliefs put the vague ramblings of the Rebecca Peters, Maurice Strongs and George Soroses of the world to shame.

But of course, as we've seen again and again, some people *have* no shame.

Yes, our military and police provide the first line of defense against domestic and foreign violence, but as the chaos following Hurricane Katrina graphically proved, these defenses are hardly fool-proof. And while the media emphasis was, of course, on the shameful reports of looters and marauders using guns to hurt the innocent and traumatized, the story has yet to be told of how many people were able to defend themselves and their families because they were armed and so had no need to capitulate in the face of chaos and temporary lawlessness.

In fact, as Katrina and other such disasters demonstrate so starkly, it is *precisely* when "the sanctions of society and laws are found insufficient to restrain the violence of oppression" that the right of the American people to possess arms is most critical.[23] As for the question of "human rights" the mantra globalists continually invoke, *there is no right more important than that of self-defense!* To deny a law-abiding citizen the means to defend himself and his family is to deprive him of his "life, liberty and property" in violation of the Fifth Amendment to the Constitution.

Of course, like any right, the Second Amendment is subject to regulation to protect the community from abuse. We don't want little children to have access to guns, for example. And society certainly has a vested interest in keeping guns out of the hands of criminals and the mentally ill. But that's a far cry from eviscerating an individual's right to possess arms altogether, as IANSA and their UN cronies want to do.

Today we face a determined yet amorphous enemy in the form of Islamist terrorists, who have specifically targeted American civilians for death wherever they are found. Al—Qaeda attacked our homeland without any provocation, killing nearly 3,000 innocent people just going about their business on a beautiful September day. Our government was taken completely by surprise on 9/11, despite years of intelligence gathering. Ever since, Federal officials have issued terrorist warnings with little specificity, warning us to be on guard at all times.

This is a new kind of war, one that hardly qualifies as a classic military confrontation between nations with organized military forces. Osama Bin Laden, who either in person or from the grave periodically updates his threats and promises of mass murder, said in his "Sermon for the Feast of the Sacrifice" in 2003:

> You should know that seeking to kill Americans and Jews everywhere in the world is one of the greatest duties [for Muslims], and the good deed most preferred by Allah, the Exalted.[24]

With armed fanatics entering our country hell-bent on slaughtering innocent civilians, our God-given right to possess and use arms in our own defense has never meant so much. Yet the globalists continue to demand that we give up the ability to defend our homes and families to meet some self-appointed committee's interpretation of what constitutes a "global norm of good behavior!" It would be laughable if it weren't so nausea-inducing.

And adding to the surreal nature of the argument, Peters and her internationalist pals want us to entrust the UN with our safety by giving them the ultimate authority to decide what firearms Americans "may" keep in their homes and on their persons.

Lest we forget, this is the *same* UN that has failed miserably in so many of its efforts to protect unarmed civilians from genocide—most notably during the Rwanda crisis in 1994 when the UN Department of Peacekeeping Operations (headed by none other than Kofi Annan) blatantly squandered a chance to destroy illegal weapons before they could be used to kill thousands of innocent civilians.[25] The unarmed masses, unable to defend themselves had, however, the "right" to be mowed down by armed thugs.

And this is the same UN whose "humanitarian" Relief and Works Agency (UNRWA)—the agency that runs the Palestinian refugee camps—lets those camps be used as bases for small-arms factories, explosives laboratories, and arms caches. Just for the sake of convenience, it even lets terrorists use UN vehicles to transport the weapons to target locations![26]

Terrorist organizations actively use UNRWA offices and schools to conduct their illegal activities, and Hamas has widespread support among the 23,000 Palestinian refugees that UNRWA has hired to work in the camps.[27]

That's some record of success. If "human rights" are so important to Kofi and his minions, why not arm some of the young, terrified girls continually being exploited for sex and worse by UN "peacekeepers?" After all, their rights—as well as their bodies—are being horribly violated on a regular basis.

Clearly, the UN can't stop genocide or break up terror cells operating in its own facilities. Nonetheless, Rebecca Peters, George Soros, and their little friends would vastly prefer it if we would forfeit our Second Amendment rights to this bungling, criminally inept group of bureaucrats and elitists.

With at least five of the current Supreme Court justices on record as being, to some degree, receptive to using international law in their interpretations of the Constitution—Justices Ginsberg, Breyer, Kennedy, Stevens, and Souter—the Supreme Court could well decide the next Second Amendment case on the basis of an artificially contrived "international norm" that denies individuals the right to own guns for self-defense. Should that happen, former Homeland Security Secretary Tom Ridge's celebrated duct tape may turn out to be the only thing we're free to arm ourselves with.[28]

We need judges who demonstrate both common sense and a willingness to adhere to the Constitution's core principles, ones who take to heart Thomas Jefferson's belief that "no freeman shall be debarred the use of arms (within his own lands or tenements),"[29] judges who set aside, with deserved contempt, the argument that gun ownership is a privilege to be denied individual citizens in the interests of some amorphous "greater good."

CHAPTER SEVEN

UNIVERSAL INJUSTICE
FOR ALL

IT IS SAID THAT all roads lead to Rome, the city where Caesars once dreamed of ruling a truly global empire. In 1998, some 2,000 NGOs came together in Rome. Calling themselves the Coalition for the International Criminal Court (ICC), these groups also have in mind world domination—they're just going about it in a different way.

Working with government officials from supportive countries and with the ever-eager assistance of the UN bureaucracy, ICC proponents argued for a permanent global court, one with universal jurisdiction to prosecute those individuals accused of the usually vaguely defined "crimes" against humanity, including genocide and "war crimes." Their efforts were rewarded by passage of the Rome Statute of the International Criminal Court (Rome Statute).

The U.S. voted against the Rome Statute in its final form because it conferred exceedingly broad jurisdiction over nonparties against their consent. It also diluted the existing powers of the Security Council on matters involving use of military power.

Indeed, the way the Rome Statute was written, Security Council authorization isn't even required before the ICC can proceed with a prosecution involving a peacekeeping mission—including those involving the U.S. military. The Security Council would be powerless to stop such prosecutions unless all 5 permanent members went along with a vote to delay it. Naturally rejecting this country's objections, the Conference adopted the Rome Statute by a vote of 120 in favor, 7 against, and 21 abstentions. Said William Pace, the "governor" of the Coalition for the International Criminal Court, with evident glee, "It frustrated the U.S. as much as any warlord in Somalia...They were extremely against it."[1]

In the same vein, an advisor to the Lebanese delegation proclaimed after the vote to approve the Rome Statute: "The United States is a bully. They have tried to destroy this important effort by denying the prosecutor true independence from the superpowers' grasp. The P-5 [Permanent Five of the Security Council] will never turn over their own people and they are the criminals using weapons of mass destruction".[2]

The International Criminal Court Assumes Power

One hundred thirty-nine states signed the treaty by the December 31, 2000 deadline. The ICC's formal jurisdiction to prosecute individuals allegedly committing covered crimes commenced on July 1, 2002, following ratification of the statute by the requisite sixty signatory states. Cleverly, the court can prosecute crimes committed on the territory of a country that has ratified the Rome Statute, even if the accused isn't a citizen of that country—or IS a citizen of a country that isn't a party to the Rome Statute!

The Assembly of States Parties—the ICC's governing body—is comprised of one representative from every country that ratified the Rome Statute. This Assembly is charged with electing judges and prosecutors; considering and deciding the court's budget; approving any additional agreements or amendments, and providing administrative oversight. It can also remove judges or prosecutors who fail to uphold the duties of their office.

In February 2003, the ICC's first eighteen judges were elected by secret ballot, using an election procedure set forth in the Rome Statute aimed at "ensuring fair gender and regional representation," merit not being considered a valid criterion apparently.[3] No judges came from overtly repressive regimes this time around.[4] However, there's no guarantee that such lively influences won't make their way onto the bench in the future.

And here's an irony. At least two of the judges who responded to a questionnaire from Human Rights Watch—one NGO—criticized the election process overseen by yet *another* NGO! What fun these people must have running around policing each other! It certainly beats being productive.

In any event, Judge Jorda criticized the election procedure, saying that "the process remains too marked by political maneuvering." Judge Song said that *"the procedural rules should be modified so that well-qualified candidates could be more easily elected."* [5] (emphasis added)

During a transition phase, three of the current judges will be replaced via election every three years. The judges then elected by *this* process are to remain in office for the full nine-year term.[6] Without procedural reforms and a requirement that judges be elected from truly democratic states, the process will clearly be open to abuse.

While the International Criminal Court is formally distinct from the United Nations, it is inextricably woven into the UN's designs for global governance, and so receives significant support from the secretary-general and various UN bodies. It can even do an end-run around the powers conferred by the UN Charter upon the Security Council, and particularly the veto powers of the five permanent members.

Only one major problem has stood in the way of the ICC's cheerleading squad—the Great Satan has both refused to join and will not recognize this make-believe court's jurisdiction over American citizens. Although Bill Clinton took time out from Oval Office hijinks to sign the Rome Statute before leaving the White House, the Senate never ratified it and President Bush has since declared that the signature is withdrawn. But this doesn't mean that the ICC can't target American travelers, or subject servicemen overseas to politicized, capricious ICC prosecution.

Wisely, we're putting our citizens first. As a condition of receiving U.S. aid, countries must sign bilateral agreements under which they agree not to arrest and turn U.S. citizens over to the ICC's jurisdiction. President Bush has signed legislation that essentially codifies this policy.

Over the years the United States had annually obtained resolutions from the UN Security Council providing immunity for U.S. troops and government personnel involved in UN peacekeeping operations. But in 2004, the ubiquitous Kofi Annan successfully rallied support against extending immunity for American peacekeeping troops from ICC prosecution. Pointing to isolated instances of prisoner abuse at the Abu Ghraib prison in Iraq, he intoned that "I think in this circumstance it would be unwise to press for an exemption, and it would be even more unwise on the part of the Security Council to grant it...*It would discredit the Council and the United Nations that stands for* rule of *law and the primacy of the rule of law.*"[7](emphasis added) In the face of mounting opposition to extending this immunity, the Bush Administration did not seek a renewal.[8]

While confirmed anti-Americans like Annan may view the ICC as a harbinger of justice and a counterbalance against American might, close inspection of the agreement reveals just how ripe for corruption the ICC really is. American citizens, from the President to the tourist, will find themselves under constant threat of politically-motivated retaliation. Constitutionally protected rights will be rendered void if the ICC has its way.

First among Equals

Under the Rome Statute, any individual may be tried and punished by the International Criminal Court for a covered crime, if the accused is from a country that ratified the agreement (and thus consented to submit to the jurisdiction of the court). But as mentioned before, here's the kicker—if the country on whose soil the alleged crime was committed has ratified the Rome Statute, *the accused may be tried and punished by the ICC, whether or not that individual is from a country that ratified the Rome Statute.*

The ICC is supposed to be a complement to a given country's criminal jurisdictions. It is not intended to supplant any nation's courts. But this, of course, is the typical sly play on words we've seen before. While member countries have an "opportunity" to investigate alleged crimes before the ICC gets involved, the ICC prosecutor may proceed with any case if he determines, *by his own discretion,* that the member country is not willing or able to "genuinely carry out the investigation" on its own.[9]

In other words, the ICC can swoop in and seize jurisdiction from a sovereign nation's courts practically any time it wants. To say that this trans-national institution runs afoul of the U.S. Constitution is putting it mildly. *Were our country to join as a party to the Rome Statute, the International Criminal Court would be co-equal to the courts and other branches of government with regard to jurisdiction over U.S. citizens for certain crimes.*

And our own government officials—including the sitting President, congressmen, senators and judges—would be required to submit to investigation, possible arrest and even trial by a "global" court for any alleged involvement in a "war crime" or "crime against humanity"—as defined not by us, but by the ICC.

Our Constitution allows the duly elected President and members of Congress to carry out their official responsibilities without fear of prosecution while in office, for both the official acts they undertake and the policies they implement in the course of performing their duties. The Rome Statute, on the other hand, specifically denies such protection to government officials of any nation subject to the jurisdiction of the ICC! Article 27 of that agreement bluntly states that it makes no difference what protections the country's domestic laws might provide to duly elected government officials:

> This Statute shall apply equally to all persons without any distinction based on official capacity. In particular, official capacity as a Head of State or Government, a member of a Government or parliament... shall in no case exempt a person from criminal responsibility under this Statute...

This sweeping authority over elected officials makes it all the more ironic that Bill Clinton—whose decision to use NATO forces against Slobodan Milosevic was called a "war crime" by the Yugoslavian leader's supporters since it lacked UN authorization—would choose to sign the agreement. Had it been in place during his tenure in office, ICC prosecutors might very well have made Clinton forget all about Ken Starr.

At the same time, what's good for the goose is evidently not good for the gander, since the ICC judges, the ICC prosecutor, the deputy prosecutors and the registrar get a free pass on anything they do in the course of *their* work for the International Criminal Court! They enjoy diplomatic immunity while in office and, even after the expiration of their terms of office, "continue to be accorded immunity from legal process of every kind in respect of words spoken or written and acts performed by them in their official capacity."[10]

Talk about gall.

In plain English, the Rome Statute would allow our elected leaders to be prosecuted by the ICC for "war crimes" defined as some imaginary violation of a conjured-up "international norm." An ICC judge or prosecutor bribed to fix a case involving a genocidal dictator, on the other hand, could be immune from any legal consequences whatsoever for this flagrant transgression of his or her responsibilities!

Of course, this all plays right into the hands of the usual suspects—the same tiresome, self-proclaimed "human rights" and "peace" activists who want to wield the ICC as a club with which to pummel the U.S. for daring to confront the true evils of the world—using *our* blood and *our* treasure without being bound to the theatrical swoonings of a sanctimonious elite.

We've already gotten a glimpse into the political Pandora's Box these activists are opening. Taking advantage of Germany's universal Code of Crimes Against International Law which, irony of ironies, grants *German* courts universal jurisdiction in cases involving war crimes or crimes against humanity—topics they clearly know a great deal about, to their enduring shame—a U.S. based "human rights" group filed a criminal complaint against Defense Secretary Donald Rumsfeld and other top U.S. officials for alleged abuses in the Abu Ghraib prison. Welcome to justice in the brave new world![11]

ICC Harm to the United States

To fully grasp the danger the ICC presents, let's assume that, following an irresponsible Senate ratification of the Rome Statute placing us under the ICC's jurisdiction, the president asks Congress for additional funding to support our troops in Afghanistan and Iraq. Congress approves. A constitutional challenge is brought by a left-wing activist group against both the Afghanistan and Iraq wars. It is rejected by a 7-2 majority of the Supreme Court. (We'll leave it to you to imagine who cast the dissenting votes.)

The supplemental money appropriated by Congress pays for smart bombs that are later used to level a suspected Taliban terrorist stronghold in Afghanistan. As is usually the case, the terrorists are hiding among civilians. In the course of the bombing, there are some unintended civilian casualties and damage to the surrounding wilderness areas. A handful of terrorists are captured by Afghan authorities as they attempt to flee and are turned over to the U.S. The prisoners are then taken into custody and sent to Guantanamo Bay for further detention and questioning.

A coalition of NGOs then brings a complaint to the ICC Prosecutor claiming that U.S. government officials and the military conspired to commit "crimes against humanity" and "war crimes" that should be prosecuted and tried by the ICC. Included in the charges are both the military action itself and interrogation of the prisoners at Guantanamo under allegedly mentally stressful and degrading circumstances. Positively delirious at the prospect, the prosecutor agrees and, after determining that the U.S. government will not investigate the clearly nonsensical charges, decides to pursue the case with the approval of the ICC's Pre-Trial Chamber.

Suddenly, a standard military operation conducted under the authority of two sovereign governments is turned on its head and characterized as a "crime." Such a charge would be laughable if only it were not so real. Under the typically vague language and sweeping guidelines that permeate the Rome Statue, the criminal charges brought and tried by the ICC could include all of the following:

- Bombing an area where civilians live—"crimes against humanity" and "war crimes" including "murder", and "intentionally directing attacks against the civilian population as such or against individual civilians not taking direct part in hostilities."[12]

- Incidental civilian casualties and harm to surrounding environment—"war crimes" including "intentionally launching an attack in the knowledge that such attack will cause incidental loss of life or injury to civilians or damage to civilian objects or widespread, long-term and severe damage to the natural environment which would be clearly excessive in relation to the concrete and direct overall military advantage anticipated."[13]

- Imprisonment and interrogation of captured suspected terrorists at the Guantanamo base—"crimes against humanity" and "war crimes" including "torture" and "other inhumane acts of a similar character intentionally causing great suffering, or serious injury to body or to mental or physical health."[14]

Even when such serious charges are made, the ICC does not need to provide the greater context in which the alleged acts took place (in this specific case, retaliation for an act of war committed on American soil). ICC prosecutors don't even need to meet an evidentiary burden in order to bring a suspect to trial—even if said suspect is a Marine acting on orders to capture a known terrorist!

The prosecutorial power the ICC has granted itself truly has no limit. The president and any congressman or senator voting for the military appropriation as well as all military personnel involved could—and probably would, given the sheer venality of our judicial "betters"—be subject to prosecution and trial by the ICC for one or more of these so-called "crimes."

But wait, there's more. Given our prior hypothetical Supreme Court decision, *in theory the seven Supreme Court justices who rejected the "peace activists" previous challenge could themselves be prosecuted by the ICC for this decision!*

Outraged yet? Here's another example. Suppose that an eager-beaver reporter from CNN is doing an investigative series on the unfolding UN peacekeeper sex scandal in the Democratic Republic of the Congo. The ICC Prosecutor has opened his own investigation. Deputy prosecutors are sent to interview witnesses, potential suspects and to gather evidence.

Suppose further that the journalist reports, based on un-named sources, that one of the ICC deputy prosecutors, a Frenchman, has received bribes and sexual favors in return for keeping a particular rape incident involving a fellow country-man secret. The unsubstantiated CNN report inflames the lo-cal population and results in repeated attacks against foreign-ers, particularly French residents and French members of the UN peacekeeping force wrongly thought to be involved in the despicable incidents. Several of the rape suspects are killed and their bodies dragged through the streets, with signs say-ing "Death to the French."

France, predictably a party to the Rome Statute, institutes a complaint in the ICC against CNN and its reporter under Arti-cle 25 (3)(e) of the Rome Statute for publicly inciting others to commit genocide through its—allegedly—baseless and in-flammatory reporting. France refers to the deliberate targeting of European nationals as evidence of genocide and cites the precedent of the International Criminal Tribunal for Rwanda's conviction of three individuals in 2003 for their role in operat-ing a radio station accused of broadcasting inflammatory statements before and during the genocide of April 1994.

After being advised that the First Amendment of the U.S. Constitution protects both CNN and its correspondent from criminal prosecution in the U.S., the ICC prosecutor decides to proceed with the case. At the same time, he reaffirms immu-nity for all of the ICC's own personnel, *including the ICC deputy prosecutor who was allegedly bribed during the course of his investi-gation.*

Scenarios like this could become all too common if we let ourselves be lulled into accepting ICC jurisdiction over Ameri-can citizens. Indeed, since both Afghanistan and the Democ-ratic Republic of the Congo, the countries cited in our exam-ples, are themselves parties to the Rome Statute, and since the "crimes" allegedly took place within their respective territo-ries, American citizens would still be at risk of being pulled into the ICC's dragnet—even if the U.S. isn't a party to the Rome Statute!

Incidentally, Iraq isn't a party to the Rome Statute. Hence, the attempt by "human rights" groups to bring their case against Rumsfeld in *Germany* under that country's universal crime law, since the ICC was unavailable.

Turning the Clock Back to 1775

The ICC's potential for abuse is boundless. In its present form—likely in *any* form—it is inherently at odds not just with common sense but with our constitutional system of government. Were the U.S. to become a party to the Rome Statute, time-honored constitutional guarantees of ordered liberty under laws made by our elected representatives would give way to a jerry-rigged international "system" of laws spawned by the obsessions of starry-eyed fanatics and implemented by unelected foreign bureaucrats. The ICC's blatant undermining of our hard-won liberties would make King George III blush. Here are but a few of the rights and constitutional protections we'll be signing away should the globalists get their way:

- *National Sovereignty*: The ICC can intervene whenever it decides that our courts have failed to act the way ICC wants. The Constitution would no longer be the supreme law governing U.S. citizens, and foreign courts would wield the power to prosecute and try American citizens for actions taking place within the U.S.

- *Separation of Powers*: The ICC houses both the judges and the prosecutor within the same governmental institution—the direct opposite of the Constitution's principle of separation of powers. Both the ICC's judges and the prosecutor are appointed by the same group of unelected State party representatives—the Assembly of States Parties. *The prosecutor would have a roving mandate to search out and investigate any act he or she believes would rise to the level of a covered crime.*

- *Right of Self-Defense*: The "crimes against humanity," "genocide," and "war crimes" statutes are so broadly defined that, in the hands of unaccountable prosecutors and judges, they can be made to include just about any act or consequence normally associated with warfare and imprisonment of enemy fighters. Due process certainly requires more than vaguely worded and amorphous standards of conduct against which to judge peoples' guilt or innocence of criminal wrongdoing.

- *Trial by Jury*: The Rome Statute has no provision for trial by jury—a basic Constitutional right under Article III and the Sixth Amendment that is afforded to persons accused of crimes in the United States. *The International Criminal Court can convict a person of the most serious of crimes on a simple majority vote.* Perhaps the Rome Statute drafters' use of the term "chamber" in describing the various panels of ICC judges was a Freudian reference to the inquisitorial "star chambers" of old.

- *Speedy and Fair Trial*: The Rome Statute does not contain the rigorous procedural protections of speedy trial, the right to confront and cross-examine all witnesses, and inadmissibility of hearsay or highly prejudicial evidence that Americans expect from their judicial system.

- *Freedom from Double Jeopardy*: If the ICC prosecutor loses a trial, he or she can appeal a verdict of acquittal, negating the accused's Constitutional protection against "double jeopardy." Indeed, even after being acquitted, the accused may continue to be detained—his or her liberties denied—while the prosecutor pursues the appeal! This gives a new meaning to the expression "if at first you don't succeed, try, try again."

- *Rule of Law*: Unlike most treaties where the parties can add reservations to conform to their domestic law requirements, this treaty prohibits any such reservations. The U.S. has entered into other international "human rights" treaties with assurances that their scope would be limited to domestic jurisprudence decisions interpreting the Fifth, Eighth, and Fourteenth Amendments to the U.S. Constitution. But the Rome Statute departs from this practice and forces nations that accept the ICC's jurisdiction to waive anything contrary in their own laws and to entrust the fate of their citizens to the ICC's decisions based on vaguely worded "norms of international human rights" law.

John Hancock and his fellow revolutionaries fought a war to end foreign control of our country. The ICC would be nothing short of a throwback to the circumstances they had to change by force of arms! Under the ICC, American citizens would be (1) subjected "to a jurisdiction foreign to our constitution and unacknowledged by our laws"; (2) "depriv[ed] of the benefits of Trial by Jury"; and (3) "transport[ed] beyond [the] Seas to be tried for pretended offences."[15]

Unfortunately, as we have seen, even though President Bush "unsigned" the agreement, it can still cause us grievous harm. Assuming that the U.S. won't be able to negotiate bilateral treaties with every ICC signatory, the ICC will inevitably by used as a tool by globalists and left-wing activists to hamstring America's pursuit of its own vital interests.

The Khan Job

The ICC also sets a precedent for even more permanent international courts, courts designed to force compliance to all sorts of outlandish utopian notions. (Of course, these courts wouldn't exist if a truly accountable democratic process was in play.) The idea of an International Environmental Court is already setting the NGO world abuzz. While recognizing that environmental protection had already been introduced in a general sort of way in the Rome Statute under the potpourri categories of either "crimes against humanity" or "war crimes," the proponents of a permanent International Environmental Court are, of course, not satisfied. They argue that there is fundamental human "right" to a healthy environment, and that the enforcement of said "right" requires a separate court devoted especially to environmental concerns. And they want a court with real teeth, not one that simply provides mediation and arbitration dispute resolution services between willing participants.

And as we now know, where there's a left-wing cause that someone is obsessive about, an NGO devoted to it can't be far behind. And lo and behold, we find The International Court of the Environment Foundation, a leading supporter of the environmental court movement. Their agenda is so radical—bordering on hysterical—that it almost makes ICC zealots sound reasonable:

> [We seek] the establishment of an International Court of the Environment as a new, specialized and permanent institution on a global level based on the following principles:
>
> - The right of access not only for the States but also for individuals, NGOs and environmental associations.
>
> - The *erga omnes* effect and authority of its decisions handed down in the name of the International Community.
>
> - On-going promotion of all initiatives aimed at strengthening existing institutions and instruments for resolving international environmental disputes.[16]

The Latin phrase *erga omnes*, which literally means "towards all" or "in relation to everyone," is worth noting. This is a concept that the "human rights community" increasingly uses to mean obligations owed to the entire international community—and binding, whether one consents or not.

Under this concept, a common set of principles of "human rights" and "humanitarian law" can be imposed, to "be observed by all and everywhere, by every State, every group of persons and every individual" worldwide—with or without the consent of the said individuals or their sovereign governments. "Observed" is a tricky word when used in this context, since all that "observation" is going to be backed by a global enforcement mechanism. [17]

While *erga omnes* may be couched in terms of "human rights," it has little to do with the inalienable rights given to us by our Creator. Conjuring up "rights" from thin air is a game anyone can play. Any subject on which a plurality of countries defines a set of rules of conduct under the guise of "human rights" means creation of just another playground in which the UN and its supplicants get to set all the rules.

For globalists, "international norms" on "human rights," which can be stretched to include virtually all spheres of human activity (including many activities that rational people would find grotesque or detrimental to society), are "binding independently of the treaties that codify them. *Consequently all States have the obligation to observe them always even if they have not ratified Conventions of human rights and humanitarian law or have withdrawn from them after having ratified them.*"[18] (emphasis added)

In other words, not just national sovereignty be damned, but if countries see the light and realize the absurdity of what's going on here, they still can't break free of the globalist snare!

Who speaks for the "human rights community?" From whose enlightened psyche is handed down to the unwashed masses the "international norms" on "war crimes" and "crimes against humanity" the ICC is to follow? Amnesty International's Secretary-General Irene Khan is among the most brazen of these candidates for martyrdom, and to utterly no one's surprise, her rhetoric is distinctly anti-American.

In the message accompanying the 2004 Amnesty International Report, for example, Khan accused the U.S. government of being "bereft of principle" and of "[S]acrificing human rights in the name of security at home."[19] But that was nothing compared to what Khan had to say in 2005. She declared the Guantanamo detention camp for suspected terrorists to be the "gulag of our times"—as blind as all of her brethren to the concept of degrees of magnitude.[20] Millions of innocents died in Stalin's gulags. Guantanamo shouldn't even be mentioned in the same breath.

Not to be outdone by this blatantly hysterical outburst, William F. Schulz, executive director of Amnesty International USA, issued nothing less than a threat to U.S. government officials in May 2005. He said that they could be subject to arrest and trial for war crimes if they left the United States.[21]

Khan, Schulz and like-minded "human rights" extremists are making a mockery of the cause they purport to serve. Yes, some abuses of detainees have occurred on our watch, but they are the exception and not the rule. We self-examine and correct what goes wrong in our systems. By harping on the inevitable mistakes that will be made during the war against terror, these Amnesty International leaders shamefully ignore the horrors the U.S. has ended, and the seeds of democracy we have sown.

Or, looking at it another way—the Taliban imposed a brutal theocracy on the Afghan population, treated millions of women like chattel, and harbored a global terrorist network until the United States and its allies liberated the nation from their grip—but *we're* the bad guys?

Saddam Hussein's Baath Party likewise ruled Iraq with an iron hand and used WMDs against its own citizens and neighbors until the American-led coalition ended its brutal reign. If *anyone* merits comparison to Stalin, it's the despots we deposed. And if anyone merits comparison to "Baghdad Bob," the buffoonish Saddam apologist who doggedly claimed that Iraq's army was beating our military and its allies when actual truth was staring him in the face, it's Irene Kahn.

When push comes to shove, Amnesty International always sides with those who hate this country. Of course, when pressed in a TV interview to substantiate Amnesty International's charges of abuse with specific evidence, Schulz couldn't do so. In fact, he ended up conceding that the detainees were not being denied food or medical care and were not being used for forced labor. Anyone who has read Solzhenit-syn would be hard-pressed to find any resemblance to Stalin's gulag. Perhaps Kahn and Schulz are just too busy being compassionate on behalf of the rest of us to be bothered with the facts.[22]

Let's look at Guantanamo. Evidence has shown that many detainees' complaints were exaggerated or made up altogether. The facts are that the detainees' religious sensitivities have been accommodated to an astounding—if not outrageous—degree, including provision of religiously correct meals, provision of prayer mats, caps, and the Koran, stencil markings in each cell pointing toward Mecca, and broadcasting on loudspeakers the Muslims' call to prayer five times daily.

While Amnesty International may be angry because they did not get personal invitations to visit the Guantanamo facility, their claims of a cover-up are ridiculous. The International Committee of the Red Cross (ICRC) has not only been given access to the facility but has proclaimed that "[T]he U.S. civilian and military authorities must be credited for engaging in continuous and frank dialogue with the ICRC, despite any diverging points of view."[23]

Khan blithely skips over the inconvenient fact that Saddam Hussein tortured and murdered hundreds of thousands of his own people, even using chemical weapons against them, until the United States and its allies acted. In her Alice in Wonderland world, the humiliation of Iraqi prisoners at Abu Ghraib by a relatively small number of American soldiers, as wrong as it was, is no better than Hussein's use of detainees at the prison as guinea pigs for outlawed chemical and biological weapons experiments.[24]

Indeed, demonstrating a total loss of moral compass (if not sanity), Khan devoted at least as much space in her forward to the *2005 Amnesty International Report* to her condemnation of the United States for bad detention conditions as she did of the

Sudanese government for the mass murders of more than two million of its own people—an unforgivable lack of perspective in someone considered the "leader" of a once-venerated organization.

Khan's on that long list of elitists who detest the United States government for standing up for the true ideals of freedom—as opposed to the current "human rights" fad of the day. If stymied by America's refusal to join the International Criminal Court, Khan's Amnesty International will no doubt join with other "human rights" activists to demand the arrest of American officials overseas, just as Amnesty's USA chief Schulz threatened.

Perhaps they'll also manage to convince some equally perspective-free federal judge like Judge Robertson to take up the vendetta against American officials they brand as "human rights" violators. For Amnesty International, the best kind of American judge is the kind that "human rights" law professor Martin Geer described as willing to "create, develop, and implement the incorporation doctrine...to take small, though important, steps towards expanding U.S. jurisprudence to effectively incorporate international human rights law for violations committed both within and outside the United States, *for citizens and aliens alike.*"[25]

Unlike the hypothetical ICC cases considered earlier, this is more than just an abstract concern. The ACLU and Human Rights Watch recently sued Secretary of Defense Donald Rumsfeld in a federal district court in Illinois on behalf of eight detainees who alleged abusive treatment while in U.S. custody. The suit claims that Rumsfeld violated the U.S. Constitution and—more critically—*international laws* including the Geneva Conventions on treatment of Prisoners of War.[26]

The allegations are little more than a sinister repackaging of charges that were aired in the press and extensively debated during the U.S. Presidential election. The American people listened, evaluated the charges, and to the slack-jawed disbelief of their intellectual and moral "superiors" around the world, re-elected George W. Bush anyway. But it's a sad day in American history when one federal judge in Illinois is asked to take the side of the enemy against the judgment of the duly elected President of the United States. How this case will wind up is anyone's guess.

Harry Truman, War Criminal?

One can only wonder what globalist traps might have snared Harry Truman for the actions that he took to end World War II. If journalist Philip Nobile had his way, Truman would have been tried for war crimes. Nobile edited a book entitled *Judgment at the Smithsonian* that contained material originally written for an exhibit in August 1995 by the Smithsonian, marking the 50th anniversary of Truman's decision to drop atomic bombs on Hiroshima and Nagasaki. This material was not included in the exhibit, due to a public outcry over its slanted content.

Nobile also wrote a piece entitled "Hiroshima Debate: Was Harry Truman a War Criminal?" in which he challenged what he called the "Nuremberg Consensus"—the prevalent view held among historians that Truman's decision, when viewed in the context of the choices he faced, was reasonable because Japan refused to surrender. Truman weighed—and rejected— the alternative of possibly losing as many as 250,000 American lives during an invasion of Japan.[27]

Nobile's argument is that Truman's actions with regard to dropping the atomic bomb should be considered war crimes, even if evaluated against the standards applied to the Nazis at Nuremberg.[28]

In point of fact, however, if one reads Truman's thoughts as expressed in his diary, it's clear that he considered the bombings an absolute last resort, used only after it was clear that Japan had no intention of surrendering:

> We were approaching an experiment with the atom explosion.
> I was informed that event would take place within a possible
> thirty days. I then suggested that after that experimental test of
> the fission of the atom, that we give Japan a chance to stop the
> war by a surrender. That plan was followed. Japan refused to
> surrender and the bomb was dropped on two targets after
> which event the surrender took place.[29]

It is absurd to equate Truman's cautious and highly deliberative decision to bring a much needed end to a devastating war with the genocidal acts of Nazi war criminals tried at Nuremberg.

Politicized globalists love to impose their holier-than-thou attitudes on the rest of us. It is outrageous that the ICC would equate the behavior of aggressor dictatorships with the rarely pretty, but nonetheless liberating, actions of the democracies that confront them. It's equally outrageous that runaway federal judges invoke vaguely defined "international human rights" legal standards that are not found in our Constitution and that step on the prerogatives of our elected leaders.

Yet even as sweeping as the ICC's powers already are, it's just one of the curbs globalists are seeking to impose on our right to use military power in pursuit of our own—and the world's—best interests.

CHAPTER EIGHT

UN GLOBALISTS THREATEN U.S. MILITARY SOVEREIGNTY

KOFI ANNAN claimed that the U.S.-led invasion of Iraq was an illegal act that contravened the UN Charter. Had supporting briefs been filed by Jacques Chirac, Amnesty International and George Soros, Annan might have had the gall to argue that only the UN Security Council had the legal authority to authorize such an action—which, of course, it did not grant in this case—and that the UN Charter required member states to cede their sovereign right to conduct military actions.

The arguments offered by anti-war globalists are worth examining in detail because they provide a window into their endlessly fascinating, and utterly naïve, thought processes when it comes to the vital area of national security.

The Legal Case under the UN Charter for the War in Iraq

The opponents of the Iraq war contend that there should have been a second Security Council measure following Iraq's failure to comply with Resolution 1441's weapons inspections requirements. They claim that Resolution 1441 did not itself contain a specific authorization for member states to use military force to enforce its terms.

And they challenge the U.S. position that Iraq's failure to comply with the conditions of the ceasefire ending the first Gulf War, or with any Security Council resolutions adopted thereafter, including Resolution 1441 (passed unanimously by the Security Council in the fall of 2002), provided sufficient justification for direct military action by the member states themselves.

In all such resolutions, they claim, including Resolution 1441, the Security Council made a point of saying that it remained "seized of the matter," which, in some interpretations, means that it as a collective body would take such steps as may be required for the implementation of its resolutions.

This line of argument was the one used by the lawyers who tried to get Donald Rumsfeld tried in Germany:

> There is only one legal basis for the use of force other than self-defense: Security Council directed or authorized use of force to restore or maintain international peace and security pursuant to its responsibilities under Chapter VII of the UN Charter.[1]

Those making this argument point to the use of a two-step process in both Korea and the first Gulf War, when Security Council resolutions were passed that specifically authorized the member states to use all means necessary to repel aggression against another country after the first resolution denouncing the aggression was ignored.[2] While acknowledging that Resolution 1441 did say that "serious consequences" would ensue if Iraq continued to be in material breach of its terms and of prior resolutions, according to the globalist contingent it was up to the Security Council—not the United States or its allies—to determine what those consequences would be.

Opponents of the Iraq war misunderstand—perhaps willfully—the actual text of the UN Charter's provisions on the powers and prerogatives of the Security Council. Contrary to their assumptions, the Security Council does *not* have exclusive jurisdiction over military decisions of the member states. The Council has "primary" responsibility under Article 24 of the UN Charter to act on behalf of the member states to try to maintain international peace and security, meaning that it shares power over the enforcement of the UN Charter's principles with the member states themselves.

In other words, the Security Council has no more than the powers conferred on it by the member states as their common agent against a menace to such peace and security. The member states do not lose their own sovereign powers to act, particularly after they have given the Security Council ample opportunity to enforce its own decisions.

But, say advocates for the Security Council's exclusive powers over the use of military force, Article 39 of the UN Charter confers such exclusive power when it says that "[T]he Security Council shall determine the existence of any threat to the peace, breach of the peace, or act of aggression and shall make recommendations, or decide what measures shall be taken in accordance with Articles 41 and 42, to maintain or restore international peace and security."

This argument again reflects a fundamental misunderstanding of what the drafters of the UN Charter actually intended to say and its application to the Iraq war. The Security Council determined that Saddam Hussein's regime posed a serious threat to peace, and that Iraq remained in breach of its obligations under a series of Security Council resolutions.

In addition, the Council had also made recommendations for non-military actions against Saddam Hussein's regime under Article 41 of the UN Charter, with which the United States cooperated. But those actions didn't work.

Article 42 of the UN Charter does grant authority to the Security Council to decide upon collective military action as the next step if the non-military measures used under Article 41 prove inadequate: "Should the Security Council consider that measures provided for in Article 41 would be inadequate or have proved to be inadequate, it may take such action by air, sea, or land forces as may be necessary to maintain or restore international peace and security."

Note, however, that *nowhere* in this language does it say that *only* the Security Council has the authority to make a military decision on behalf of all the member states. Article 42 is a grant of *discretionary* authority to the Security Council from the member states to coordinate a military enforcement action on their behalf. *Nowhere does it compel the member states to get permission from the Security Council before using force themselves to accomplish the purposes of the United Nations if the Security Council fails to make a decision.*

There are many precedents for military action undertaken without any UN Security Council involvement at all, including military action by the United States and its NATO allies in Kosovo. Despite berating the U.S. constantly for "unilateralism," France acted precisely the same way, intervening in the affairs of the sovereign Ivory Coast without any Security Council authorization.

Indeed, the one place where the UN Charter specifically refers to any superior authority of the Security Council to entities outside of the United Nations with respect to military enforcement decisions is in Article 53, which deals with "enforcement actions" taken under "regional arrangements or by regional agencies." *In other words, when the drafters of the UN Charter meant to confer exclusive or superior authority upon the Security Council vis-à-vis other entities, they said so.*

With respect to decisions involving military matters, the UN Charter says specifically that the Security Council has superior authority over any regional organizations of states (something ignored by NATO in Kosovo, which was undertaken without UN sanction).

However, the UN Charter does not—and indeed cannot—take away the sovereign right of each member state to make the ultimate decision as to how to defend its own citizens. *What the member states have agreed to do is to work through the United Nations to the extent possible and to act consistently with the principles and purposes of the United Nations.* Indeed, since the Security Council thankfully still does not have a permanent standing army at its own disposal under agreements with the member states, all the United States and the United Kingdom—two of the original *Great Powers* and founding members of the UN—needed to do under Article 106 of the UN Charter was to "consult with one another and as occasion requires with other Members of the United Nations with a view to such joint action on behalf of the Organization as may be necessary for the purpose of maintaining international peace and security." By jointly ending Saddam Hussein's continuing threat to international peace and security once and for all and bringing freedom to the Iraqi people after extensive consultations with the other member states, the U.S., the United Kingdom and their allies did just that.

The anti-war globalists ignore the fact that the United Nations had for twelve long years tried to contain the threats to peace posed by Saddam Hussein's regime. Significantly, the U.S. worked through the UN to do so.

The result? The Oil-for-Food scandal, for starters. After Iraq's defeat in the first Gulf War and its agreement to the ceasefire terms approved by the Security Council, Iraq continued to defy the UN's will (expressed in 16 legally binding resolutions) on the most fundamental issues regarding weapons of mass destruction and genocide against its own civilians.

Hussein mocked the arms inspections process, making it impossible for the UN inspectors to conduct thorough inspections. Indeed, he forced the inspectors out in 1998. Only under threat of U.S. military action did he let them return four years later, but his pattern of deception continued. When given one final chance by the Security Council in 2002 to come clean on his entire weapons program, Hussein played games instead.

As to Hussein's horrific acts of genocide, upwards of 250,000 Shiites were most likely killed by his regime in the aftermath of the first Gulf War. Thousands of Kurds and Turkomans in the northern part of Iraq were also killed and more than a million were displaced from their homes.[3]

The give-peace-a-chance globalists confuse the ceasefire that *suspended* hostilities after the first Gulf War with a *permanent* peace that never occurred. The lawyers trying to stop Saddam's removal on the basis of violating the terms of the ceasefire stated that "[f]ollowing the formal cease-fire recorded by Resolution 687 in 1991, there has been no Security Council resolution that has clearly and specifically authorized the use of force to enforce the terms of the cease-fire, including ending Iraq's missile and chemical, biological, and nuclear weapons programs. Such a resolution is required for renewed use of force."[4]

These lawyers conveniently forget that the United States was an *individual* party to the ceasefire under which Saddam was permitted to remain in power, having entered into the Safwan Accords with Iraq on March 3, 1991, signed by U.S. Army General H. Norman Schwarzkopf and a representative of the Iraqi government. The U.S.-led coalition routed Saddam Hussein's forces and laid down non-negotiable demands for letting the despot remain in power, which he unconditionally accepted. The Security Council effectively ratified this ceasefire agreement via Resolution 687, which imposed continuing obligations on Iraq to eliminate its weapons of mass destruction in order to restore international peace and security. Hussein, of course, thumbed his nose at it all.

As Tony Blair's Attorney General Lord Goldsmith explained in remarks to the British Parliament laying out the legal case for the Iraq war, "Resolution 687 suspended but did not terminate the authority to use force" that the Security Council had previously authorized against Iraq under Resolution 678 "to eject it from Kuwait and to restore peace and security in the area…A material breach of [r]esolution 687 revives the authority to use force under [r]esolution 678."[5]

The first Gulf War coalition countries, led by the United States, implemented the Security Council's mandate to oust Iraq from Kuwait and to restore peace and security to the area. They put their troops' lives on the line to turn back Iraq's aggression, well aware that they might have to do so again, given Saddam's vile and venal nature. The ceasefire that suspended the first Gulf War allowed Saddam to stay in power, but included detailed conditions relating to inspection and destruction of Iraq's weapons of mass destruction, conditions that Hussein continually refused to meet. It makes no sense to expect that the coalition countries that fought the first Gulf War would stand idly by while Iraq violated the terms of the ceasefire by building up its military and WMD arsenal.

And there is *no* credible legal constraint preventing the U.S. and its coalition partners from taking all appropriate military actions to protect themselves against this real possibility, *before* having to face weapons of mass destruction on the battlefield—or in New York, or London. And despite the mandated "no-fly zones" established to protect the Kurds in the north and the Shiites in the south from mass slaughter, Saddam Hussein's troops continually fired on patrolling U.S. and British aircraft. Given those circumstances, *the United States had every right* under both international law *and* under Article 51 of the UN Charter (preserving each member state's inherent right to use military force in self-defense) to defend itself by removing the threat posed by Saddam Hussein once and for all.

Despite all of this, Hussein was given one final chance to live up to his obligations voluntarily. Security Council Resolution 1441, which found Saddam Hussein's regime to be in material breach of its obligations under the previous Security Council resolutions, gave Hussein yet another in a long line of opportunities to redeem himself. The resolution warned of "serious consequences" if his regime remained in breach. After more months of inspections and Iraq's submission of a materially incomplete accounting of its weapons program, there was legitimate international consensus that Hussein's regime continued to be in breach of its obligations to the United Nations.

Given the circumstances, the United States and its allies had not just the right, but the duty, to finally remove this threat to peace and human rights. This was not the kind of war of conquest or territorial expansion that violates the United Nations Charter's core principles—far from it. For its part, the U.S. wants to get out of Iraq as soon as possible so that the Iraqi people can take charge of their own destiny. In taking military action to enforce the Security Council's own resolutions against a serial aggressor and committer of genocide, the United States and its allies actually saved the United Nations from demonstrating the same impotence that destroyed the League of Nations.

The Korean Precedent

Demonstrating their usual willingness to ignore actual facts, globalists have tried to rewrite the circumstances leading up to the Iraq war. It's the only way to reach the bogus conclusion that President Bush acted illegally in deciding to remove Hussein from power.

And in that rewriting, they spin the facts surrounding the *Korean* War, which they cite as a precedent supporting their position that "[p]ast Security Council resolutions authorizing use of force employed language universally understood to do so," which did not exist in the case of Iraq.[6]

In truth, the facts surrounding the passage of the Security Council resolutions dealing with North Korea's invasion of South Korea in June 1950 squarely contradict their position.

To be sure, there *were* two Security Council resolutions. The first resolution passed by the Security Council on June 25, 1950 simply called upon North Korea to remove its forces from

South Korea and end its aggression. *It contained nothing regarding the use of force to repel the aggression.* A second resolution was passed two days later, authorizing military action by the member states against North Korea using the diplomatic turn of phrase: "recommends that the Members of the United Nations furnish such assistance to the Republic of Korea as may be necessary to repel the armed attack and to restore international peace and security in the area."

On the surface, this looks like just the two-step Security Council authorization process that Iraq War opponents say was missing before the U.S.—led invasion of Iraq. But that's a superficial analysis. In fact, the second Korean resolution was rushed through the Security Council on the afternoon of June 27, 1950, while the Soviet Union's representative to the Security Council was out of town, thereby avoiding a possible veto. But more to the point, *President Truman did not wait for the Security Council to pass the second resolution authorizing military force before sending the military into action.*[7]

In a critical meeting held at Blair House before the second resolution was adopted, President Truman made the final decision to order U.S. air and sea forces to provide cover and support for South Korean troops. Truman met with key Congressional leaders the next day to advise them of this decision.

According to an eyewitness account, a participant pointed out the possibility that the Russians would rush to the Security Council next day and cast a veto against the second resolution authorizing the use of force against North Korea. The participant told Truman that even under those circumstances, the U.S. would still take the position that we were free to act in support of the Charter. "The President said that was right. He rather wished they *would* veto."[8] (emphasis added)

At the end of the meeting, the president said to those remaining behind, "Now, let's all have a drink. It's been a hard day. I have hoped and prayed that I would never have to make a decision like the one I have just made today. I saw nothing else that was possible for me to do except that. Now, with this drink, that's out of my mind. In the final analysis I did this for the United Nations. I believed in the League of Nations. It failed. Lots of people thought that it failed because we weren't in it to back it up. Okay, now we started the United Nations. It was our idea, and in this first big test we just couldn't let them down. If a collective system under the UN can work, it must be made to work, and now is the time to call their bluff."[9]

In a teleconference between the Pentagon and General MacArthur held later that evening, Truman's instructions lifted all restrictions on the use of Far East Command Navy and Air Force in support of the South Korean forces. *The instructions referred to the Security Council resolution adopted on June 25th as the basis for so acting—even though, as we have seen, that resolution contained no authorization for the use of force.*[10]

At noon the next day, Truman made a public statement regarding U.S. policy in Korea and elsewhere in the Far East. The military die had been cast the night before, when the president moved decisively forward without waiting for the second Security Council resolution, much less any Congressional authorization. Truman made it clear that he'd have gone ahead unilaterally even if the second resolution never passed. Acting with courage, Truman was willing to go it alone if necessary to save the principles on which the United Nations was founded.

As for the establishment of a truly multinational force, that just wasn't in the cards. Seventeen countries sent forces to Korea, but as usual the U.S. assumed the lion's share of the burden. The British organized what they called the Commonwealth Division. The French, preoccupied in Indochina, sent only a token force. South Africa sent a squadron of fighter planes, and Canada, Australia, and New Zealand contributed troops.

Some responses are funny in retrospect. Saudi Arabia said that they had nothing to send to Korea beyond a company of camel cavalry which would not be useful on Korea's terrain. And it was reported that a Central American country would be willing to supply "if you can accept them, 1,000 naked, untrained men."[11]

Regarding the Korean situation and the Security Council's involvement, this much is clear from the historical record: With the United States leading the way, the UN Security Council officially condemned North Korea's aggression against South Korea and called for North Korea to remove its forces immediately. North Korea ignored the Security Council's plea. Truman was determined to repel the attack—with or without specific Security Council authorization—but he certainly wanted a second Security Council resolution calling upon the member states to contribute in support of South Korea if he could get it. A second Security Council resolution *was* passed, but *not before Truman had already committed U.S. military forces to action totally on his own authority.*

And Truman did so without prior Congressional authorization either. The United States took on the military burden with scant help from a small group of other member states. Even more so than Iraq, this was very much an American war.

Assistant Secretary of State for UN Affairs John Hickerson was deeply involved in the deliberations leading up to the President's decision and the enactment of the Security Council resolutions. He said:

> I think Mr. Truman is quite right that the interest of the United States and its allies, and of the free world was so great in defeating this aggression against Korea that it had to be done. And if, through some sort of legal mechanism one operation was blocked, then another operation would have to be found to do it.[12]

Like Truman, George W. Bush was prepared to work through the United Nations to bring an aggressive dictator to account. In the end, he decided to take the actions necessary to protect the principles for which the United Nations is supposed to stand. He made the final decision to send our military forces into Iraq, along with the United Kingdom and the other countries comprising the "coalition of the willing," even though the Security Council did not pass a follow-up resolution to Resolution 1441 specifically authorizing the use of military force.

Despite his opponents' carping, the president acted in accordance with the United Nations Charter and the authority already granted by 12 years' worth of prior Security Council resolutions which Saddam Hussein chose to ignore.

The UN has been actively involved in Iraq, effectively ratifying the coalition's actions and granting the United States and the UK broad authority as "occupying powers" in Security Council Resolution 1483, passed in May, 2003. The United Nations assisted with the nationwide Iraqi elections held on January 30, 2005. By all accounts, the election was a success. And the Iraqis are free at any time to ask American and British troops to leave.

Provide for the Common Defense

Beyond the purely legal basis for forcibly removing Saddam Hussein, there's an even more compelling issue at stake. The record of democracies, certainly from World War II onward, is one of *reaction against* unprovoked aggression, not *initiation* of wars of conquest or territorial expansion. Democracies are rarely aggressors, if only because a truly functioning democracy has built-in checks against the arbitrary exercise of power.

A functioning democracy derives its legitimacy and authority from the consent of the governed, as demonstrated through a fair and inclusive voting process and respect for the rights of all persons. It has legal systems that set limits on governmental power and provides ways for citizens to influence its representatives' decisions. There is a common ethos under which its institutions operate, including the principle of the rule of law.

The United Nations, on the other hand, is anything *but* a functioning democracy. It is little more than a collection of sovereign states with disparate interests and political systems that accords the same voting rights to dictatorships that it does to democracies. Dictators have no respect for the bedrock principles of freedom or respect for individual rights—if they did, they wouldn't be dictators.

And of course, dictators couldn't care less about what the UN says or does unless their own survival is at stake. Raw power is their raison d'être, and they do not hesitate to manipulate the processes of the UN to their advantage.

Nearly 60 years since its founding, the UN has still not reached an acceptable definition of "aggression" and "terrorism," let alone figured out how to deal with them effectively. Even genocide is often excused or ignored by the UN staff in order to avoid rocking the boat. As we've seen, among those ignoring such horrors is Kofi Annan, the man now overseeing the organization.

In the Middle East, terrorists have declared a war on democracy and self-government, which they condemn as infidel practices offensive to their medieval notions of divine rule. "[W]e vow to wash the streets of Baghdad with the voters' blood...To those of you who think you can vote and then run away, we will shadow you and catch you, and we will cut off your heads and the heads of your children."[13] Were the UN actually living up to its original ideals, it would be devoting its energies to universalizing the struggle against this virulent form of fascism, one that threatens to behead children because their parents have the temerity to cast a vote in a free election.

This struggle is inextricably tied to the battle for *real* human rights, not abstract ones, and for the dignity of *every* life.

But some people just don't get it.

How can any rational democracy entrust its security to a "world organization" that has not only consistently failed to halt grave threats to peace, but allows overt aggressors to pervert its founding principles to suit themselves? Whether it's in Rwanda, where UN leaders deliberately ignored warnings of an impending genocide, or in the Middle East where the UN has consistently and repeatedly rewarded aggression against Israel, the United Nations is incapable of enforcing collective security in a lawless world. A feeble yet once extant willingness to distinguish between right and wrong has given way to accommodation to the enemies of freedom at all costs—and all the better if the monetary portion of those costs are borne by the United States.

As former Israeli UN Ambassador Dore Gold observed, the United Nations has no "unique legitimacy" with which to sanction the use of force to deal with threats to international peace and security. This is because all the UN is, ultimately, is the collective will of a group of disparate states with varied interests, including many authoritarian regimes.[14] The United Nations is truly less than the sum of its parts.

In our country, Congress and the president are vested with the Constitutional responsibility to protect us against foreign threats. They determine the point at which aggressive acts must be countered by words—or by force. The president has exclusive power to act as the commander-in-chief of the armed forces of the United States. Congress has the power to define and punish "offenses against the Law of Nations," to declare war and appropriate money for the support of the military. *These powers to provide for the common defense of the American people are not delegable under our Constitution to any world body or subject to the veto of any other country.* Period!

The notion of "collective security" embodied in the UN Charter was seen by its original architects—the Allies who had defeated the Axis powers at such a horrific cost—as the preferred means to deter Hitler-type aggression. The United Nations was intended to help direct the pressure of world opinion against clear-cut aggression and to provide a framework for repelling it. Its architects never contemplated being forced into a choice of either prodding the organization to act against clear-cut aggression or standing by and doing nothing.

The thoughtful men who wrote the UN Charter emphasized that the United States would join the United Nations as a sovereign nation fully intent on retaining control of its own destiny. No serious consideration was *ever* given to creating a world organization with sovereign authority in its own right— at least not by serious thinkers.

"You had to keep your eye all the time on not putting too much limitations on American sovereignty," said Durward V. Sandifer at the San Francisco conference that established the United Nations. "That's the reason the United States was just as ardent an advocate of the veto as the Russians were."[15]

As President Truman demonstrated by committing American forces in South Korea before the Security Council resolution specifically authorizing the use of force was actually adopted, the United States was not about to subject itself to UN control to the detriment of this country's vital interests. The Constitution of the United States requires no less.

Korea and Iraq are hardly the only instances in U.S. history where national security interests came into conflict with international consensus. More than two hundred years ago, twenty-one crewmembers from two American ships were taken hostage by Barbary pirates and held for ransom. Thomas Jefferson, then United States minister to France, opposed paying the ransom, even though it had been customary for countries in Europe to do just that.

In his own words, Jefferson "endeavored to form an association of the powers subject to habitual depredation from them. I accordingly prepared, and proposed to their ministers at Paris, for consultation with their governments, articles of a special confederation."[16] His goal: to harness the collective will of the international community "to compel the piratical States to perpetual peace."

While a number of smaller European states were interested in a collective effort to tame the pirates, the effort fell through because France and England found the ransoms a small price to pay for a right-of-way through pirate waters. Jefferson, on the hand, saw clearly that appeasement in the face of ongoing aggression could only result in even bolder acts of violence. If history shows us anything, it shows us that appeasement does not ensure peace, but endangers it.

The United States and other countries continued to pay "protection money" to pirates from Algiers, Morocco, Tunis and Tripoli until Thomas Jefferson became president. Then, Jefferson not only refused to honor Tripoli's demands for more money, but answered its subsequent declaration of war against the United States with a show of force.

President Jefferson had to endure four long years of criticism over the war against the Barbary pirates, but he remained determined to "effect a peace thro' the medium of war." Full success eluded him, but his strategy would later be vindicated when the U.S. won enough naval victories to convince the enemy to negotiate and end the extortion. Europe went right on appeasing the Barbary pirates, paying them off for fifteen more years.[17]

In a harsh world full of evil people and regimes, military force is sometimes the only option out there. If the nations of the world acting in concert are either unwilling or unable to take forceful action against aggressors deemed threats to this country, the president and Congress have the ultimate Constitutional responsibility to do so on their own.

The Constitution's Supremacy Clause, as we have seen, places the Constitution above all laws and treaties regarding the governance of the American people. As the written compact under which the American people govern themselves, it embodies the source of the nation's sovereign authority.

There is *nothing* in the text of the UN Charter—nor was it ever its authors' intent—to challenge the Constitution's supremacy over American citizens or to condition UN membership on surrender of our ability to determine our own course.

And the last thing we need at this critical historical pass is to outsource our national security to the corrupt, bungling, "see no evil, hear no evil" institution that the United Nations has become.

CHAPTER NINE

UN GLOBALISTS THREATEN U.S. DOMESTIC SOVEREIGNTY

THE GLOBALISTS, of course, aren't content with just try-ing to suborn our foreign policy decisions to the UN's, or to subject our duly elected leaders to the compulsory jurisdic-tion of the play-actors peopling their manufactured "interna-tional court." Even stripping the U.S. treasury by way of "global taxes"—or "assessments" or "duties" or "moral obliga-tions" or "ransom" or whatever phrase globalists use to cloak their intentions—would not satisfy these do-gooder parasites. They want also to use the UN and its endless whirl of lushly catered "forums" and "seminars" and "summits" and "re-treats" to develop ways of imposing their often fanatical world views on the rest of us—whether we care to be so enlightened or not.

Never mind that the United Nations was designed as an organization made up of sovereign states, or that the Charter specifically stipulated that the UN is not allowed to "intervene in matters which are essentially within the domestic jurisdic-tion of any state."[1] The Charter establishes a framework for *organized cooperation*—not top-down coercion—among member states to address issues of common concern that transcend national boundaries. The UN is not a sovereign entity with the "right" to mandate its preferred solution.

The Economic and Social Council within the UN, for example, was authorized to set up a number of commissions to aid in the solution of international social, economic, cultural, and humanitarian problems and make recommendations; but that is the extent of its authority. Indeed, this is precisely the assurance that Senator Tom Connally, one of the key Charter negotiators, gave to the U.S. Senate in a speech before its vote to ratify the Charter:

> In their respective fields the commissions will initiate studies and make reports. They may also make recommendations in respect to such matters to the General Assembly and to the member states. Neither the commissions nor the Economic and Social Council *will have any authority or power to impose upon any state any regulation or provision whatsoever. The final choice and decision in respect to all such recommendations will remain with each individual state.*[2] (emphasis added)

Congress and the president may conduct our foreign policy in cooperation with other countries, but they retain the authority vested in them by the Constitution to decide exactly how and to what extent the United States *will* cooperate. Thus, President Truman stated as one of the key foreign policy tenets of his 1946 State of the Union Address that "full economic collaboration between all nations, great and small, is essential to the improvement of living conditions all over the world, and to the establishment of freedom from fear and freedom from want."

These are laudable and desirable goals that all people of goodwill share. We must work together to create practical solutions to these very difficult problems. But, as we've pointed out before, there's a huge difference between cooperation and coercion. And there's an equally huge difference between committed individuals teaming up with the like-minded to share information and ideas, and having those ideas—so many of them utterly nonsensical or draconian, born of the same tired, tyrannical dogmas that start revolutions—forced upon the rest of us without our consent.

Covenant of Control

Unbowed by either criticism or well-earned derision, the UN establishment has poked deeply into issues traditionally associated with the internal affairs of each member country, including education, housing, medical care, and treatment of the disabled. Much of this has happened under the auspices of the International Covenant on Economic, Social and Cultural Rights ("CESCR"), which the United States ratified back in 1977 during Jimmy Carter's thankfully short presidency.

The aptly named "covenant" is an expression of goals and aspirations of the member states toward which they pledged to work. It provides for "international assistance and coopera-tion" toward the improvement of basic conditions in the member states, while leaving it up to each member state to de-vise its own legislative measures as it deemed appropriate.[3]

"International cooperation" in this case includes *sharing* of information, *consultation*, and getting *recommendations* from the Economic and Social Council. The Council is also charged with *monitoring* how well the member states are doing, and *report-ing* its findings to other specialized UN agencies, the Commis-sion on Human Rights, and the General Assembly as it deems appropriate. But again, the power to *monitor* a situation and perhaps *rebuke* a country in writing for not acting on some rec-ommendations is a far cry from actually *punishing* a country for not living up to some vague promise it made.

Acknowledging this, the covenant contains *no compulsory enforcement provisions. Nor does it provide a basis for interference in the political or judicial mechanisms of each member state.*

Enter the Committee on Economic, Social and Cultural Rights, the body of "independent experts" that monitors the covenant's implementation by its state parties. The committee took upon itself the right to issue its *own* interpretation of the provisions of the covenant, commenting on what it regarded as the "elements" of the "rights" stated therein. Those elements included which groups had standing as aggrieved parties; the "entitlements" ensuing from each right; and the "justiciable" aspects of each right.[4]

For example, the committee expounded on the covenant's "recognition" of a "core right" to adequate housing as including oh-so-much-more than basic habitability. The committee in its wisdom concluded that "[A]dequate housing must be in a location which allows access to employment options, health-care services, schools, child-care centres and other social facilities" and that "[T]he way housing is constructed, the building materials used and the policies supporting these must appropriately enable the expression of cultural identity and diversity of housing."[5]

One wonders how many of the committee members have actually built a house or a business. It's one thing to visualize a perfect world, and quite another one to fund, organize and build it. Only people with zero practical knowledge of the *real* world could conjure up something so utterly unattainable, and then seek to force others to make their nonsensical dreams come true.

Undaunted by reality, the committee went far beyond anything found in the actual Covenant itself by claiming that the "right to housing should be ensured to all persons irrespective of income or access to economic resources" and *told* the state parties to "establish housing subsidies for those unable to obtain affordable housing."[6]

The committee then devoted a whole detailed "Comment" on the "rights of the disabled," even though the covenant itself does not refer explicitly to persons with disabilities.[7] In yet another classic example of overreach, this committee of unaccountable wonks and insufferable do-gooders wrote its own rules defining what it considers to be disability-based discrimination, how the work place and transportation should be made accommodative to the disabled, the kind of financial assistance that should be provided to the disabled, affirmative action to overcome past acts of discrimination against the disabled, etc.

Laudable goals all, but ones *exclusively* within the province of each member state's own legislative and judicial process. In our country, Congress has defined the standards for helping the disabled, most notably in the Americans with Disabilities Act of 1990. Our courts, including the Supreme Court, have rendered judicial interpretations of this law.

ADA funding has been lavish and lawsuits copious, providing a crystal-clear preview of what the globalists have in mind when it comes to social policy. As for results, well, who cares if individuals are helped or hindered? The *group* is the thing. Individuals are expendable.

We do not need a UN committee to add its own pie-in-the-sky, let's-hold-hands-and-sing-Kumbaya opinion of how the United States should address the issues regarding the disabled within its borders. Yet, the United Nations General Assembly has gone even one step further in this case and established the compactly titled *Ad Hoc Committee on a Comprehensive and Integral International Convention on the Protection and Promotion of the Rights and Dignity of Persons with Disabilities.*[8]

The resolution, written with the typical economy of language so prevalent when zealots come together in common cause, "invites States, relevant bodies and organizations of the United Nations system, including relevant human rights treaty bodies, the regional commissions, the Special Rapporteur on disability of the Commission for Social Development, as well as intergovernmental and non-governmental organizations with an interest in the matter to make contributions to the work entrusted to the ad hoc committee, based on the practice of the United Nations."

Based on this effluent flow of verbiage, the General Assembly decided to proceed with the drafting of such a convention in June of 2003. This, in turn, led the ad hoc committee to establish a working group to prepare a draft text, which would be presented to the member states as the framework for negotiation (a 7-step process of meetings, all underwritten at the expense of programs that might actually physically impact real people in need). The United States was not represented in the working group.[9]

Using the working group's draft text, the ad hoc committee has conducted sessions since May 2004 with the member states to finalize the separate Convention devoted exclusively to the rights of the disabled—a spin-off, if you will, from the wellspring of the International Covenant on Economic, Social and Cultural Rights.

All this drafting is hard work, so it's a good thing that the UN is providing funds to the miscellaneous NGOs involved. Why use member state contributions to fund practical programs that might help the disabled "on the ground"—when sitting around a big table yakking with your Great and Good friends while waiting for cocktail hour to arrive is even more satisfying?

And yet with all that yakking, the ad hoc committee couldn't even reach a universally agreed-upon definition of "disability"—the very subject of the convention they were asked to draft! One would think that definitions come *first* when it comes to creating programs to deal with—well, what's been defined. But logic never stops NGOs from their Very Important Work of trying to separate the developed nations from their money.

So, even though they lacked a definition of what "disabled" means, our intrepid "human rights" warriors plunged on nevertheless. Why should minor details, such as not being able to actually define the problem being addressed, get in the way of an ad hoc committee's agenda?[10]

In other words, the committee went ahead anyway. It included in its draft the obligation of member states to adopt legislative, administrative and other measures to give effect to the convention, to nullify or amend any laws considered inconsistent with the convention, and to ensure that their national constitutions "embody the rights of equality and non-discrimination on the ground of disability" as will some day be defined in the convention—once they get around to it.

No doubt, there will be a permanent committee established along the lines of the committee on Economic, Social and Cultural Rights that will issue its interpretations of the convention's requirements and seek to impose these interpretations on the member states' domestic processes.

We are seeing the same surreal story being played out in other policy spheres such as education, labor, and reproductive rights. In every instance, with the active encouragement and assistance of unaccountable NGOs, the United Nations establishment is using the Economic and Social Council and its committee on Economic, Social and Cultural Rights to *set and enforce international standards on domestic policy issues.*

And just think: *this committee, which can't even define the problem it was created to address,* could become a model for *other* committees set up under *other* conventions on whatever *other* issues the globalists choose to pursue!

If this were not enough, active consideration is also being given to setting up an official complaints mechanism in the Committee on Economic, Social and Cultural Rights, turning it into an adjudicatory body to determine whether an economic, social or cultural right has been violated according to its interpretation. In a joint submission presented by an international coalition of NGOs, including the Centre on Housing Rights and Evictions, the International Commission of Jurists, Food-first Information and Action Network, and International

Women's Rights Action Watch, the NGOs endorsed the idea of an official complaints mechanism that "would provide individuals and groups with access to an international adjudicative procedure."

Individuals who consider themselves victims of Covenant "violations," or representatives acting on their behalf, would be empowered "to seek and obtain remedies for specific violations of rights contained in the covenant."[11] And in this instance we have a specific example of how these NGOs plan to subject sovereign nations to nothing less than death by a million lawyer-induced paper cuts:

> The regional and international [forums} with a quasi-judicial character arguably offer the most promising venues for securing justice and interpretations that actually change governments' behavior. To date, we have used the Inter-American Commission on Human Rights (three cases, one pending) and the UN Human Rights Committee (which oversees compliance with the International Covenant on Civil and Political Rights) (one case pending). We believe that seeking favorable interpretations from the quasi-judicial mechanisms of the European human rights system, the African system, and other UN individual complaint mechanisms will be particularly important in the next 3-5 years.[12]

This from a leaked strategy memo prepared by the George Soros-backed Center for Reproductive Rights. No doubt they are pinning their hopes on Supreme Court Justices like Ginsberg, Breyer and Kennedy to finish the job and incorporate these *"favorable interpretations"* into decisions defining what our own Constitution really *should* mean.

One waits with baited breath to see what happens when the policies of some international commission enforcing environmental violations clashes with one enforcing the rights of, say, indigenous people whose means of cultural expression includes deforestation or sacrificing a rare swamp beetle. Since by that time Rebecca Peters will have seen to it that there will be no pistols, and so no duel at the center of the UN Plaza, what other mechanism might these groups use to solve their differences? A boxing ring in the middle of First Avenue? Talk about the reality show from hell!

It's obvious that all of this current and prospective Busy Work on the part of the Committee on Economic, Social and Cultural Rights, and other committees modeled after it, interferes with the United States' control over its own domestic policy-making process. These unaccountable UN committees are clearly violating the UN Charter's own provision against interference in each sovereign member state's domestic policies when they issue "binding" opinions, trumpeting nonsensical interpretations of "international norms" as if they were laws.

Yet they are getting away with their stealth power grabs because the only people paying the slightest attention to their pontifications are, of course, the very NGOs who directly benefit from the erosion of national sovereignty.

CHAPTER TEN

FREEING THE CONSTITUTION FROM THE GLOBALISTS' DEATH GRIP

D ESPITE ITS ORIGINS as a benign organization of sovereign member states brought together to cooperate on solving common problems where possible, the United Nations celebrates its 60th anniversary by attempting to redefine itself in a way that has put the organization on a direct—and potentially disastrous—collision course with this country's ability to control its own affairs.

UN leadership is intent on building up an entrenched globalist bureaucracy with legal authority over a host of policy issues, funded by usurious global taxes. And it's embarking on this fantasy voyage with the active support of thousands of well-funded NGOs and self-proclaimed "world leaders," all wielding self-serving and often breathtakingly ludicrous—and contradictory—agendas.

Despite incompetent and corrupt management, a woeful record of failure in peacekeeping efforts, and an entrenched habit of ignoring real problems until they boil over, the globalists would have us believe that the United Nations label is some sort of "Good Housekeeping" seal of approval that we must all genuflect towards.

The UN Secretariat shovels many millions of dollars from annual member state contributions (over one-fifth of which comes from the United States) to fund dozens of meetings and summits and seminars and to create reams of reports justifying more power for the UN establishment and its associated forums. On issue after issue, UN bureaucrats, NGOs, and their powerful supporters follow the same pattern.

As we've seen, the UN apparatus is used to build up an illusory, manufactured "groundswell of support" for some often draconian, impractical, mindless reform by accrediting and funding world-wide networks of unaccountable non-governmental organizations. The NGO leaders, ever modest about their roles as self-appointed guardians of human welfare, the planet and indeed the universe, do their part by creating long, vaguely worded, objective-sounding "research" reports that create the perception of a world crisis. (Sadly, the quality and language of these reports often makes it tough to take them seriously, meaning that the genuine human crises the reports are supposed to be addressing aren't taken seriously either.)

And, of course, the solutions—based as they often are on solving undefined problems—transcend the capability or willingness of traditional nation-states to handle. Angered by this "recalcitrance," the anointed decide that only a permanent global institution vested with enforcement powers and budgets of their own can force sovereign nations to heel.

Along the way, the UN's entrenched bureaucracy refuses to take sides against perpetrators of aggression in order not to upset the countries they need to garner majority support for their programs—and to counterbalance the perceived hegemony of the United States. Demonizing the U.S. is, of course, part and parcel of lending credence to the UN's obsessive belief that transnational power is better than evil national sovereignty.

U.S. out of the UN?

As tempting as it may be to simply withdraw from the UN, to kick them out of the valuable real estate they're occupying and build condos, such actions would be counterproductive. Withdrawal will simply fuel more anti-Americanism, provide easy propaganda points for our adversaries, and aggravate tensions with the allies who aren't leaving.

Nor would withdrawal end the dangers that present and future UN spin-offs such as the International Criminal Court, or a future World Environmental Court or International Tax Organization, pose to the U.S., since we obviously cannot just walk away from the global economic, political and military matters affecting us.

So the U.S. can't quit the UN (although drop-kicking Bolton's "top ten floors" would be awfully satisfying).What we can—and must—do, is contain it. *Let it serve as a safety valve for disgruntled countries and NGOs that have no other forum in which to express their gripes—and maybe as the source of an exceedingly rare good idea—while preventing it from exercising any real powers at odds with our national sovereignty.*

By staying in the United Nations and using our Security Council veto power and financial clout, we're actually better placed to rein in its obscene and obsessive excesses. We need to keep shining the light on its stealthy, secretive ways, and keep the focus on the original intentions of the UN's founders.

That we need to beat the globalists is incontestable. The best way is to demand that the UN adhere to the original values proclaimed in its Charter. Through a series of reforms, partnerships and pressure, we can dismantle the UN—not as an institution, but as a power base for the globalist agenda.

The globalists are well-organized and well-funded—often by anti-American groups and foundations operating right here at home—but they can be defeated. We must save the United Nations from the worst instincts of those who would twist this mission to serve their own agendas. So in that spirit, here's an agenda of our own:

1. Encourage the spread of democracy and the creation of Democratic States.

We must continue to spread democracy. Not only is it the right thing to do, but it's the surest road towards more responsible behavior on the part of the member states now ruled by autocrats. Countries whose people have a stake in economic growth and prosperity will have an investment in demanding more reasoned decisions from the UN, as opposed to using it as a propaganda forum.

Some anti-war critics charge that democracy is an institution that Western nations have no business trying to push on the rest of the world. But the evidence of democracy's worldwide appeal proves otherwise. Between 1972 and 2002, the number of countries classified as "free" by Freedom House jumped from forty-three to eighty-nine.[1] Democracy is spreading throughout the world. Even in the Middle East, there is an incipient movement toward democracy in various Arab lands—"a strong commitment to Islamic ideas does not hinder the embrace of democratic principles" as long as they reflect the local cultures and values.[2]

Indeed, we find Grand Ayatollah Ali-Muhammad Sistani, the revered leader of Iraq's Shiite clergy, telling his followers that taking part in the elections and building a democratic system are religious duties. In the wake of the U.S.-led liberation of Iraq, we have witnessed Palestinian presidential elections, Saudi local elections, Egyptian presidential reforms and Lebanese street protests that eventually ousted Syrian control.

And history shows that democracies don't start wars.

Starting all over with a permanent coalition of democratic countries to *replace* the United Nations is one possibility. But this is not likely to work, because too many democracies like France, Germany and Belgium wouldn't abandon the UN for fear of alienating their third-world client states and their own political constituencies. Equally important as far as they're concerned, they also regard the UN as a vehicle for restraining U.S. power.

But the United Nations itself may turn more towards a truly democratically-oriented agenda as more of its member states become functioning democracies. A hopeful sign is the establishment of the UN Democracy Caucus, a group of democratic nations committed to working within the United Nations to strengthen democracy—the surest route towards ensuring "human rights." But this development must be reinforced, since the members don't vote as resolutely against the *real* rights abusers, as the non-democratic member states vote to protect them.

2. Create multilateral alternatives to the UN.

We must change the terms of the debate about the proper role for the United Nations. Too often we hear the windy argument that to support the principle of multilateralism, one must wholeheartedly support the United Nations as its only legitimate manifestation.

French President Jacques Chirac said "[T]here is no alternative but the United Nations" in his speech before the UN General Assembly in September 2003. During the 2004 Presidential campaign, Democratic nominee John Kerry said that "[W]ithin weeks of being inaugurated, I will return to the UN and I will literally, formally rejoin the community of nations and turn over a proud new chapter in America's relationship with the world."[3]

Chirac and Kerry both have it wrong. Multilateralism and the United Nations are hardly one and the same. The United States has never left the community of nations. Beneficial multilateralism is really about cooperation among countries working towards a common goal that produces net positive results against that stated (and defined) goal. As University of Kiel (Germany) international relations professor Joachim Krause put it:

> In its broadest sense, multilateralism can be defined as international cooperation among more than two states, designed to solve international problems and to deal with conflicts resulting from perceived or actual anarchy in international relations...In most cases, it has been functionally oriented and either global or regional in scope.[4]

The United Nations is obviously the largest multilateral institution in the world since its membership spans the globe. However, in some instances, its very size—and its large number of autocratic member states—are handicaps, because they dilute a sense of common purpose at a level that really means something.

With some exceptions—fanatical Islamic terrorists and rogue dictators come to mind—everyone would answer "yes" if asked whether they favored peace, freedom from oppression, and a healthy life for all. The rub comes in reaching agreement among diverse peoples with diverse histories and life experiences as to exactly what these words and phrases mean contextually—and how these ephemeral goals are to be made manifest.

There will always be disagreements over which goals should take priority, and how best to achieve them. *Striving for either the perfect solution or for the least common denominator by global consensus often keeps us from reaching fast and practical solutions to manageable problems.* Not to mention that, when global elitists are on the case, practical solutions are going to be in short supply.

When the United Nations is prevented by its own procedures from taking effective action to combat a widely acknowledged threat like Saddam Hussein, the choice is not between UN multilateralism and U.S. unilateralism. Indeed, in the case of Iraq, France's threatened veto of a resolution authorizing collective military action was a far more unilateral act than the United States' leadership of a coalition of states to do the job that France shirked.

True world consensus would have brought Saddam Hussein to his knees long before, and at far less human cost. Looking behind the curtain to see how the UN decision-making machinery actually works, we see how the interplay of international realpolitik and the customary self-interested dealings among states makes such consensus impossible. When collective security is at stake, we need a viable alternative.

The U.S. remains among the most dedicated multilateralist countries in the world. We know that international cooperation is not just desirable, but necessary when it comes to fighting common threats such as global terrorism. And we are working with our allies in Europe and Asia to deal diplomatically with the nuclear threats posed by North Korea and Iran.

Free trade also requires concessions on our part in order to achieve a win-win outcome with our trading partners. But intelligent cooperation does *not* mean acquiescence to whatever other countries think, just because they think differently.

We contribute disproportionately to the United Nations. We work through NATO, the Organization of American States and alliances with Asian countries. We actively support the World Bank, the International Monetary Fund, the Global Environmental Facility, public-private partnerships such as the Global Alliance for Vaccines and Immunizations, and legions of multilateral relief agencies. We are hardly "going it alone."

It's time to break with the romantic fiction that sees the UN as the only claimant to multilateral "legitimacy." With our partners and allies, we must devise new forms of multilateralism that address the world's new realities, instead of going back to the tainted UN well over and over. Professor Krause has suggested, for example, a multilateral organization that serves to coordinate Western efforts to modernize the Middle East—a "Middle Eastern Transformation Agency to plan and oversee various programs to bring about economic, political, and social reforms in the region."[5]

This could include, as Rep. Henry Hyde has suggested, a comprehensive economic development program for the Middle East similar to the Marshall Plan that rebuilt Western Europe after WW II. Such a program can help stimulate intra-regional free trade and other economic ties between a Palestinian state and Israel to their common benefit, laying a foundation of common interests among influential blocs of moderates in both communities that will make them strong stakeholders in a genuine peace.

We should also assemble coalitions of countries on particular issues of common interest. This is a proven strategy. We can strive for more common ground on economic and environmental issues with emerging global players like China and India. We should forge partnerships with the Sub-Sahara African countries by standing with them to combat ethnic cleansing, demonstrating real commitment to fighting AIDS and other diseases and by working cooperatively to stimulate economic growth in the developing world–the best anti-poverty program of all. How about, for example, agreeing to remove trade barriers to exports of African agricultural products that are grown on lands for which the farmers tilling those lands are provided secure, formally recognized legal title by their governments? This is but one example of a practical, reciprocal and measurable action, not a wealth redistributionist scheme via incomprehensible "covenants," "treaties" and 'Millennium

Outcome" documents that do nothing but expand NGO and UN bureaucrat egos- and bank accounts.

In short, the failure of the UN's brand of multilateralism isn't the failure of multilateralism, per se. And this country's embrace of alternative forms of multilateralism, ones designed address specific problems that the UN has proven incapable of solving, is not unilateralism, as the critics of U.S. foreign policy suggest. We are not abandoning the United Nations. *We are opening the multilateralism market up to competition, and it's high time we did.*

3. Challenge UN overreach with Security Council vetoes and strong financial pressure.

We must use every lever available to aggressively spotlight the constant, grabby overreaching of the UN Secretariat, General Assembly, the Economic and Social Council and any and every other UN body. This includes forcing every General Assembly resolution and treaty impacting collective security issues to a Security Council vote, where the U.S. can exercise its veto power. It means enforcing the Congressional limitations on appropriations for the UN budget on items that violate the edict against UN interference in the domestic affairs of the member states. We should challenge any attempt by member states to cut off the U.S.'s voting rights, simply because we are withholding American contributions to UN agencies that refuse to abide strictly by the limitations on their authority as set forth in the very Charter that governs them.

4. Protect U.S. soldiers from ICC prosecution.

Continue the Bush Administration's policy of bilateral arrangements with countries that have chosen to ratify the International Criminal Court Rome Statute. Any country that won't pledge not to initiate or assist in any ICC prosecution of

American soldiers participating in a peacekeeping operation should face reprisals, including a cut-off of all foreign aid.

Nor should we participate in any UN peacekeeping operation, unless given immunity from ICC prosecution. Here's one hopeful sign—the Security Council's recent authorization for the ICC to handle prosecutions of Sudanese human rights atrocities includes protection from ICC investigation or prosecution for United States nationals and members of the armed forces of states that are not parties to the Rome Statute. But this is just a start. U.S. policy should be "no ICC immunity— no troops or logistical support." Period.

5. Smash global taxation.

Mohamed El-Ashry, currently the Senior Fellow of Ted Turner's UN Foundation, told this author that the global tax issue is very much alive, and that he himself had been asked to chair a portion of a meeting called by French President Jacques Chirac to discuss a proposed tax on aviation fuel. He said that global taxes are the "only way you can raise additional resources" required to fund the UN's myriad programs on poverty and other causes—which makes sense, of course, only if you feel that these programs are worth funding. To El-Ashry's way of thinking, we shouldn't have a choice in that determination, since our "betters" have already done the heavy mental lifting for us.

He believes aviation fuel and international financial transactions taxes are "fair" because everyone's favorite boogeyman, "the rich," are the only people who'll have to pay them— assertions that are, of course, demonstrably false.

But, demonstrating at least a vague understanding of how the world works, El-Ashry also said that, for global taxes to be implemented by treaty, the U.S. must support the idea.

Through his past leadership of the Global Environmental Facility, El-Ashry should know first-hand how the United

States steps up as a donor to worthy causes. But the actions we take on this front are voluntary ones. *Imposition of global taxes on American citizens violates the United States Constitution.* Such impositions cannot be allowed to stand.

The president must refuse to submit, and the Senate refuse to ratify, *any* treaty or protocol that includes a provision on global taxes or whatever euphemism is being bandied about to disguise the globalists' intentions. We must refuse to accept *any* treaty which establishes a mechanism under which the member states agree to enact legislation for the purpose of collecting taxes for remittal to a global fund.

If globalists seek to punish Americans by imposing global taxes on our domestic activities—for example, our patterns of Internet or energy usage—the U.S. should challenge the tax before the World Trade Organization as the equivalent of a discriminatory tariff. We should take all other appropriate action against the offending parties.

It's hard to overstate the dangers here. Take the example of a tax discriminating against Americans, this time in the energy arena. Some signatories to the Kyoto Protocol want to impose a global carbon tax scheme structured in a manner that would penalize the United States for not agreeing to the global-warming treaty. Under this scheme, any American product imported into a Kyoto signatory country could be assessed a special import tax (i.e., a tax on the energy consumed within the United States to produce the imported product) before it could be sold to that country's consumers.

Meanwhile, any products exported from the same country to the United States would receive an indirect subsidy from the home country in the form of an energy cost rebate, on the theory that the exporter had incurred higher costs than their American counterparts in complying with the Kyoto Protocol. The net effect is to punish the United States with trade reprisals for exercising its sovereign right under the U.S. Constitution and UN Charter not to join a treaty with which it disagrees.

If the globalists try to impose such global taxes on American citizens—taxation without representation—we should be prepared to retaliate in kind against the exports of the countries leading this shameless cabal. And if any instrumentality of the United Nations is used to aid and abet such a global tax scheme, we should immediately withhold our funding.

6. Demand effective UN budget reforms and discipline.

The UN's final regular budget for 2004-2005 has been set at $3.6 billion.[6] This is nearly a billion dollars higher than the UN regular biennium budget adopted for 2002-2003[7] The UN's budget increases are out of control—even Congress takes more than two years to grow its budget by 40%!

Although UN management is slowly implementing some reforms, on Kofi Annan's watch it has fallen far short of what it promised to do. Waste and inefficiency are still rampant. The General Accounting Office concluded that UN management still does not systematically monitor and evaluate program performance, so that it can actually eliminate ones that don't work.

Overall, while the GAO noted some improvements and some programs in various stages of implementation, it found that only 38% of the sixty-six major reform initiatives in the UN's promised 2002 reform agenda have been instituted.[8]

The United Nation's leadership must accelerate and strengthen on-going UN budget and management reforms, require rigorous zero-based budgeting processes for every funded project, along with demonstration of results against measurable objectives. That's how it works in the real world (if not in Congress).

Managerial deadwood in the United Nations bureaucracy should be eliminated, with performance-based evaluations and compensation replacing the status quo that is driven by seniority, cronyism, political correctness and geographic distribution. New financing needs should be met by establishing priorities and strict redeployment of resources from lower-priority activities to those of higher priority, rather than adding yet another layer of resources to the existing ones and seeking new funding.

Duplicative activities should be eliminated. Committees should be subject to sunset provisions. Any biennial budget proposal that is found to make mainly editorial changes to the programs contained in previous budgets—simply regurgitating in slightly altered form the previously used text from years past—should be summarily rejected.[9] We should continue to insist that an American representative sit on the member state budget committee.

The UN's audit capability should be strengthened, not just beyond what Annan has called for, but with independent outside audits supplementing an adequately funded internal audit and inspection function. Earlier this year, a bipartisan task force chaired by former House Speaker Newt Gingrich and former Senate Majority Leader George Mitchell, recommended that the UN establish an "Independent Oversight Board (IOB) that would function in a manner similar to a corporate independent audit committee.[10] The Volcker committee recommended much the same thing—all falling on deaf ears at the Millennium+5 General Assembly summit meeting. But we must press on if the UN is to have any chance of escaping the morass in which it finds itself. If that means withholding some funds until the UN gets serious about reform (as some in Congress have suggested), so be it.

In order to work, an independent oversight board would need the authority to set the budget and direct the work of the UN's internal audit group without interference. The results of all audits would be made available to all member states on a regular and timely basis under guidelines, as the Gingrich-

Mitchell Task Force recommended, that "meet, at a minimum, the freedom of information flow between U.S. investigative agencies and the Congress."[11] Low standards indeed.

And the auditors' recommendations should be implemented promptly, with regular progress reports distributed to all member states. The secretary-general and his management team must instill, and be role models for, a culture that has zero tolerance for even the slightest hint of conflict-of-interest, misuse of funds or other wrong-doing. The cloak of secrecy surrounding internal investigations must be removed once and for all. Any further lapses in proper behavior or managerial oversight should result in severe sanctions, up to and including removal from office without pay.

When it comes to budget discipline, despite talking the talk, the secretary-general shows precisely the opposite inclination in this open-ended statement of the UN's expanded mission:

> The millennium development goals and the commitments agreed upon through the global conferences define critical objectives for the international community. *The Organization must enhance its capacity to provide global direction with respect to these objectives...ensure that there is comprehensive follow-up to the global conferences, including the International Conference on Financing for Development and the World Summit on Sustainable Development.* The United Nations convenes conferences and meetings, and produces a vast variety of reports and documents, on a daily basis. These are not marginal activities of the Organization, but reflect a central and fundamental aspect of how the world's most inclusive multilateral institution conducts its business. [12]
> (emphasis added)

So even the secretary-general admits that the UN's fundamental purpose is to constantly meet, convene and generate reams of documents without ever setting any meaningful performance benchmarks or creating any realistic objectives for completion! And yet he wants more and more money to do what, precisely? Put on more meetings?

Perhaps the most telling evidence of the UN's penchant for extravagance is a memo that the secretary-general's chief-of-staff wrote to senior UN managers, warning them not to engage in lavish entertaining during the 2002 environment summit in Johannesburg, since it was inconveniently taking place in the midst of the famine plaguing southern Africa. This warning was issued against the backdrop of the prior UN World Food Summit held in Rome. Apparently, discussing how to cut world hunger in half is hungry work itself, because attendees came under heavy criticism for the elaborate feasts they enjoyed.[13] Maybe the participants felt that they could only understand the full dimensions of hunger by indulging in its polar opposite.

It is time to break this vicious cycle by aligning expectations and budget priorities with what is both useful and reasonably obtainable.

7. Demand NGO accountability.

Thousands of non-governmental organizations are officially accredited by the United Nations, with formal consultative status. As Annan stated, "[T]oday, a major United Nations gathering without the involvement of civil society in all its various forms is scarcely imaginable... Many United Nations treaty bodies now routinely consider alternate reports from non-governmental organizations alongside the official reports from Governments."[14]

These NGOs are accountable to no one, except perhaps to their often equally fanatical donors. And for the most part, they tend to represent only one point of view on a given subject—inevitably the "progressive" point of view that pushes for more coercive UN involvement in their agenda. Lashing out at the United States and at business participation in UN matters, for example, the UN's non-governmental Liaison Service Development Dossiers web site contains the following diatribe:

> In the United States, communities have suffered their own version of structural adjustment for 15 years. During that time, the U.S. domestic social budget has been destroyed. The priority for many NGOs and community groups now is to build a progressive movement over the next 20 years from the grassroots up...NGOs are concerned that the UN considers non-profit business organizations to be on a par with NGOs. For some NGOs, these business groups have no place in international policy dialogue, since they do not represent the public interest...[15]

Whether non-profit or for-profit, business groups have *every* right to be involved in international policy dialogues that might affect them! In direct contrast to so many NGOs with their unanchored utopian schemes, these groups bring real-world experience and perspective to the table. Far from "not representing the public interest," they represent *exactly* those who create jobs and prosperity, something which few NGOs can lay claim to. Just how is that not in the public interest? Most have accountability policies that are far more stringent than those of their critics.

We should insist, as a condition of accreditation, and of the right to participate in UN meetings, the publication of regular independent audits of NGO finances and performance. We should also insist that the meeting minutes of all accredited NGOs be open to regular public inspection and that other governance reforms be instituted, including an independent watchdog. And every issue should be represented by accredited NGOs across the political spectrum to ensure that all points of view are heard.

As summed up by Jeffrey E. Garten, Dean of the Yale School of Management:

> NGOs have had too much of a free ride in identifying themselves with the public interest. They have acquired the high ground of public opinion without being subjected to the same

public scrutiny given to corporations and governments. It is time that companies and governments demand more public examination of NGOs.[16]

The U.S. government should more aggressively monitor the NGOs to whom it provides funding, or with whom it contracts for services, and cut them off if they unfairly attack U.S. policies. The NGOs are entitled to say whatever they want, but the American taxpayers should not have to subsidize those actively working against this country's best interests.

And particular governmental attention must also be paid to whether major U.S. foundations that actively underwrite groups attempting to undermine American sovereignty should be entitled to tax-exempt status or government grants.

8. Require unbiased research on significant policy issues.

To put it mildly, Jeffrey Sachs' Millennium Development Project research report has been found wanting when viewed from a policy perspective. It is little more than an advocacy piece masquerading as serious research. The report reflects few facts, but plenty of hot air in the form of Sachs' own elevated preference for a massive income redistribution program in which the more developed countries are "asked" to finance the development of poorer countries on faith.

For obvious reasons, no one asked an economist coming from, say, a Chicago School of Economics angle to run the numbers and make sure they added up. The report is all about Sachs and so lacks any serious discussion of alternative programs for catalyzing growth, such as the innovative ideas of Peruvian economist Hernando De Soto. Yet it's being touted as the undisputed basis upon which to achieve the UN Millennium Development goals! Fallacious assumptions, questionable data and seriously flawed research are a sure path not just to erroneous conclusions, but to catastrophically costly policy failure, in both monetary and human terms.

It should be noted that the quality of Jeffrey Sachs' research has been questioned in the past. A *New York Times* profile in 2002 mentioned a report drafted by a committee that he led, which was criticized for claiming that that $101 billion spent on "health" could result in 8 million lives saved a year and potential annual income gains of $186 billion.[17]

According to the *New York Times* article, "[E]xperts said his claims were not backed by the airtight statistics that most economic and medical journals demand." Sachs responded to this criticism by saying that he was only seeking to "entrance" policymakers by the orders of magnitude involved.

Excuse us, but it's the job of snake-charmers and street performers to "entrance." Economists are supposed to present observers with something of more concrete value than the sight of a cobra rising from a woven basket, or a mime pretending to smell a flower. Sachs presented his "entrancing" numbers as if they were precise estimates based on economically sound assumptions and methodology. They weren't.

If his reputation as a researcher is to regain its luster, Sachs should withdraw his "smoke and mirrors" Millennium Development Project report, enlist an economist with more free market leanings as co-director and obtain certification of any report's research quality through unbiased peer review *before* re-submitting his report to the secretary-general or the General Assembly. Sachs can thereby make an actual positive contribution by serving as a role model for truly objective, constructive research.

9. Demand exhaustive treaty evaluation.

Traditionally, treaties were written pacts among two or more sovereign states settling a conflict or otherwise addressing the resolution of a specific inter-relational issue. Under the United Nations umbrella, treaties—in UN-speak often referred to as conventions, covenants or protocols—have been increasingly used as instruments to establish "global norms" and their resulting institutions. As we've seen, these treaties have intruded further and further into areas that historically have been the exclusive domains of sovereign governments. In short, these treaties have become the insidious cornerstone of the movement toward global governance.

So it's more critical than ever that the President and Senate analyze the implications of every word in every treaty they consider for U.S. participation. Is the objective of the treaty clearly stated, with means of implementation and measurements of performance narrowly tailored to reach achievable results? Are the benefits and burdens distributed fairly without disproportionately penalizing the United States?

Does the treaty set up a permanent governing authority and, if so, what are its mandate, jurisdiction and operational procedures? Do any treaty provisions conflict with Constitutional provisions or any current domestic legislation?

This doesn't mean that the U.S. must get its way on every issue, but it *does* beg the question, why is the U.S. involved *at all* in negotiations over *anything* where the end result, if ratified by our elected representatives, means "global" control over American resources and tax dollars? We are constantly being bombarded by "treaties" and "agreements" and "covenants" and the like that collectively, if ratified, would create a morass of "international codes of conduct" accompanied by international bureaucracies to enforce them. Since we know all this, perhaps it's time to "just say no" to treaties for a while.

Were we to enter into such agreements just to placate world opinion, we might win grudging—and very temporary—praise from the secretary-general and a few world leaders. But that's hardly a valid reason for becoming a slave to the whims of the fanatics and zealots who infest the UN and so many NGOs.

10. Enforce judicial restraint.

We have seen how some federal judges have overstepped their judicial role and sought to impose their own moral views and policy preferences, rather than interpret the law. Globalists, of course, look for just such judges when shopping around their cases— fellow travelers who might be moved to incorporate "international norms" into interpretations even if they conflict with the text and animating principles of the Constitution itself.

It's a stealth tactic, and a dishonorable one, too, since globalists are using unelected judges to incorporate concepts and interpretations into American law that would, quite frankly, be squashed in any kind of legitimate debate.

As of this writing, John Roberts has just been sworn in as Chief Justice of the U.S. Supreme Court. And if he stays true to his word, globalists are going to have a *lot* harder time trying to manipulate our legal system on the way to truncating our freedoms.

According to an article in *The Australian*, "The man nominated to replace the recently deceased William Rehnquist told U.S. senators this week he did not believe foreign law should bear on the deliberations of the nation's highest court. His views are consistent with the Bush administration's narrow view of the U.S. justice system and its suspicion of global treaties on issues such as human rights."

The article continues, "Roberts expressed support for the contention that U.S. judges should only consider local law— despite the fact many foreign superior courts, including the High Court of Australia, refer to the U.S. Supreme Court's decisions in their judgments at various times."

During his confirmation hearings, in fact, Roberts hit the nail on the head when it comes to the dangers of bringing foreign precedents into American courts—so much so, that his comments are worth noting in detail:

The president who nominates judges is obviously accountable to the people. Senators who confirm judges are accountable to people. And in that way, the role of the judge is consistent with the democratic theory.

If we're relying on a decision from a German judge about what our constitution means, no president accountable to the people appointed that judge and no Senate accountable to the people confirmed that judge. And yet he's playing a role in shaping the law that binds the people in this country. I think that's a concern that has to be addressed.

The other part of it that would concern me is that, relying on foreign precedent doesn't confine judges. It doesn't limit their discretion the way relying on domestic precedent does.

Domestic precedent can confine and shape the discretion of the judges. Foreign law, you can find anything you want. If you don't find it in the decisions of France or Italy, it's in the decisions of Somalia or Japan or Indonesia, or wherever.

As somebody said in another context, looking at foreign law for support is like looking out over a crowd and picking out your friends. You can find them. They're there.

And that actually expands the discretion of the judge. It allows the judge to incorporate his or her own personal preferences, cloak them with the authority of precedent—because they're finding precedent in foreign law—and use that to determine the meaning of the constitution.

And I think that's a misuse of precedent, not a correct use of precedent."[18]

Heartening words, indeed. During any judicial nominating process, it is vital to inquire how the candidate would approach such questions—and to weed out those who do not commit to a strict constructionist approach to Constitutional interpretation.

However, experience has shown that it's difficult to predict how judges will actually approach a case when it is brought before them. Just look at the disappointing course that Justice Kennedy has taken on the relevance of foreign law and "international norms" to Constitutional interpretation! Therefore, we should also consider using Congress' power to limit the jurisdiction of the federal courts, assigning cases involving claims that have any basis in international treaties or other international law sources to a single court equipped to handle them—for example, the Federal Circuit Court of Appeals (whose jurisdiction already includes the U.S. Court of International Trade, U.S. Claims Court, and the Court of Veterans' Appeals and Patent Appeals). In this case, the Federal Circuit would become the court of first instance to hear the claims, with appeal only to the Supreme Court.

Congress has the Constitutional power to establish the lower federal courts. It can also limit the jurisdiction of these courts. And except for the original jurisdiction of the Supreme Court specified in the Constitution that does not apply to the type of claims we are discussing, Article III, Section 2 of the Constitution gives Congress the power to make "such exceptions, and under such regulations" as Congress finds necessary to Supreme Court jurisdiction.

In other words, Congress has the authority to make exceptions to Supreme Court jurisdiction in the form of general rules and based upon policy and Constitutional reasons other than the outcomes of a particular line of cases.[19]

Using this approach and following the pattern of analogous legislation that has been proposed in the past, the following Congressional solution is recommended to appropriately limit the courts' jurisdiction:

> *No district federal court or state court shall adjudicate any claim involving, or base in whole or in part any decision, order, final judgment, or other ruling that defines any Constitutional or statutory rights or obligations or that requires the appropriation or expenditure of money, or imposition of taxes upon, an international treaty, covenant, convention, or protocol, including reliance on regulations, rules, decisions, interpretations, norms or policies of any international body.. The Court of Appeals of the Federal Circuit shall be the exclusive federal court for the origination of such claim and then only upon the condition that such Court (and the Supreme Court, upon appeal of a decision by the Court of Appeals of the Federal Circuit) shall not issue any decision, order, final judgment, or other ruling that requires the appropriation or expenditure of money or imposition of taxes in connection therewith that interferes with the legislative functions of Congress or that relies in whole or in part on any foreign or international law that conflicts with the original text and history of any provision of the U.S. Constitution. A violation by a Federal court justice or a judge of these jurisdictional limits shall be an impeachable offense, and a material breach of good behavior subject to removal according to rules and procedures established by the Congress.*

It's a sad commentary that we must consider mandating that courts adhere to the original text of the Constitution! Yet it's becoming increasingly necessary to reinforce the principle that the legitimacy of American law does not depend on conformance to any body of law or norms outside of the Constitution.

Unless controlled, the courts may follow the path that Thomas Jefferson warned about when he said: "[T]he germ of dissolution of our federal government is in the constitution of the federal judiciary; an irresponsible body...working like gravity by night and by day, gaining a little to-day and a little to-morrow, and advancing its noiseless step like a thief, over the field of jurisdiction...."[20]

Judges who incorporate "international norms" into their interpretations in contradiction to Constitutional textual and historical evidence should be subject to possible impeachment and removal from office.

11. Demand more from ourselves...and from others.

The United Nations was a bold experiment. Generations of American school children, including this author, learned of its noble mission and grew up believing in it. And the UN has done much good over the years when focused on immediate needs—coordinating international contributions to disaster relief and addressing health crises or critical food shortages, for example.

However, as the globalists have usurped control and begun using the UN as the flagship of their secretive NGO navy, the better to bombard us with incomprehensible, sprawling treaties and omnipotent transnational courts, it's clear that Harry Truman's creation isn't living up to its promise...or promises.

The UN has continually shrunk back in the face of evil, preferring to debate what "evil" means, or whether or not it even exists, instead of confronting it.

Evil is rampant and recurrent in this world. It appeared in the concentration camps of the Holocaust, the gulags of the Soviet Union, the killing fields in Cambodia, the horrific attacks of 9/11 and the mass graves of Saddam Hussein's regime. Trite, silly phrases like "Don't be evil," "Visualize World Peace" and "I'm a tree-hugger, I pine for yew" make for catchy bumper stickers, but are hardly appropriate for use as the philosophical underpinnings for *any* government, much less a world government. Yet it's on this level of profundity—or lack thereof—that so many globalists seem to operate.

In their fairy-tale world of Very Important Thoughts, the use of military force to end a brutal dictatorship in Iraq in order to provide a chance for human dignity and freedom has no better moral standing than that same brutal dictator's use of military force to do the very opposite. "Disgusting" is too mild a word to describe such beliefs.

Time and time again, the United States has sacrificed blood and treasure to confront evil and defeat it. Those who are intent on using the United Nations to "contain" America's global influence conveniently forget that the United States military has been an instrument for endless good in vanquishing the totalitarian evils of fascism and communism—without keeping the spoils of war for itself.

Much has already been written about the UN's moral failures and institutional shortcomings. The main purpose of this book is not to dwell on the UN's past, but rather to raise serious questions about where the left-wing "progressive" ideological cabal controlling the UN today is planning to take it in the future.

The United Nations is no more than the sum of its member states. It can't just paper over conflicting interests and agendas on fundamental issues of war and the global economy, and no cosmetic reforms can change this fundamental fact.

But the alternative—to yield more sovereign power in the name of global governance to the UN and its associated unelected international forums—is sheer insanity. It pits utopian dreams in the form of universal policy prescriptions, implemented through undemocratic processes, against a tried and true constitutional democracy that has been an overwhelming force for good for over 200 years.

Those who want to turn the UN into a global governance authority of its own operate on the premise that "international law" is a talisman that can resolve every problem. They believe that national sovereignty, irrespective of whether its source lies in the Constitution of a functioning democracy, should be swept aside. In the minds of Kofi Annan, Jacques Chirac, Maurice Strong, George Soros, their allies and fellow travelers, there is no real distinction between the sovereignty of an autocratic nation and a democratic one since the citizens of both are ultimately "citizens of the world" who should be subject to global laws.

But a legal and political system only works when all under its jurisdiction share a common set of values and a process that is directly accountable to the people who will be subject to the rules created by the system. That is not possible within the governance structures that the globalists are trying to devise. Their path leads to totalitarianism, albeit "with a human face." The death of millions has proved time and time again not only that this route doesn't work, but that it is an abomination.

President Harry Truman wisely ignored the siren songs emanating from the globalists of his day, many of whom were *already* recommending the establishment of an international judiciary, funded by a global tax, with the power to create and enforce new principles of its own. Bad ideas die hard; exhausted by two world wars, the desire of people of good will to create a "new world order" is perhaps understandable. But it makes no more sense today than it did sixty years ago when Walter Lippman observed that the idealistic Woodrow Wilson's gravest error was "forgetting that we are men and thinking that we are gods." Today, it is the globalists who believe they are gods.

The United Nations Charter and the United States Constitution are compatible if both are interpreted according to their core principles. We can continue to work through the United Nations when it makes sense, or we can choose other forms of multilateral cooperation when that makes better sense.

However, we must not allow manufactured, cynical pronouncements of "global norms of good behavior" and "global governance" fads to override *our* nation's ability to control its own destiny under the glorious and brilliantly conceived Constitution that so many have given their lives to defend.

NOTES

Introduction

1. David Brooks, "Loudly, With a Big Stick," *New York Times*, April 14, 2005.
2. *Google Corporation*, "Ten Things Google Has Found to Be True," http://www.google.com/corporate/tenthings.html

Chapter One

1. Townsend Hoopes and Douglas Brinkley, *FDR and the Creation of the UN* (Yale University Press, 1997), Chapter 1.
2. Ibid.
3. Ibid., 2, quoting in Walter Lippman, *U.S. War Aims* (Boston: Little, Brown and Co, 1944), 181-82.
4. Ibid., 20, 56.
5. *Truman Presidential Museum and Library*, Letter from John Ross Delafield to President Harry S. Truman, April 18, 1945, http://www.trumanlibrary.org/whistlestop/study_collections/un/large/index.php.
6. *United States Senate Historical Office—Oral History Project*, Interview with Francis O. Wilcox, Chief of Staff, Senate, Foreign Relations Committee, 1947-1955, Interview #1 at the Legislative Reference Service by Donald A. Ritchie, February 1, 1984, http://www.senate.gov; FDR and the Creation of the U.N, *supra* at 202.
7. *Truman Presidential Museum and Library*, Note from Secretary of State Edward R. Stettinius Jr. to Matthew Connelly, May 23, 1945, http://www.trumanlibrary.org/whistlestop/study_collections/un/large/index.php.
8. *World Federalist Movement*, "Frequently Asked Questions," http:// www.wfm.org/index.php/pages/2.
9. Robert Muller, "5000 Plus Idea Dreams for a Better World," *Robert Muller.org*, http://robertmuller.org/. As for Dr. Muller's University for Peace, which is sponsored by the United Nations as a model for education in the 21st century, Dr. Muller and his adherents believe that it sits on a sacred mountain called Mount Rasur from which a civilization of peace and nature will spread to the entire world. According to Dr. Muller's "Prophecy of Rasur" (the god of indigenous children), this god spoke to the children of the village of Quisar at the base of Mt. Rasur, the site of the University for Peace from which a new civilization of peace would spread. throughout the world. He told the children that the Great Spirit was in every animal, leaf and grass they see and that it is also in them.
10. Natalie Steinberg, "On Gongos and Quangos and Wild NGOs," *The World Federalist Movement*, December 2001, http://www.wfm.org/index.php/docu ments/460; Professor Peter Willetts, "What is a Non-Governmental Organization," *UNESCO Encyclopedia*, (London: City University, 2002).
11. Claude Salhani, "To the Ballots, Citizens", *Washington Times*, April 15, 2005,

http://washingtontimes.com/upi-breaking/20050415-090129-2026r.htm

12. Seven principles for globalization (Source: Speech by French President, Jacques Chirac, Paris, January 7, 1999):
- Collective responsibility and collective action
- Equity
- Solidarity—to avoid exclusion of people or nations
- Diversity
- Safety first, environmentally and otherwise (do no harm)
- Liberty and respect for human rights
- Complementarity and subsidiarity

13. Speech by French President Jacques Chirac, "To the VIth Conference of the Parties to the United Nations Framework Convention on Climate Change," The Hague, November 20, 2000.

14. Speech by French President Jacques Chirac, "New Year Greeting to the Diplomatic Corps Speech," Paris, January 8, 2004.

15. James Gustave Speth, *Red Sky at Morning* (Yale University Press 2004), 178.

16. James Gustave Speth, "A New Paradigm: Bring It On!", Environmental Law Institute Award Dinner Millennium Celebration, Washington, D.C., October 26, 1999, http://yale.edu/forestry/popup/events/fall99/10_26envlaw.html

17. Thalif Deen, "UN to Put Global Taxes Centre Stage," *Global Policy Forum,* July 8, 2004, http://globalpolicy.org/finance/alternat/2004/0708globaltax.htm.

18. *Center for Global Development*, Landau Report to President Jacques Chirac, December 2004, http://cgdev.org/docs/landau%20report.pdf.

19. Sobhy Mujahid, "Call For Incorporating Sharia Into International Law," *IslamOnline.net*, April 30, 2004, http://islam-online.net/English/News/2004-04/30/article05.shtml.

20. Bernard Lewis, "What Went Wrong," *Perennial*, 2003.

21. Some globalists try to argue that, because treaties are specifically referred to in the Constitution's Supremacy Clause (Article 6) as part of the supreme law of the land and that the reference is followed almost immediately by the phrase "anything in the constitution or laws of any State to the contrary notwithstanding," treaties are superior to the Constitution itself. The Supreme Court has dismissed this argument out of hand: "This [Supreme] Court has regularly and uniformly recognized the supremacy of the Constitution over a treaty."—Reid v. Covert, October 1956, 354 U.S. 1, at 17.

Chapter Two

1. *Independent Inquiry Committee*, "Third Interim Report issued by the Independent Inquiry Committee into the United Nations Oil-for-Food Program," August 8, 2005, http://www.iic-offp.org/documents/Third%20Interim%20Report.pdf. At a minimum, according to the committee's first interim report, Sevan's conduct in running the Oil-for-Food Program demonstrated a "grave and continuing conflict of interest" that had "seriously undermined the integrity of the United Nations." "First Interim Report issued by the Independent Inquiry Committee into the United Nations Oil-for-

NOTES

Food Program" (February 3, 2005); "Hearing Before the Committee on International Relations House of Representatives, The Oil-for-Food Program: Tracking the Funds" (November 17, 2004), http://www.house.gov/international_relations/108/96930.pdf.

2. *United Nations,* Statement attributable to the spokesman for the secretary-general on reimbursement of Benon Sevan's legal expenses, March 22, 2005, http://un.org/apps/sg/sgstats.asp?nid=1359. See also "UN Will Not Pay for Legal Fees of Official Implicated in Iraq Oil-for-Food Probe," *UN News Centre,* March 28, 2005.

3. *Independent Inquiry Committee* "Second Interim Report by the Independent Inquiry Committee into the UN Oil-for-Food Program," March 29, 2005.

4. *UN News Centre,* "Annan Says Exoneration by Iraq Oil-for-Food Report 'great relief'," March 29, 2005.

5. Ibid.

6. Ibid.

7. Jacques Chirac, "U.S. Action Brought Crisis," *CNN.com,* September 23, 2003, http://cnn.com/2003/U.S./09/23/sprj.irq.un/.

8. Dore Gold, *Tower of Babble,* (Crown Forum, 2004), 135-153.

9. *Frontline,* "The Triumph of Evil," transcript of interview with Iqbal Riza, January 26, 1999, http://pbs.org/wgbh/pages/frontline/shows/evil/etc/script.html.

10. *Pioneer Press,* "Kofi Annan was Aware of Tutsis' Peril," May 4, 1998, http://geocities.com/CapitolHill/Lobby/4621/rwanda1.html.

11. Benny Avni, "Annan Holds Full Staff Meeting to Address Multiple UN Scandals," *The New York Sun,* April 6, 2005.

12. Stewart Stogel, "Staff Blasts Organization," *NewsMax,* June 15 2004. Details a UN survey, reporting on the United Nations Organizational Integrity.

13. Ibid.

14. *United Nations Office of Human Resources Management,* http://un.org/Depts/OHRM/salaries_allowances/salary.htm.

15. Barbara L. Schwemle, "Salaries of Federal Officials: A Fact Sheet," Congressional Research Service, January 11, 2005.

16. Linda Fasulo, *An Insider's Guide to the UN,* (Yale University Press, 2004).

17. *General Accountability Office,* "United Nations: Reforms Progressing, but Comprehensive Assessments Needed to Measure Impact," February 13, 2004, GAO-04-339.

18. *United Nations,* "Press Conference By Secretary-General Kofi Annan at United Nations Headquarters," December 14, 1998, http://www.un.org/News/Press/docs/1998/19981214.sgsm6837.r1.html.

19. "Report of the Secretary-General In Larger Freedom: Towards Development, Security and Human Rights for All," March 21, 2005.

20. *UN News Centre,* "Annan to Present on Monday New Report on Building Better and Safer World," March 18, 2005.

21. Ronald Baily, "International Man Of Mystery: Who Is Maurice Strong?" *The National Review Online,* September 1, 1997, http://nationalreview.com/01sept97/bailey090197.html. For good background discussion, see also Henry Lamb, "Maurice Strong: The New Guy in Your Future," January, 1997, http://http://citizenreview online.org/august_2002/maurice_strong.htm.

22. Agenda 21, Chapter 33, Section 33.18.

23. Ibid, Chapter 5, Sec. 5.3.

24. Maurice F. Strong, "Remarks by Maurice Strong on the Occasion of the 25th Anniversary of the UN Conference on Environment and Development," *Earth Council,* June 5, 1997, http://ecouncil.ac.cr/about/speech/strong/sweden.htm.

25. "Working Group III: Governance from Commission on Sustainable Development acting as the preparatory Committee for the World Summit on Sustainable Development, Third Session," April 30, 2002, http://johannesburg sum mit.org/html/.../ngo_comments_governance_rev2.doc.

26. Maurice Strong, "Stockholm to Rio: A Journey Down a Generation," quoted in "UN Reform—Restructuring for Global Governance," *Eco-Logic* (July/Aug 1997), http://iahf.com/world/un-refm.html).

27. For details on what the Commission on Global Governance had to say, see http://itcilo.it/actrav/actrav-english/telearn/global/ilo/globe/gove.htm

28 http://libertymatters.org/chap2.htm

29. *CalgarySun.com,* "The Mind behind Kyoto," 2001, http://calgarysun.com/cgi-bin/niveau2.cgi?s=Lifestyles&p=66719.html&a=1.

30. Judi McLeod, "When the Big Hand Says Thirteen Moon Calendar," *Canada free press.com,* August 27, 2004, http://torontofreepress.com/2004/cover082704.htm.

31. Maurice F. Strong, "Where on Earth Are We Going?" (Texere LLC, 2000), 225.

32. Maurice F. Strong, "Hunger, Poverty, Population and Environment," April 7, 1999, http://thp.org/reports/strong499.htm.

33. *The Earth Charter Initiative,* http://earthcharter.org/innerpg.cfm?id_menu=19.

34. Dyan Machan, "Saving the Planet with Maurice Strong," Forbes, January 12, 1998, quoted on *Global Policy Forum,* http://globalpolicy.org/finance/docs/machan.htm

35. Ibid. See also Pranay Gupte "Embroiled in a United Nations Scandal is an 'International Man of Mystery,'" *The New York Sun,* April 29-May 1, 2005.

36. Ibid.

37. Judi McLeod, "Environmental Car Salesman of 2005: Maurice Strong, Meet George W. Bush," *Canadafreepress.com,* January 4, 2005, http://canadafreepress.com/2005/cover010405.htm.

38. The Ark of Hope Homepage, http://www.arkofhope.org/

39. Richard Clugston, "The Earth Charter and Good Globalization, Presented at the Earth Charter Community Summit," September 28, 2002, http://earthcharter usa.org/rick_speech.htm.

40. Ibid.

41. For Jeffrey Sachs' discussion of America's barbarism and his equating of abuses at the Abu Ghraib prison to the beheading of an American hostage see "The March to Barbarism," from web site of Project Syndicate, an international association of newspapers which receives support from George Soros' Open Society Institute, http://project-syndicate.org/contributors/contributor_comm.php4?id=2, (May 2004).

42. Ibid.

43. Elizabeth Becker, "Banker Presses Aid for Poor to Fight Terror," *New York Times,* April 22, 2004.

44. Jeffrey Sachs, "Defeating Terrorism through Global Prosperity," *Project Syndicate,* October 2001. Written very shortly after the tragedy of 9/11, Sachs referred to the United States as the "developed world's stingiest donor" and blamed

"American stinginess" as the cause of "high costs to U.S. security." In other words, if only America had been a more generous donor, the terrorist attack on September 11th may never have happened. See also Jeffrey Sachs, "The Decline of America," *Project Syndicate*, March 2004. In this fine piece, Sachs accused the Bush Administration of "thuggish behavior," said that U.S. military spending shows how America can be "a force for great ill" and predicted America's "inevitable decline."

45. Jeffrey Sachs speech to the World Bank on concerning the needs of "Environmentally and Socially Sustainable Development," *World Bank's B-SPAN*, March 1, 2004. Appears on the web casting service that presents World Bank seminars, workshops, and conferences on a variety of sustainable development and poverty reduction issues via streaming video.

46. *Probe International*, "Times of Zambia," July 7, 2004, http://odiousdebts.org/odiousdebts/index.cfm?DSP=content&ContentID=10806.

47. *United Nation Department of Public Information and Non-Governmental Organization*, "Millennium Development Goals: Civil Society Takes Action," September 8-10, 2004, http://undpingoconference.org/.

48. Jeffrey D. Sachs, http://www.results.org/web site/article.asp?id=1624, June 15, 2005. Telephone press briefing with Jeffrey Sachs Discussing the Upcoming G-8 Summit

49. Maurice Strong, "Where on Earth Are We Going?" (Texere LLC, 2000), 216, 229, 230. In this volume, Strong recounts his observations on the Rio Earth Summit; Alan Larson "U.S.-EU: A Major New Commitment," *Small Earth Times*, March 18, 2002, http://globalpolicy.org/socecon/ffd/conference/2002/0318useu.htm. Alan comments on the Monterrey summit and is quoted by Roman Rollnick and Jay Newton.

50. International Conference on Financing for Development, Report of the UN Secretary-General, August, 2003, http://un.org/esa/ffd/Documents2003.htm. The specific U.S. undertaking to increase its development aid only to 0.15 percent of its GNP by 2006 (contradicting Sachs' claim that the U.S. made a specific commitment to the 0.7 percent target he favors) is referenced in "Implementation of and Follow-up to Commitments and Agreements made at the conference." The U.S.'s achievement of its undertaking ahead of schedule is documented in Final Official Development Assistance for 2003. *Organization for Economic Cooperation and Development*, http://oecd.org/statisticsdata/0%2C2643%2Cen_2649_33721_1_119656_1_1_1%2C00.html. See also Roman Rollnick and Jay Newton, "U.S.-EU:A Major New Commitment," *Small Earth Times*.

51. Brett Stephens, "Our Man in the Twilight Zone," *Wall Street Journal Opinion Journal Online*, Sept 17, 2005.

52. Jeffrey D. Sachs, "The Development Challenge," *Foreign Affairs*, March/April 2005.

53. Brett Stephens, "Our Man in the Twilight Zone," *Wall Street Journal Opinion Journal Online*, Sept 17, 2005.

54. "Final Official Development Assistance for 2003," supra.

55. *Economic Cooperation and Development Assistance*, "Conflict Prevention and Peace Building: What Counts as ODA," March 3, 2005, http://www.oecd.org/Long Abstract/0,2546,en_2649_201185_34535174_1_1_1_1,00.html.

56. Carol Adelman, "Aid and Comfort," *Tech Central Station*, August 21, 2002,

http://techcentralstation.com/082102N.html.

57. Ibid.

58. Donald G. McNeil, Jr., "New Vaccine Said to Offer Hope Against Deadly Bacterium," *The New York Times*, March 25, 2005.

59. Yaw Sophism, "A Case For Remittance Policy In Ghana," *GhanaHomePage*, December 12, 2003, http://www.ghanaweb.com/GhanaHomePage/features/artikel .php?ID=42857

60. "International Monetary Fund, World Economic Outlook: Chapter 2—Two Current Issues Facing Developing Countries" (April 2005).

61. Charles W. Corey, "Africa Must Look Inward For Development, Ghanaian Economist Says," http://usinfo.state.gov/af/Archive/2005/May/09-833863.html.

62. Jeffrey D. Sachs, *The End of Poverty*, (New York: The Penguin Press, 2005), 306-307. In this book, Sachs claims that if every donor country were to increase their level of foreign aid to 0.5 percent of GNP, the United States would be responsible for paying 51% of the total increase, or approximately $38 billion (at 302). But this does not appear to jibe with two tables in Professor Sachs' Millennium Project report. Table 17.5 compares the estimated gaps between the actual assistance commitments of the developed countries that are members of the Development Assistance Committee and what it would take to meet commitments of 0.44 percent and 0.54 percent of Gross National Income in 2006 and 2015 respectively. In 2006, the gap for the United States between assistance and its actual assistance commitment is estimated to be $32.2 billion. The same gap for 2015 is estimated to be $51.5 billion. Now consider Table 8 of the report which projects what it calls the "plausible development assistance needs to meet the Millennium Development Goals" and the gap between existing development assistance needs and existing commitments. The projected total development aid gap for 2006 is $48 billion. The projected total development aid gap for 2015 is $74 billion. Put these two tables together and one can see what the report's authors are trying to do. They are using ostensibly objective data to make the case that the United States' so-called commitment gap ($32.2 billion and $51.5 billion for 2006 and 2015 respectively under these assumptions) is responsible for three-fourths of the total world-wide development aid gaps ($48 billion and $74 billion for these same years). Whatever the real figures, Sachs expects the U.S. to pay the bulk of the cost of his global redistribution plan through increased taxes if necessary.

63. Jeffrey D. Sachs, "Investing In Development," http://www.unmillennium project.org/

64. The Professor Sachs interview is reported in IRIN/Anthony Mitchell (Addis Ababa, July 28, 2003). The war fatalities data were compiled in a web site of "Major Episodes of Political Violence 1946-2002," Monty G. Marshall Director, Center for Systemic Peace.

65. *Transparency International,* "Transparency International Corruption Perceptions Index 2003," October 9, 2003, http://transparency.org/cpi/2003/ cpi2003.en.html. The site charts levels of corruption in 133 countries. See also *IRINnews.org* "Ethiopia: Corruption Reportedly Worsening," http://irinnews.org/report.asp?ReportID=37106& SelectRegion=Horn_of_Africa&SelectCountry=ETHIOPIA.

66. Jeffrey D. Sachs, "The End of Poverty", supra at 315.

67. John Cassidy, "Always With Us? Jeffrey Sachs' Plan to Eradicate World Pov-

erty," supra; http://earthinstitute.columbia.edu/about/director/documents/SMF7.pdf.

68. Janine R. Wedel, "The Harvard Boys Do Russia," supra.

69. ABC Radio National Background Briefing, "Russia: Six Years of Privatisation," August 2, 1998,

70. *The CIA World Factbook*, "Ethiopia," December 18, 2003, http://www.mc library.edu.mn/worldfactbook2003/geos/et.html#Econ

71. Roger Bate, "Analysis: Is Aid Worthwhile," *United Press International*, August 31, 2002, http://upi.com/view.cfm?StoryID=20020831-010635-1581r.

72. "Remarks of Congressman Jim Kolbe, Chairman of the House Foreign Operations Subcommittee, Before the Advisory Committee on Voluntary Foreign Aid," October 9, 2002. In these remarks Congressman Kolbe cites a number of relevant statistics.

73. "Report of the International Conference on Financing for Development Monterrey, Mexico, March 18-22, 2002," Statement by Mike Moore from World Trade Organization web site, http://wto.org/english/news_e/spmm_e/spmm81_e.htm.

74. Thilo Thielke, "For God's Sake, Please Stop the Aid!", *Der Spiegel*, July 4, 2005, http://service.spiegel.de/cache/international/spiegel/0,1518,363663,00.html.

75. Richard C. Holbrooke, "The Role of the United Nations in American Foreign Policy," *Council on Foreign Relations*, July 4, 2005, http://cfr.org/pub8094/richard_c_holbrooke/the_role_of_the_united_nations_in_american_foreign_policy.php.

Chapter Three

1. UN Press Release SG/SM/7249/Rev.1: Secretary-General Says 'Global People-Power' Best Thing For United Nations In Long Time, Needing Response In Partnership With Civil Society (text of a statement delivered by Secretary-General Kofi Annan at the World Civil Society Conference in Montreal, Canada, on December 8, 1999).

2. Seán Ó Siochrú, "Global Governance of Information and Communication Technologies: Implications for Transnational Civil Society Networking Version 1.0," *Social Science Research Council*, November, 2003, http://www.ssrc.org/programs/itic/. See also, Natalie Steinberg "Background Paper On Gongos And Quangos and Wild NGOs," *World Federalist Movement*, December, 2001, http://www.wfm.org/index.php/base/main.

3. *Global Policy Forum*, "About GPF," http://www.globalpolicy.org/visitctr/about.htm

4. Global Civil Society 2001, Frances Pinter, "Chapter 8 Funding of Global Civil Society Organisations," from The Centre for the Study of Global Governance web site, http://www.lse.ac.uk/Depts/global/Yearbook/yearbookcontributors.htm.

5. Michael Albert, "What Are We For?" *Global Policy Forum*, September 6, 2001, http://www.globalpolicy.org/globaliz/econ/2001/0906gbz.htm.

6. *The Association for Progressive Communications*, "About the APC," http://www.apc.org/english/about/index.shtml

7. Professor Peter Willetts, "What is a Non-Governmental Organization," UNESCO Encyclopedia (2002).

8. Jennifer Butler, "New Sheriff in Town: The Christian Right Nears Major Victory at the United Nations and for Faith and Family Christian Right Advocacy at the

United Nations," *Political Research Associates*, http://publiceye.org/magazine/v16n2/PE_Butler2.html.

9. Laura Peek and Liz Chong, "Update 4: Greenpeace Tries to Stop Oil Trading; Kyoto Protest Beaten Back By Inflamed Petrol Traders" *Times Online*, February 17, 2005.

10. Speech by French President Jacques Chirac to The VIth Conference Of The Parties To The United Nations Framework Convention On Climate Change The Hague, (November 20, 2000).

11. William D. Nordhaus and Joseph G. Boyer, "Requiem for Kyoto: an Economic Analysis of the Kyoto Protocol," February 8, 1999.

12. Margo Thorning, "The Kyoto Protocol: Impact of Climate Change Policy on U.S. Economic Growth and Environmental Quality," *American Council for Capital Formation*, October 6, 1998, http://www.accf.org/publications/testimonies/test-kyoto-impact98.html

13. Ministry of Environment & Forest, Press Release, "Government Decides to Ratify Kyoto Protocol on Climate," *Government of India Press Information Bureau*, August 7, 2002, http://pib.nic.in/archieve/lreleng/lyr2002/raug2002/07082002/r070820027.html.

14. *Associated Press*, "Kyoto Accord Goes Into Effect," http://www.foxnews.com/story/0,2933,147741,00.html

15. James Pinkerton, "Tony Blair Pulls the Plug on Kyoto at Clinton Summit," Sept. 16, 2005, Tech Central Station.

16. Alan Oxley, "Howard Vindicated on Kyoto Strategy," Australian Financial Review, December 20, 2005, Opinion Sec. Alan Oxley is the former ambassador to the General Agreement on Trades and Tariffs and Chairman of the Australian APEC Studies Centre.

17. William Echikson, "EU Shifts Focus On Environment To Growth Plans," *Wall Street Journal*, February 2, 2005.

18. *Center for Reproductive Rights*, "Step-by-Step Guide Using the UN Treaty Monitoring Bodies to Promote Reproductive Rights" www.crlp.org/pdf/pub_bp_stepbystep.pdf

19. Peggy Kalas, "Why We Need a Global Approach, A briefing from the World Federalist Movement & the International NGO Task Group on Legal and Institutional Matters," *International Environmental Dispute Resolution*, August 2002.

20. Ibid.

21. *Associated Press*, "Environmental Court Would Assess and Punish Environmental Crimes Green Meeting in Brazil to Propose Environmental Court," September 14, 2004.

22. Agenda 21, Chapter 38, Section 8.1.

23. Speech by Hon. Christopher H. Smith of New Jersey In The House Of Representatives (December 8, 2003) with submission to the Congressional Record of Center for Reproductive Rights documents including, "International Legal Program Summary Of Strategic Planning Through October 31, 2003 Memo #1-International Reproductive Rights Norms: Current Assessment."

Chapter Four

1. Peter J. Spiro, "The New Sovereigntists: American Exceptionalism and its False Prophets," *Foreign Affairs*, November/December 2000.

2. Anne-Marie Slaughter, "The Real New World Order," *Foreign Affairs*, September/October 1997.

3. "Shelter is a Basic Human Right, says Court of Appeal," May 21, 2004, *Shelter.org*, http://shelter.org.uk, england.shelter.org.uk/home/home-624.cfm/pressrelease listing/1/pressrelease/85/.

4. *Roper v. Simmons*, 03-633 (2005).

5. *Lawrence v. Kansas*, 539 U.S. 558 (2003).

6. Associate Justice Ruth Bader Ginsburg, "Looking Beyond Our Borders: The Values of a Comparative Perspective in Constitutional Adjudication," *Remarks for the American Constitutional Society*, August 2, 2003.

7. Alexander Hamilton, *The Federalist No. 83*.

8. *Dred Scott v. John F.A. Sandford*, 60 U.S. 393 (1856); *Plessy v. Ferguson*, 163 U.S. 537 (1886).

9. Stephen Breyer, Associate Justice, Supreme Court of the United States, "Harvard University Tanner Lectures On Human Values 2004-2005," November 17-19, 2004.

10. Ibid.

11. Patti Waldmeir, "Breyer urges U.S. attention to foreign law," *Financial Times*, August 9, 2005.

12. *Knight v. Florida*, 528 U.S. 990, 993-999 (1999) (Breyer, J. dissenting from denial of certiorari).

13. *Sierra Club v. Morton*, 405 U.S. 727 (1972).

14. Jim Allison, "Congressional Debates: Religious Amendments, 1789," *The Constitutional Principle—Separation of Church and State*, http://members.tripod.com/~candst/

15. Ibid.

16. Ibid.

17. *McCreary County v. American Civil Liberties Union of Ky.*, 03-1693 (2005); *Van Orden v. Perry*, 03-1500 (2005).

18. *Bureau of the Committee of Religious NGOs at the United Nations*, Conference on Interfaith Cooperation for Peace, June 22, 2005, http://www.un.org/docs/ecosoc/ meetings/2005/22June2005.html

19. Joe Woodard, Religious Analyst, "The UN Quietly Wages War on Religion," *The Calgary Herald from LifeSite News*, (August 23-26, 2001), http://www.dailycatholic .org/issue/2001Aug/aug23gc1.htm,

20. Ibid.

21. *Rasul v. Bush et al.*, 03-334 (2005).

22. *Al Odah v. United States et al.*, 03-343 (2005).

23. Ruth Wedgwood, "Judicial Overreach," *Wall Street Journal*, November 16, 2004, Op-ed.

24. *Hamdan v. Rumsfeld*, Civil Action No. 04-1519, (Memorandum Opinion U.S. District Court for the District of Columbia at 18).

25. "Convention (III) relative to the Treatment of Prisoners of War," Geneva, 12 August 1949, Article 17" (emphasis added).

26. Ibid., Articles 25, 30, 52, 53, 60.

27. Abraham Lincoln to Winfield Scott, Letter, Arrest of Maryland Legislature, April 25, 1861, *Ashbrook Center for Public Affairs*, http://teachingamericanhistory.org /library/index.asp?document=413

28. Abraham Lincoln, Reply to Erastus Corning and Others regarding resolutions concerning military arrests and suspension of habeas corpus, June 1863, *Ashbrook Center for Public Affairs*, http://teachingamericanhistory.org/library/index.asp?document=612

29. *Hamdan v. Rumsfeld et al.*, 04-5393 (D.C. Cir. 2005).

30. *Grutter v. Bollinger* 539 U.S. 306 (2003). See also the remarks of Justice Ruth Bader Ginsburg to the American Society of International Law, April 1, 2005, *American Society of International Law*, http://www.asil.org/events/AM05/ginsburg050401.html,

31. Pew and Belden, Russonello and Stewart, *Americans and the World Public Opinion on International Affairs: United Nations*, "General Attitudes towards the UN," http://www.americans -world.org/digest/global_issues/un/un1.cfm.

Chapter Five

1. Harry Alonso Cushing, ed., *The Writings of Samuel Adams*, Volume III, 1773-1777, referencing a diary entry by a Mr. Hutchinson for September 6, 1775, http://www.gutenberg.org/

2. Samuel Johnson, "Taxation No Tyranny—An Answer To The Resolutions And Address Of The American Congress," *The Works of Samuel Johnson*, (Pafraets & Company, Troy, New York, 1913; volume 14, pages 93-144).

3. John Hancock, "Freeing America From Old World Despotism," 1776, Document Number: GLC639.12, *Gilder Lehrman Institute of American History* from http://gil derlehrman.org/search/display_results.php?id=GLC00639.12

4. "Deliberations of Constitutional Convention," August 13, 1787, http://www .constitution.org/dfc/dfc_0813.htm.

5 James Madison, Letter to John Adams, August 7, 1818, *Library of Congress*, http: //lcweb2.loc.gov/cgi-bin/query/r?ammem/mjmtext:@FIELD(DOCID+@lit(jm080158)).

6. Agenda 21, Chapter 33, Section 33.18, http://www.un.org/esa/sustdev/docu ments/agenda21/.

7. Interview, Secretary-General Boutros-Ghali, January 14, 1996, *BBC Radio 4*.

8. Boutros-Ghali, Lecture at Oxford University, January 15, 1996, *United Nations Press Release SG/SM/5870/Rev.1* from http://www.un.org/News/Press/docs/1996/19960 112.sgsm5870.html.

9. "NGO Paper 1 New Financial Mechanisms for Sustainable Development—Green Taxes for Global Needs," http://csdngo.igc.org/finance/fin_pos_paper1.htm

10. James A. Paul and Katarina Wahlberg, "Global Taxes for Global Priorities," March 2002, *Global Policy Forum*, http://www.globalpolicy.org/socecon/glotax/general/ glotaxpaper.htm.

11. See *Tobin Tax Initiative*, http://www.tobintax.org

12. Ibid., with link to http://tobintaxcall.free.fr

13. "U.S. Congress Concurrent Resolution on Taxing Cross-border Currency Transactions to Deter Excessive Speculation," (H.Con.Res.301), sponsored by Congressman Peter DeFazio (D-OR) and Senator Paul Wellstone (D-MN), introduced April 11, 2000.

14. "Global Taxation and the United Nations: A Review of Proposals," *Congressional Research Service*, May 3, 2002.

15. Anthony B. Atkinson, *"New Sources of Development Finance: Funding the Millennium Development Goals,"* September 20, 2004, *Global Policy Forum*, http://www .globalpolicy.org/socecon/glotax/general/.

16. Press Release GA/10006, *"General Assembly Adopts $2.63 Billion Budget For 2002-2003,"*December 24, 2001, http://un.org/News/Press/docs/2001/GA10006.doc.htm; UN General Assembly, Fifty-seventh Session, Item 114 of the Provisional Agenda, Programme Budget for the Biennium 2002-2003, *"Implementation of Projects Financed from the Development Account, Report of the Secretary-General,"* August 28, 2002, from UN web site, http://un.org/ga/57/document.htm

17. UN Press Release GA/AB/3663, "Budget Committee Briefed on Latest Developments in Plan to Refurbish United Nations Headquarters," http://globalpolicy.org/ finance/docs/2005/0317hqrefurb.htm

18. Pranay Gupte, "Embroiled in a United Nations Scandal Is An 'International Man of Mystery', *The New York Sun*, Weekend Edition April 29-May 1, 2005.

19. UN Press Release GA/AB/3579, October 23, 2003, http://www.un.org/News/ Press/docs/2003/gaab3579.doc.htm

20. "UN Audit Found Early 'Oil-for-Food' Problems," *Fox News*, May 20, 2004.

21. "Third Interim Report issued by the Independent Inquiry Committee into the United Nations Oil-for-Food Program," August 8, 2005.

22. "UN Audit Found Early 'Oil-for-Food' Problems," *Fox News*, May 20, 2004.

23. "Second Interim Report issued by the Independent Inquiry Committee into the United Nations Oil-for-Food Program," March 29, 2005.

24. "UN Audit Found Early 'Oil-for-Food' Problems," *Fox News*, May 20, 2004.

25. "Second Interim Report issued by the Independent Inquiry Committee into the United Nations Oil-for-Food Program," March 29, 2005

26. David R. Sands, "GAO Denied Access to Oil-for-Food Audits," *The Washington Times*, April 29, 2004.

27. Kevin Baumert, "Global Taxes and Fees: Recent Developments and Overcoming Obstacles," May 1998, *Global Policy Forum*, http://www.globalpolicy.org/ socecon/glotax/baumert.htm

28. "Public Law 106-113, 106th Congress an Act Making Consolidated Appropriations for the Fiscal Year Ending Sept. 30, 2000, and for Other Purposes, Sec. 561."

29. "Public Law 106-113, Sec. 406".

30. John Dickinson, "Liberty Song," 1768, http://chronicles.dickinson.edu/ency clo/l/BostonChronicle1768-2.jpg

Chapter Six

1. *International Action on Small Arms*, "Regulation of Civilian Possession of Small Arms and Light Weapons, Biting the Bullet—Briefing 16," http://www.international-

alert.org/pdf/pubsec/BB_Briefing161.pdf. Biting the Bullet is a joint project of International Alert, Saferworld and the University of Bradford to inform and promote the development and implementation of the UN Programme of Action on small arms.

2. *Justice Department*, "Whether the Second Amendment Secures an Individual Right, Memorandum Opinion for the Attorney General," (August 24, 2004). This memorandum, prepared by the Justice Department, provides an excellent in-depth history and analysis of the Second Amendment.

3. Tony Mauro, "Scholar's Shift in Thinking Angers Liberals," *U.S.A Today*, http://www.saf.org/TribeU.S.A.html.

4. *International Action on Small Arms*, http://www.iansa.org/about.htm.

5. *International Action on Small Arms*, http://www.iansa.org/documents/govern ance/consultation_eng.doc.

6. *Amnesty International*, "Global Arms Trade Dangerously Unregulated—New Report: Amnesty International, Oxfam, IANSA Launch Global Control Arms Campaign," http://amnesty.org.il/data/arms1003.html (October 9, 2003).

7. Rebecca Peters, "Statement by Rebecca Peters, Soros Senior Justice Fellow/ International Alliance for Women, to the 7th Session of the UN Commission on Crime Prevention & Criminal Justice," http://www.tf.org/tf/violence/firearms/Intl/women5w p2.shtml.

8. Dr. James B. Lawson, "The Great Australian Gun Law Con: How Effective Were the Gun Bans? New National Gun Laws—Are They Cost Effective?" *Institute of Public Affairs Review* (December 1999), http://members.ozemail.com.au/~confiles/law son.html

9. *International Service for Human Rights*, "United Nations Conference on the Illicit Trade in Small Arms and Light Weapons in all its Aspects," http://ishr.ch/About UN/ReportsandAnalysis/UNConf-lightarms2001.htm. Statement by the President of the Conference after the adoption of the Programme of Action to Prevent, Combat and Eradicate the Illicit Trade in Small Arms and Light Weapons in All Its Aspects.

10. *People's Daily*, "UN Negotiators Agree on Small-arms Trade," http://english .people.com.cn/english/200107/22/eng20010722_75570.html.

11. *International Action on Small Arms*, http://iansa.org/un/bulletin.htm#no4.

12. *Justice Department*, "Whether the Second Amendment Secures an Individual Right—Memorandum Opinion for the Attorney General supra 10."

13. James Madison, *"The Federalist,"* No. 39.

14. *United States v. Miller*, 307 U.S. 174 (1939).

15. Alexander Hamilton, *"The Federalist,"* No. 29, 183-185.

16. James Madison, *"The Federalist,"* No. 46.

17. *Adams v. Williams* 407 U.S. 143, 150 (1972) (Douglas, J., dissenting).

18. *Printz v. United States* 521 U.S. at 938-39 (Thomas, J., concurring).

19. David B. Kopel, "The Supreme Court's Thirty-Five Other Gun Cases: What The Supreme Court Has Said About The Second Amendment," *Saint Louis University Public Law Review* (1999), http://www.davidkopel.com/2A/lawrev/35finalpartone.htm

20. *United States v. Emerson*, 270 F.3d at 203 (5th Circuit 2001).

21. *Silveira v. Lockyer*, 312 F.3d 1052, as amended, 328 F.3d 567, reh. denied, 2003 WL 21004622 (9th Cir. 2003).

22. *U.S. Constitution*, Amendments 4 and 5; Articles 1, 2 and 4.

23. William Blackstone, *Commentaries on the Laws of England: The Rights Of Persons*, (Chicago: University of Chicago Press, 1979), 139.

24. Osama Bin Laden, "Bin Laden's Sermon for the Feast of the Sacrifice (March 5, 2003)," *The Middle East Media Research Institute*, http://memri.org/bin/articles.cgi?Area=jihad&ID=SP47603.

25. Dore Gold, *Tower of Babble*, (New York: Crown Forum, 2004).

26. Mitchell G. Bard, "Myth and Fact: UNRWA & Terrorism," *United Jewish Communities*, 2004, http://ujc.org/content_display.html?ArticleID=128376.

27. David Bedein, "How the West Weakens Israel," *FrontPageMagazine.com*, http://frontpagemag.com/Articles/ReadArticle.asp?ID=10331.

28. Frank James and Rick Pearson, "Ridge Defends `Duct Tape' Tip: Homeland Agency Plans More Advice," *Chicago Tribune*, February 14, 2003.

29. *The University of Virginia*, "Thomas Jefferson on Politics & Government: The Right to Bear Arms," http://etext.virginia.edu/jefferson/quotations/jeff1500.htm#Arms.

Chapter Seven

1. *TerraViva Online*, "ICC a Pesky Itch under U.S. Warhorse's Saddle," http://ipsnews.net/fsm2003/27.01.2003/nota1.shtml.

2. Floy Lilley, "Reports from Rome, Creation of the International Criminal Court The Superpower The World Loves To Hate," *Sovereignty International, Inc.*, http://sovereignty.net/p/gov/rome7-6.htm.

3. *Human Rights First*, "Election of ICC Judges and Prosecutor," http://humanrightsfirst.org/international_justice/icc/election/elections.htm.

4. Ibid.

5. Ibid.

6. Ibid.

7. Warren Hoge, "Annan Rebukes U.S. for Move to Give its Troops Immunity," *New York Times*, June 18, 2004.

8. Warren Hoge, "U.S. Drops Effort to Gain Immunity for Its Troops," *New York Times*, June 23, 2004.

9. *Rome Statute of the International Criminal Court*, Article 18(3).

10. *Rome Statute of the International Criminal Court*, Article 48(1) and (2).

11. *Deutsche Welle*, "Rumsfeld Sued for Alleged War Crimes," http://www.dw-world.de/dw/article/0,1564,1413907,00.html.

12. *Rome Statute of the International Criminal Court*, Article 7(1)(a) and Article 8(2)(b)(i) and (2)(b)(ii).

13. *Rome Statute of the International Criminal Court*, Article 8(2)(b)(iv).

14. *Rome Statute of the International Criminal Court*, Article 7(1)(a)(f) and (k) and Article 8(2) (b)(xxi)."

15. Ibid.

16. *International Court of the Environment Foundation*, http://icef-court.org/icef/about.htm.

17. *Jude Ibegbu*, "Genocide Mass Killings and Right of United Nations to Humanitarian Intervention," http://etrurianet.it/jude/human.HTM.

18. Ibid.

19. Irene Khan, "Why Human Rights Matter," *Amnesty International*, http://web
.amnesty.org/report2004/message-eng.

20. Irene Khan, "Forward to Amnesty International 2005 Report," *Amnesty International*, http://web.amnesty.org/report2005/message-eng.

21. Jim Lobe, "Rights: Give Rumsfeld the Pinochet Treatment, Says U.S. Amnesty Chief", *International Press Service*, May 25, 2005, http://ipsnews.net/new_nota.asp
?idnews=28823.

22. William Schulz, Hardball interview with Chris Matthews, *MSNBC.com*,
http://www.msnbc.msn.com/id/8073301/.

23. Michelle Malkin, "Gitmo: The Truth," *New York Post*, June 2, 2005, quoting
"Inside the Wire" by Erik Saar who served as an army sergeant at Guantanamo for six
months and wrote first hand about his experiences there. For the International Committee of the Red Cross statement regarding its dialogue with U.S. civilian and military authorities, see Letter to the Editor from Antonella Notari, Spokesperson for the
International Committee of the Red Cross, Wall Street Journal (May 24, 2005).

24. *GlobalSecurity.org*, "Intelligence: Abu Ghurayb Prison" http://www.global
security.org/intell/world/iraq/abu-ghurayb-prison.htm.

25. Martin A. Geer, "Human Rights and Wrongs in Our Own Backyard: Incorporating International Human Rights Protections Under Domestic Civil Rights Law—A
Case Study of Women in United States Prisons," Harvard *Human Rights Journal* Vol.
13 (Spring 2000).

26. *American Civil Liberties Union*, "The Lawsuit Against Donald Rumsfeld Over
U.S. Torture Policies," http://aclu.org/SafeandFree/SafeandFree.cfm?ID=17572&c=206.

27. *Truman Presidential Museum and Library*, "Chronology regarding Truman and
the A-bomb from August 2-10, 1945," http://trumanlibrary.org/whistlestop/study_col
lections/bomb/large/documents/fulltext.php?fulltextid=21.

28. Philip Nobile, "Hiroshima Debate: Was Harry Truman a War Criminal? Applying the Nuremberg Standards to Ourselves," *TomPaine.com*, http://tompaine.com/
feature.cfm/ID/3428.

29. *Truman Presidential Museum and Library*, "Pages from President Truman's diary regarding June 18, 1945 meeting," http://www.trumanlibrary.org/whistlestop/stu
dy_collections/bomb/large/documents/fulltext.php?fulltextid=10.

Chapter Eight

1. Michael Ratner, John Burroughs, Peter Weiss, and Andrew Lichterman, "The
United Nations Charter and the Use of Force Against Iraq," *Lawyers Against the War*,
October 2, 2002, http://www.lawyersagainstthewar.org/legalarticles/ratner.html.

2. Ibid.

3. Gold, *Tower of Babble*, ca. chapter 5.

4. Ratner, et al, "The United Nations Charter and the Use of Force against Iraq."

5. Lord Goldsmith, "Written Answer on Iraq Advice," *BBC News*, March 18,
2003, http://news.bbc.co.uk/1/hi/uk_politics/vote_2005/frontpage/44921 95.stm.

6. Ratner, et al, "The United Nations Charter and the Use of Force against Iraq."

7. Dean Acheson, "'Princeton Seminar' Comment," *Truman Presidential Museum
& Library*, February 13, 1954, http://trumanlibrary.org/whistlestop/study_collections/

NOTES

korea/large/korea62650.htm.

8. Dean Acheson, "Memorandum of Conversation by Philip C. Jessup," *Truman Presidential Museum and Library*, June 26, 1950, http://trumanlibrary.org/whistlestop/study_collections/korea/large/korea62650.htm.

9. *Truman Presidential Museum and Library*, "Oral History Interview with Assistant Secretary of State for UN Affairs John Hickerson," June 5, 1973, http://trumanlibrary .org/oralhist/hickrson.htm#oh3.

10. Ibid.

11. Ibid, supra.

12. Ibid.

13. Dexter Filkins, "Insurgents Vowing to Kill Iraqis Who Brave the Polls on Sunday," *New York Times*, January 26, 2005.

14. See, for example, the excellent discussion in Gold, *Tower of Babble*.

15. Richard D. McKinzie, "Oral History Interview with Durward V. Sandifer," *Truman Presidential Museum & Library*, March 15, 1973, http://trumanlibrary.org/ oralhist/sandifer.htm#oh1. Sandlifer was an international lawyer who served as secretary-general and chief technical expert for the U.S. delegation to the UN conference in San Francisco.

16. Gerard W. Gawalt, "America and the Barbary Pirates: An International Battle Against an Unconventional Foe," *Library of Congress*, http://memory.loc.gov/ammem/collections/jefferson_papers/mtjprece.html.

17. Ibid.

Chapter Nine

1. *Charter of the United Nations*, Article 2, Principles 1 and 7, http://www.un.org/aboutun/charter/chapter1.htm.

2. Tom Connally, transcript of speech to the U.S. Senate, *New York Times*, June 28, 1945.

3. *International Covenant on Economic, Social and Cultural Rights*, Article 2, Section 1, http://www.unhchr.ch/html/menu3/b/a_cescr.htm.

4. *Office of the High Commissioner for Human Rights*, "CESCR General Comment 3," December 14, 1990, http://unhchr.ch/tbs/doc.nsf/(symbol)/CESCR+General+comm.ent+3.En?OpenDocument.

5. Ibid.

6. Ibid.

7. *Office of the High Commissioner for Human Rights*, "CESCR General Comment 5," December 9, 1994, http://unhchr.ch/tbs/doc.nsf/0/4b0c449a9ab4ff72c12563ed0054f17d?Opendocument.

8. UN General Assembly Resolution 56/168, "Comprehensive and integral international convention to promote and protect the rights and dignity of persons with disabilities," *UN Global Programme on Disability*, December 19, 2001, http://www.un.org/ esa/socdev/enable/disA56168e1.htm.

9. *UN Global Programme on Disability*, "Report of the Working Group to the Ad Hoc Committee," http://www.un.org/esa/socdev/enable/rights/ahcwgreport.htm. According to the UN Global Programme on Disability's "Enable" web site, the work-

ing group was comprised of the following governments, NGOs, and national human rights institution: Cameroon, Canada, China, Colombia, Comoros, Ecuador, Germany, India, Ireland, Jamaica, Japan, Lebanon, Mali, Mexico, Morocco, New Zealand, Philippines, Republic of Korea, Russian Federation, Serbia and Montenegro, Sierra Leone, Slovenia, South Africa, Sweden, Thailand, Uganda, Venezuela Disability Australia Limited, Disabled Peoples' International, Disabled Peoples' International (Africa), European Disability Forum, Inclusion International, Inter-American Institute on Disability, Landmine Survivors Network, Rehabilitation International, World Blind Union, World Federation of the Deaf, World Federation of the Deafblind, World Network of Users and Survivors of Psychiatry South African Human Rights Commission.

10. *Landmine Survivors Network*, "Convention Document Legal Analysis," http://rightsforall.org/docs/LSN_commentary.doc. In the "Draft Articles for a Comprehensive and Integral International Convention on the Protection and Promotion of the Rights and Dignity of Persons with Disabilities" produced by the Working Group to the Ad Hoc Committee, there is no definition of the term "disability." It was left blank with a footnote that reads: "Many members of the Working Group emphasized that a convention should protect the rights of all persons with disabilities (i.e. all different types of disabilities) and suggested that the term 'disability' should be defined broadly. Some members were of the view that no definition of 'disability' should be included in the convention, given the complexity of disability and the risk of limiting the ambit of the convention. Other delegations pointed to existing definitions used in the international context including the World Health Organisation's International Classification of Functioning, Disability and Health (ICF). There was general agreement that if a definition was included, it should be one that reflects the social model of disability, rather than the medical model."

11. *International Commission of Jurists*, "Joint Submission Presented by the Centre on Housing Rights and Evictions, the International Commission of Jurists, Foodfirst Information and Action Network and International Women's Rights Action Watch Asia-Pacific on Behalf of the International Coalition for an Optional Protocol to the International Covenant on Economic, Social and Cultural Rights," December 2004, http://icj. org/IMG/pdf/submission.pdf.

12. Hon. Christopher H. Smith, "Documents Reveal Deceptive Practices by Abortion Lobby," *Congressional Record*, December 8, 2003, available at http://www.c-fam.org/ pdfs/SecretLegalDocuments.pdf. Representative Smith of New Jersey submitted documents from the Center for Reproductive Rigths to the Congressional Record.

Chapter Ten

1. Michael McFaul, "Democracy Promotion as a World Value," *The Washington Quarterly*, (The Center for Strategic and International Studies and the Massachusetts Institute of Technology, Winter 2004-05), 148-149.

2. Ibid, 151.

3. *NBC News' Meet the Press*, April 18, 2004.

4. Joachim Krause, "Multilateralism: Behind European Views," *The Washington Quarterly*, (The Center for Strategic and International Studies and the Massachusetts Institute of Technology, Spring 2004).

5. Ibid.

6. UN General Assembly Fifty-ninth Session, Resolutions Adopted by the General Assembly on the Report of the Fifth Committee (A/59/448/Add.2) Revised Budget Appropriations for the Biennium 2004-2005 from UN web site, http://daccess-ods.un .org/access.nsf/Get?Open&DS=A/RES/59/277%20A-C&Lang=E,http://un.org/News/Press/docs/2004/ga10323.doc.htm

7. Ibid.

8. *United States General Accounting Office*, "United Nations: Reforms Progressing, but Comprehensive Assessments Needed to Measure Impact," February 2004, supra, http://www.gao.gov/new.items/d04339.pdf.

9. See the complaints of the United States and Eurpean Union representatives in response to a 2006-2007 budget outline report, November 10, 2004, http://unis.unvienna. org/unis/pressrels/2004/gaab3647.html.

10. *The United States Institute of Peace*, "Report of the Task Force on the United Nations: American Interests and UN Reform," June 2005, http://www.usip.org/un/ report /index.html. This report was produced at the direction of Congress by a bipartisan task force headed by Newt Gingrich and George Mitchell.

11. Ibid.

12. *United Nations*, "Report of the Secretary-General, Strengthening the United Nations: An Agenda for Further Change," September 9, 2002, http://un-ngls.org/ Strenghening_United_Nations_an_agenda_for_further_change.pdf.

13. *BBC News*, "UN Ban on Feasts During Famine," August 6, 2002, http://news .bbc. co.uk/1/hi/world/africa/2176653.stm.

14. *United Nations*, "Report of the Secretary-General, Strengthening the United Nations: An Agenda for Further Change," supra 10.

15. *UN Non-Governmental Liaison Service Development Dossiers*, http://un-ngls.org/ documents/publications.en/develop.dossier/dd.04/04.htm#04 and http://un-ngls.org/ documents/publications.en/develop.dossier/dd.04/05.htm#05

16. *SustainAbility*, "The Accountability and Governance of NGOs in the 21st Century," April 3, 2003, http://sustainability.com/programs/pressure-front/ accountability/3%20April%20Issues%20Paper.pdf.

17. Daniel Altman, "Jeffrey Sachs, an Economist On The Move," *The New York Times*, November 30, 2002.

18. Michael Cameron, "Roberts Gives His Verdict, Rejecting Foreign Laws," *The Australian*, September 16, 2005.

19. Alexander Hamilton, "The Federalist No. 80," *The Federalist Papers*.

20. Thomas Jefferson, letter to Charles Hammond, August 18, 1821, from the University of Virginia Library Electronic Text Center, http://etext.lib.virginia.edu/ jefferson/quotations/jeff1270.htm.